Overview and Critique of

Piaget's Genetic Epistemology 1965-1980

Overview and Critique of

Piaget's Genetic Epistemology 1965-1980

Rita Vuyk

1981

ACADEMIC PRESS

A Subsidiary of Harcourt Brace Jovanovich, Publishers
London · New York · Toronto · Sydney · San Francisco

British Library Cataloguing in Publication Data

Vuyk, Rita
 Overview and critique of Piaget's genetic
 epistemology, 1965-1980.
 Vol. I
 1. Piaget, Jean   2. Knowledge, Theory of
 3. Child psychology
 I. Title
 155.4'13   BF721   80-41465

ISBN 0-12-728501-6

Typeset by DMB (Typesetting), Oxford
Printed by St. Edmundsbury Press, Bury St. Edmunds

Volume I

Piaget's Genetic Epistemology 1965-1980

''Au terme d'une carrière il vaut
mieux être prêt à changer de
perspective que d'être condamné
à se répéter sans plus.''

Jean Piaget, 1976 (**99**)

Foreword

Rita Vuyk's study will certainly find a prominent place among the many works, both eulogistic and critical, devoted to Jean Piaget. It deserves such a place because of the careful consistency with which the author has carried out the task she set herself, i.e. to understand in detail and to set forth objectively the most recent (and as it happens the most complex) developments in the thought of Jean Piaget.

Rita Vuyk has followed Piaget's scientific production faithfully and with considerable discernment from 1965 up to his latest publications and his last manuscripts; thus, with the disappearance of the great Genevan savant, her work has become a book in honour of Piaget as much as a book about Piaget. Volume I, which the author herself considers to be simply descriptive and which lays no claim to uncovering the links in the progression of Piaget's thought, presents an excellent analysis of the texts produced during the period under discussion and clearly demonstrates Piaget's unrelenting pursuit of new facts and new theoretical insights. Oriented towards the future until the very end in his search for the psychological mechanisms that underlie the creation of new ideas, Piaget, in some of his most recent writings and in the light of new data, also reexamined a number of problems that had occupied his mind for many years, such as the reasons that lead to the construction of notions of conservation.

The period analysed by Rita Vuyk is a period of both epistemological synthesis and exploratory experimentation (carried out with the International Centre of Genetic Epistemology in Geneva) on the psychological processes of discovery, whose epistemological implications have not yet been fully spelt out.

The author's scientific career only recently brought her into direct contact with the Centre for Genetic Epistemology; her achievement in expounding Piaget's thought with exceptional clarity is therefore all the more remarkable. It is not easy to explain the role Piaget attributed to the phenomenon of phenocopy in the light of modern neo-Darwinism: it takes considerable insight to situate the hypothesis of functional continuity between vital adaptation and the norms of knowledge within a coherent epistemological framework; nor is it easy to elucidate the progressive elaboration of Piaget's equilibration theory and its heuristic fecundity for an understanding of the progress of knowledge. Yet the author is very much aware that these issues cannot be evaded in any serious discussion of the scientific value of Piaget's genetic epistemology, which is both interdisciplinary and constructivist.

Volume I is certain to be of great interest to all those who are not yet familiar with the latest work of Piaget and his close collaborators. Volume II goes further and gives a highly pertinent overview of the various criticisms that have been made of Piaget's work. As such it constitutes an excellent tool for further evaluation and elaboration, and provides refreshing new insights into the problems raised by various critics, even for those who were Piaget's close collaborators. With admirable judgement Rita Vuyk has made a choice of criticisms and arranged them in an original referential framework without ever losing sight of the essential. What matters is not the age of acquisition of certain concepts, for example, but the scientific status of the explanations, the falsifiability of the hypotheses, and Piaget's renewal of the structural models, in particular the cybernetic model.

Although this book could only have been written by someone who was intellectually in tune with the general trend of the Piagetian *oeuvre*, Rita Vuyk kept to scientific objectivity throughout and maintained her reserve on certain specific points.

I have had the pleasure on many occasions of discussing her project with her, and have benefited from the necessity of becoming aware of the presuppositions implicit in the theoretical basis of our work. Piaget himself expressed his interest in discussing with Rita Vuyk various points that had remained obscure in his writings as well as a number of modifications adopted since his earlier publications: "It is a rare pleasure to encounter an intelligent critic of one's ideas".

Most regrettably, Piaget himself was not able, as he intended, to write this Foreword, to which he would surely have brought all the personal warmth and subtle humour of which in discussions with colleagues as with his critics he possessed the secret.

November 1980   Bärbel Inhelder

Preface

This book is written by a psychologist for psychologists, but *not* about a psychologist. Though Piaget is also a psychologist, I am convinced that one can only understand and evaluate his theory if one takes his claim to be a genetic epistemologist seriously. In consequence the epistemological implications of his theory have been stressed throughout the book, while all possible applications have been left out.

In the first volume of this book I have tried to summarize Piaget's more recent theorizing as faithfully as possible. However, compressing some thousands of pages into a bare three hundred and organizing the material beyond a sequence of summaries of his books, already implies a personal touch even if all personal comments are avoided. "Compressing" has also had two other consequences: details of experiments have had to be left out and the ensuing abstract presentation makes the book difficult to read. It certainly does require some previous knowledge of Piaget's theory though all definitions of terms can easily be found by using the index. Furthermore, the presentation is something like a "smoothed curve of experimental data". All the passages annotated in my copies of his books as being incomprehensible, nonsense, contradictory, etc. have been deleted from the overview. In reading the "smoothed" main trends of his theory, one can easily get the impression that I never saw the many problematic details. This would be far from correct, but as I explain in Chapter 1 I am convinced that many of these details are irrelevant for the evaluation of his theory and the future development of his constructivism.

Considering Piaget as a genetic epistemologist has also had consequences for the second volume, in which critical arguments against Piaget are reviewed. Issues like "Is psychology a legitimate means for answering epistemological questions?" and "Is Piaget's use of logic justified?" become far more important than some of the experiments concerning details of the theory, though not all the experiments have been neglected. Furthermore, and this is essential, once Piaget's theory is seen as a defence of constructivism-structuralism-interactionism-functionalism against other epistemologies, the discussion really concerns the implicit or explicit epistemologies of his critics with their resulting psychologies. Hence attacks on Piaget's theory have been embedded in short overviews of the theoretical backgrounds of his critics. I have tried to make these objective, but it will be clear to any reader that my sympathies are on the side of constructivism. I believe that constructivist theories going beyond Piaget are of the utmost importance and therefore they have been elaborated more extensively than one might expect in a critique of Piaget's theory. As the theoretical and epistemological backgrounds of Piaget's critics may not interest all readers, the arguments themselves have been given in bold print, while the final chapter, i.e. Chapter 24, summarizes the main trends. In consideration of this approach Volume II should really have been written by a team of authors. However, this went beyond my organizational capacity. I have tried to solve the problem by asking each of several authors to summarize his own theory and asking others to comment on my text before publication, and then including their reactions in the final text. Though the end result is therefore some kind of a joint venture, the final responsibility is evidently mine.

Of all the persons who have helped me to write this book Professor Jean Piaget is of course the most important one. His first reaction to my venture was "J'admire votre courage", and from then on he has been most helpful. Having given me permission to use his manuscripts that were in press, he has also patiently answered my endless questions on these manuscripts as well as on his views expressed in earlier publications. During recent years he has refused to write forewords to "Piagetian" books and therefore his kind offer to write a foreword for this one was a most flattering exception. But he evidently had to wait till the manuscript was nearly finished and at that time a severe illness prevented the fulfilment of his promise. Still, I am very thankful for his interest and his kind intention.

But Piaget has not been the only one from the "School of Geneva" to help me. Bärbel Inhelder and Guy Cellerier were willing to read many parts of the manuscript, encouraging and criticizing at the same time, while a number of other "Genevans" gave me some of their time as well.

Nearly all the authors to whom I sent chapter sections regarding their own work have given me their comments and are acknowledged in the text. My Dutch colleague, Nico Frijda, showed unusual patience whenever I gave a cry for help because I had got stuck once more, and he even managed to find time to read successive versions of some of the chapters. I am very grateful for his help, as well as for that of some younger psychologists, Rex Boswinkel and Ab Weerman, whose critical comments on Volume I showed me how obscure some of my passages were for the type of readers I was writing for.

Last, but certainly not least, I would like to mention another young psychologist, Gijsbert Erkens who—with endless patience and perseverance—did all the dull jobs inherent in the writing of a book: finding articles and books that might be relevant (far more than I could ever use!), making summaries, checking my quotations, correcting proofs, etc. Any author will appreciate how valuable and time-saving such help is. Though the speed with which books and articles on Piaget are published and the slowness with which they become available in the Netherlands probably made me miss some publications, their number would have been far more extended without his untiring help.

I do hope that readers who find the book helpful or interesting but react critically to parts or aspects of it, will send me their comments. If ever the book is up-dated in a second edition these might help me to improve the text.

1082 KJ Amsterdam   Rita Vuyk
The Netherlands
May 1980

A Guide to Reading this Book

The topics of Volume I and Volume II

Chapter 2 gives a short overview of recent developments of Piaget's theory. These developments are then elaborated in Volume I. As readers of Piaget's publications know, and as I have mentioned in the foregoing, he is not always as clear as the reader might wish. Summarizing a more or less unclear text without adding a personal interpretation evidently implies the risk of writing a "difficult" text—to use a euphemism. The reader may therefore well feel frustrated at times. I can do no more than offer my excuses for unclear passages. On the other hand many Piagetians will feel that there is no need to read paragraphs on assimilation/accommodation and such well-known topics. However, Piaget has given new definitions recently (**96**) that are important for understanding his latest notions.

Psychologists may be mostly interested in Piaget's recent views on well-known topics (Chapter 11). It is possible to read this chapter without all the foregoing text but the paragraphs on abstraction and the chapter on equilibration are required for a full understanding.

Volume II contains the main arguments against Piaget's theory. If it had been written parallel to the content of Volume I it would have become a very slender volume. It is indeed astonishing how many critics still use Piaget's early books without trying to find out whether he has changed his point of view or not. However, such a limitation would have left out the whole discussion on stages and a lot of that on conservation, formal operations, etc. So I have included critical arguments against older notions but using recent critical publications and trying to go into the main issues. However, even the main issues have led to a great number of publications. As limitations of space made it impossible to include everything I would have liked to include, I have concentrated on genetic epistemology, discussions about general issues concerning this science and Piaget's core-concepts. The use of recent publications has made me leave out many important discussions, e.g. that between Bruner and Piaget.

As for the psychogenesis of knowledge I have tried to find central themes and theoretical solutions of Piaget's critics, referring readers to overviews of experiments instead of giving them myself. Where I mention experiments I have preferred to discuss a few of them in some detail to illustrate the problems involved. Even so the reader will repeatedly encounter the phrase: "due to limitations of space...". Due to all the restrictions mentioned the final selection of critics and their theoretical background is a very personal one.

Cross-references between Volumes I and II are given in small print, at the beginning of a chapter and in the text where relevant. Thus the reader is not obliged to read all of Volume I first but may turn to relevant critical arguments whenever his main interest is directed at the critique.

Some practical points

In Volume I Piaget's text has been summarized in normal-sized print. Relatively long quotations have been indented as well as examples. To differentiate the two as clearly as possible the word "example" has been printed before examples. All the examples given have been taken from Piaget's publications. Small print gives cross-references as well as my personal comments.

In Volume II small print indicates cross-references and expressions of my appreciation for authors who have kindly helped me. The latter have been included in the text instead of the Preface because experience shows that many readers do not read the Preface.

The list of references in Volume I only contains publications by Piaget and contributions of Piaget to discussions, interviews, etc. They are given in the chronological order of the original publications followed by the title, etc. of the translation into English. Because of the great number of publications in the same year the usual system of 1965a, 1965b, etc. has been replaced by numbers. In Volume II the same system has also been used for the sake of consistency. In the text these numbers are printed in bold type. Where two pages are mentioned (separated by /) the first refers to the original and the second to the translation. With one exception (74) the original is in French, the translation in English. Where only one page reference is given, a glance at the list of references will show whether this is a French or English publication.

There is one index in Volume II. As the page numbers allow the reader to see at a glance whether the text can be found in Volume I or II, this need not cause any difficulties. Where Piaget is referred to in Volume II his name has been added. Definitions given in the text can be found under the concept which has been defined or under the heading "Definitions". To facilitate finding them in the text they have been printed in italics.

Contents of Volume I

Foreword vii
Preface ix
A Guide to Reading This Book xii

A ‖ Introduction

1 Introducing Genetic Epistemology, Piaget, Some Critics, and Myself

theory of knowledge

1.1 The Genesis of Genetic Epistemology 4
1.2 Piaget: A One-Man Interdisciplinary Team . . 5
1.3 Criticizing Piaget's Writings . . . . . (7)
1.4 My Own Point of View 7
    1.4.1 Piaget's Writing 7
    1.4.2 Piaget's Theory . . . . . . (9)

2 Conservation and Transformation Within Piaget's Theory

2.1 In Defence of a Constructivist Genetic Epistemology . 10
2.2 The Two Phases of Genetic Epistemology . . . 11
    2.2.1 The Study of Structures 11
    2.2.2 The Study of Functioning 12

B ‖ Genetic Epistemology

3 Piaget's Genetic Epistemology as an Interdisciplinary Science

3.1 Scientific Epistemology 21
    3.1.1 The Development of Scientific Epistemologies . 21
    3.1.2 The Main Characteristics of Scientific
           Epistemologies 22

3.2 Philosophy and Epistemology 24
3.3 Genetic Epistemology and its Methods . . . 25
    3.3.1 The Historico-Critical Approach . . . 26
    3.3.2 The Psychogenetic Approach 27
    3.3.3 Common Mechanisms in the Development of
         Sciences and of Cognitive Psychogenesis . . 28
3.4 Genetic Epistemology and other Sciences . . . 29
    3.4.1 Genetic Epistemology and Sciences Giving
         Data and Theories about Man
         ("les sciences de l'homme") 30
    3.4.2 Genetic Epistemology and Sciences offering
         Models 33
3.5 A Summarizing Description of Genetic Epistemology . 36

4 Piaget and Other Epistemologies

4.1 Piaget's Classification of Epistemologies . . . 38
4.2 Piaget's Overview of Other Epistemologies and his
    Arguments against them 38
    4.2.1 Metascientific Epistemologies 38
    4.2.2 Parascientific Epistemology (Husserl) . . . 41
    4.2.3 Scientific Epistemologies 42
    4.2.4 Nativism and Maturationism 44

5 The Core-Concepts of Piaget's Epistemology

5.1 Constructivism, Realism and Interactionism . . . 46
    5.1.1 Constructivism 46
    5.1.2 Realism 49
    5.1.3 Interactionism 51
5.2 Structures and Procedures 52
    5.2.1 Structures 53
    5.2.2 Procedures 58
    5.2.3 Structures and Procedures 59
    5.2.4 The Final Question: "Do Structures Exist?" . . 60
5.3 Action, Functions, Equilibration 62
    5.3.1 Action, Action Schemes and Operations . . 62
    5.3.2 The Functions of Assimilation and
         Accommodation 64
    5.3.3 Equilibration 67
    5.3.4 Organization 68
5.4 The Driving Forces of Development 70

C ‖ The Psychogenetic Construction of Knowledge

6 Piaget's Way of Tackling Problems of Cognitive Development

6.1 General Aspects of Research 75
   6.1.1 Verification and Experimentation in
          Psychology 75
   6.1.2 Explanation 77
6.2 Piaget's Research on Cognitive Development . . 80
   6.2.1 The Usual Type of Experimentation . . . 80
   6.2.2 Training Experiments 85

7 The Object in the Subject-Object Interaction

7.1 Physical Reality and Knowledge 87
   7.1.1 The Figurative Aspect of Knowledge . . . 88
   7.1.2 Causality 100
7.2 Other Subjects and Knowledge 111
   7.2.1 Egocentrism 112
   7.2.2 Social Transmission 113

8 The Subject in the Subject-Object Interaction

8.1 Understanding and Transforming 118
   8.1.1 Introducing Abstraction and Generalization . . 118
   8.1.2 Introducing Conscious Thought 120
   8.1.3 The Development of Abstraction and
          Generalization 123
8.2 Correspondences and Morphisms 136
   8.2.1 Introducing Correspondences, Morphisms
          and Categories 136
   8.2.2 The Development of Correspondences and
          their Relation with Transformations . . . 137
8.3 Success and Understanding 141

9 A Model for Development: Equilibration

9.1 What is in Equilibrium with What? 144
   9.1.1 Assimilation and Accommodation . . . 144
   9.1.2 Affirmation and Negations 145
9.2 What Causes Disequilibrium? 147

9.3 Reactions to Disequilibrium   149
    9.3.1 Non-Adaptive Reactions to Disequilibrium   .   .   149
    9.3.2 Adaptive Reactions to Disequilibrium:
         Regulations and Compensations   .   .   .   150
9.4 Improving Equilibration   156
    9.4.1 Improving Equilibration in General   .   .   156
    9.4.2 Details of the Interaction Between Subject
         and Object in Equilibration   .   .   .   157
    9.4.3 Progressive Compensations   .   .   .   163
9.5 Is Equilibration Empirically Verifiable?   .   .   .   165
9.6 Does the Theory of Equilibration Describe or
    Explain?   167

10 The Highest Level of Equilibration: Differentiations
    and Integration

10.1 Differentiation and Integration in Generalization   .   .   170
10.2 The Possible and the Necessary   172
    10.2.1 The Mechanisms Leading to New
          Possibilities   174
    10.2.2 The Mechanisms Leading to Necessity   .   .   177
    10.2.3 The Relationship Between the Possible and
          the Necessary and its Development   .   .   .   179
    10.2.4 The Relationship Between the Possible,
          the Necessary and Operations   .   .   .   182
10.3 Dialectics   183
    10.3.1 The Dialectic of Predicates, Concepts,
          Judgements and Inferences: a Genetic
          Study (**113**)   185
    10.3.2 Dialectics in General   187

11 A New Look at Old Friends

11.1 Stages   190
    11.1.1 The Six Stages of Infant Development   .   .   191
    11.1.2 Stages in the Experiments   .   .   .   191
    11.1.3 The Main Stages of Development   .   .   .   192
11.2 The Sensorimotor Stage   194
    11.2.1 Is the Process of Equilibration the Same
          as in the Later Stages?   194
    11.2.2 The Permanent Object   200

11.3 The Pre-Operational Stage 203
    11.3.1 Identity 204
    11.3.2 Mathematical Functions 206
    11.3.3 Empirical Reversibility (= Revertibility) and
           Operational Reversibility (= Reversibility) . 208
    11.3.4 What is ''Pre-Operational'' About the
           Pre-Operational Child? 209
11.4 The Stage of Concrete Operations 211
    11.4.1 Conservation 212
    11.4.2 Class-Inclusion 219
    11.4.3 Seriation and Transitivity 221
    11.4.4 Logico-Arithmetical Structures . . . 224
    11.4.5 Logico-Geometrical Structures . . . 225
11.5 The Stage of Formal Operations 226
    11.5.1 The Nature of Formal Operations . . . 226
    11.5.2 Recent Research on Formal Operations . . 228

D ‖ The Biological Foundation of Knowledge

12 Organic and Cognitive Regulations

12.1 Piaget's Guiding Hypothesis 234
12.2 Structures and Functions 234
    12.2.1 Structural and Functional Isomorphisms . . 234
    12.2.2 A Comparison of the Functions and Structures
           of the Organism and Cognition . . . 236
12.3 Structures and the Brain 243

13 Biological and Cognitive Phenocopies

13.1 Piaget's Critique of Lamarckism and
    Neo-Darwinism 245
    13.1.1 Lamarckism 245
    13.1.2 Neo-Darwinism 247
13.2 Piaget's Theory of Evolution 248
    13.2.1 Phenocopies 248
    13.2.2 The Cognitive Equivalent of Phenocopies . 251

References 255
List of Translations 263

Contents of Volume II

A′ ‖ Introduction

14 What and How to Criticize

B′ ‖ Genetic Epistemology

15 Philosophy, Epistemology and Genetic Epistemology
16 Genetic Epistemology as an Interdisciplinary Science
17 Critique of Piaget's Core-Concepts

C′ ‖ The Psychogenetic Construction of Knowledge

18 The Object in the Subject-Object Interaction
19 The Subject in the Subject-Object Interaction
20 The Processes of Development
21 New Attacks on Old Enemies
22 Critique of Piaget's Way of Tackling Problems

D′ ‖ The Biological Foundation of Knowledge

23 Biology and Knowledge

E′ ‖ Piaget's Open System

24 Conclusion

References
Index

A | Introduction

1 Introducing Genetic Epistemology, Piaget, some Critics and Myself

☐This chapter has no strict counterpart in Volume II. Chapter 14 introduces the attacks on Piaget's theory and some other relevant chapter sections of Volume II are mentioned in small print within the present chapter.

Piaget's whole life as a scientist has been dominated by two preoccupations which he describes as follows,

"the search for the mechanisms of biological adaptation and the analysis of that higher form of adaptation which is scientific thought, the epistemological interpretation of which has always been my central aim" (**109**, p.XI)

These preoccupations are linked by the study of the psychogenesis of knowledge. Thus Piaget is a psychologist but only in so far as this science helps him to answer epistemological questions concerning the development of knowledge. This gives us a very vague and preliminary description of *"genetic epistemology"* as *a science studying the conditions that make the development of knowledge possible.* I shall elaborate this in Chapter 3. For the time being it should show us that this book emphasizes genetic epistemology, taking Piaget's claim that he is a "genetic epistemologist" seriously.

However, before having a closer look at Piaget's genetic epistemology —specifically the development of his theory from 1965 on—it might be worthwhile to summarize the genesis of genetic epistemology. This summary will be followed by a description of the way Piaget works and writes, because many criticisms are not directed at his theory but at his style of writing. Finally some remarks about my own point of view are given. As I cannot offer a theory of my own, I think that my point of view has no importance. However, experience has taught me that some readers will be irritated by Volume I if I try to leave myself completely out of the picture. Thus this chapter forms a rather personal and unscientific introduction that is totally uncharacteristic of the "scientific" 'exposé of Piaget's theory in Volume I and the overview of critiques in Volume II.

1.1 The Genesis of Genetic Epistemology

Piaget's autobiography clearly shows how his early work was influenced by his French-speaking background and French type of secondary school ("lycée"). When still an adolescent schoolboy Piaget studied philosophy and psychology under the stimulating, thought-provoking guidance of the logician Reymond. Though Piaget had already published a number of articles on his detailed research on molluscs (particularly pond snails), his interest now turned to philosophy, specifically epistemology. Under the influence of Reymond he decided to specialize in biological philosophy (**15**, p.14/p.7). However, Piaget's plans soon became more ambitious after his biological studies and he felt he wanted to write a general book on the theory of knowledge seen from a biological standpoint. His biological background had made the young Piaget a scientist and therefore he decided—against the advice of his mentor Reymond—to begin by studying experimental psychology during a couple of semesters in order to analyse the relations between organic life and knowledge (**15**, p.15/p.8).

Piaget was allowed to work in the institute of the late Binet during 1919-1921, and when the Swiss psychologist Claparède invited him in 1921 to come to Geneva he thought that studies in child psychology might be useful for a period of some five years. In a sense this intention was carried out, because his appointment in 1925 to Reymond's chair in Neuchâtel meant a teaching load of psychology, philosophy of science, sociology and a philosophy seminar. Piaget hoped that all this would bring him closer to epistemology.

When he returned to Geneva in 1929 it was as Professor of the History of Scientific Thought, but he also continued his research in child psychology. Though the latter extended over far more than the five years of his original planning, Piaget has never given up his ideal of a genetic epistemology, in which psychology would be the link between his two interests.

His ideal took a more realistic shape when he used the results of his research for writing a three-tome work on genetic epistemology, published in 1949-50. This book already showed that genetic epistemology could not only link biology and psychology to epistemology, but was also truly interdisciplinary. Such interdisciplinarity has always remained a characteristic of Piaget's work.

☐The interdisciplinary aspect of Piaget's work is criticized in 16.1.

1.2 Piaget: A One-Man Interdisciplinary Team

The interdisciplinary nature of genetic epistemology might have become less pronounced or have been limited to fewer sciences if Piaget's own interests had not extended over so many domains of science.

Having started his career as a biologist, he kept up his interest in those problems of biology that are linked to his epistemological approach. After turning to psychology, Piaget was a biologist, epistemologist and psychologist. Then his interest turned to logic, mathematics and physics, because the history of these sciences was essential for his historico-critical method, and because of the models logic gave to genetic epistemology. Finally he wrote about cybernetics and artificial intelligence. If Piaget was asked how he possibly became such a "generalist", he answered that he rather had an "encyclopedic ignorance", but that the interdisciplinary Centre d'Epistémologie Génétique, founded in 1956, gave him a chance to learn from everybody. Watching how he learned, taught others to learn as well (**74**, p.50(English)/p.97(French)).

☐A critique of his "encyclopedic ignorance" is given in 16.3.

In fact, though Piaget himself is a sort of one-man interdisciplinary team, his work is only possible because he has been head of the Centre since 1956. This is so important that a brief description of Piaget's style of working there seems required.

At the Centre a number of specialists from different disciplines cooperate. Piaget chooses a central topic and frame for the work to be done that year. Every week there is a meeting of the team, guests, interested collaborators and assistants. After an introduction by one of the participants, there is a general discussion which is very productive because the same general topic and often the same concepts, e.g. causality, are elaborated from the point of view of different disciplines (**108**, p.114ff). All those years Piaget led the discussions without being handicapped by too much technical knowledge (**108**, p.116). When the reader of one of his books wonders why Piaget never quotes details of publications, the answer is usually that the topic was discussed in this team. This way of working is so self-evident for him that he quotes in a recent book, "As Henriques said...", leaving the reader wondering who Henriques might be.

While the topic of the year is thus discussed theoretically from many viewpoints, assistants are working on experiments. Their experiences and preliminary results are regularly reported in the group, thus giving Piaget a chance to know what is going on and to evaluate this together with the other members of the team. At the end of the year there is a symposium and then Piaget begins to work on the preliminary reports and the protocols, writing up the results in a book.

When analysing the protocols, Piaget is very much influenced by his search for something new. Every experiment within a series on the same topic is carefully explored until he finds a new aspect of a former notion or a totally new idea. This is acceptable when it is consistent with the main trends of his theory. After this the publication of these detailed analyses is important in order to allow for verifications. Though Piaget emphasizes this need of verification, he does, in fact, write to clarify his own ideas without taking the reader into account— not to mention the translator. Many years ago Piaget said that he would have written differently if he had realized that his books would be translated. Yet, he never changed his very long and complicated sentences, with an unlimited use of parentheses, or his tendency to make new words without giving a clear definition, etc.

However, not all of what is often considered Piaget's vagueness, is determined by his lack of interest in the reader. Piaget does not believe in the value of passive absorption of what a teacher communicates. He wants his "pupils" of whatever level to think for themselves, and to make their own discoveries (e.g. **103**, p.132). In a discussion with Bringuier (**200**) one of Piaget's team-members, Rafel Carreras, made a very nice comparison. If one puts a transparent piece of paper on top of a photograph and then traces the photograph with a pencil, one has the feeling of succeeding very well. Yet, when the paper is taken off, one sees that essential parts are missing. What Piaget gives others, even his collaborators, is the tracing, and not the photograph. Another reason for giving an incomplete image is that Piaget thinks in very large units. He has ideas about fundamental issues but he does not parcel them out into elements that are small enough for others to absorb (as Cellerier says in the same discussion, **200**, p.120). His collaborators in the Centre and the University are able to help each other in reconstructing a "photograph", though not necessarily the one Piaget had in mind. And this is exactly what he hopes for. In 1976 he wrote that he was convinced that he had given a general skeleton of a theory that was nearly evident, but still full of lacunae. Filling in these lacunae would then lead to many differentiations that might be integrated in the whole without contradicting the major principles and the broad outline of the system (**98**, p.223).

A look at the work of Piaget's "school" clearly shows that his collaborators and followers are indeed hard at work at filling in the holes while keeping within the general framework of a constructivist theory: Inhelder and her team are concentrating on strategies, Cellerier on the integration of Piagetian constructivism and artificial intelligence, Sinclair and her team on psycholinguistics, Gillièron on methodological research, Mounoud and Montangero on infant research, etc. In fact, to do justice to Piaget's importance this book should have included a third volume on these developments, but limitations of space and time made that impossible.

1.3 Criticizing Piaget's Writings

As Volume II shows, one can criticize Piaget's theory on many levels. For the time being I shall only mention the superficial complaint, found in many publications, that Piaget writes too much, that his writings are unclear, that there are many contradictions between parts of different publications or even within the same book, that he writes whole books instead of concise articles, and so forth.

Finally we find the complaint that his theoretical writings are generally so repetitive, prolix and opaque that they defy translation; they can only be transliterated (Johnson-Laird, **302**).

1.4 My Own Point of View

1.4.1 Piaget's Writing

Having spent some years on a staple diet of Piaget's own publications in order to exclude an influence from other points of view or interpretations, I can heartily agree with anyone who complains about his style of writing. It is relatively easy to understand the main trends of his theory, but one often becomes confused when trying to understand every single paragraph. I think that Droz and Rahmy gave excellent advice when suggesting that the average reader could just skip problematic paragraphs. Mentioning Droz and Rahmy takes me to the next point, that of translations. Their book is called *Lire Piaget* (**227**). The title of the translation, *Understanding Piaget*, is hopelessly misleading. Droz and Rahmy do tell the reader how to find his way in the labyrinth of Piaget's publications, but they give no help for understanding his theory. This is just one example of a disservice often done by publishers, causing disappointment to the reader whose expectations are not met. While this aspect of translations might easily be avoided, the difficulty of translating Piaget is a far greater obstacle for readers who cannot read the original. Translators should be versed in Piaget's theory, and in both French and English. As even those translators who combine the three conditions repeatedly make slips, one can see what happens when a translation is hastily and superficially done by someone less capable. Any reader of a recent translation who comes to the conclusion that at the time of writing Piaget was really becoming very old, may be reassured that the original is as ''clear'' as any of his books ever were.

I would like to add another point on Piaget's writing style which is related to his concentration on one specific topic and his constant search for something new, on the one hand, and to his disregard for his readers, on the other. I am referring to his tendency to make general and positive statements that go beyond what he would say if he was thinking more profoundly about the topic. His reader, without a profound knowledge of Piaget's work, may well take these strong pronouncements too literally.

> **Illustration:** When Piaget and Inhelder wrote that the child is ''completely'' egocentric (**9**), this was never meant to be taken literally, as Piaget's other writings on egocentricity clearly show. However, the experiment on the model of three mountains, which was intended to study the child's understanding of perspective, not of egocentricity, began to lead a life of its own. ''Is the child so egocentric?'', ''Is the child able to understand an easier version of the task at an earlier age?'', etc.

In summary, my opinion is that there are many passages in Piaget's publications that are vague, contradictory, too strongly expressed, etc. But the problem is to know when this weakness of his writing invalidates his theory and when it is indeed no more than a style of writing causing his readers extra difficulties. When ''contradictions'' are real, they should surely be exposed, but contradictions in different books may well be due to a change in point of view or to overgeneralization. Anyone doing Piagetian research should therefore study all of Piaget's writings on a topic, admittedly a hard job considering that his French books have no index. As for translations, I think that any serious student, either pro- or anti-Piaget should be able to find someone who can read French. Many quite incomprehensible paragraphs are only incomprehensible because of serious errors in the translation. I am convinced that any of the justified criticisms of Piaget's style of writing do not invalidate his theory. In other words, any scientific evaluation should carefully distinguish between occasions where Piaget's tendency to jump to conclusions and to overgeneralize weakens or invalidates his theory and those passages where he was carried away by enthusiasm. Admittedly it is sometimes difficult to draw the line between the two.

1.4.2 Piaget's Theory

I shall go into the critique of Piaget's theory in Volume II, so I shall just give some personal remarks here. I am convinced that Piaget asks the right questions. However, this is no guarantee that the answers are right and it is certainly not my intention to defend Piaget's theory at any cost. He would not like that, though he sometimes gives the impression of having an easy answer to every attack. Having an open mind for theoretical and/or empirical weaknesses means that one should, on the one hand, show up misrepresentations and misinterpretations that do not justify the attack built on them. On the other hand, the more interesting issues, that go much deeper than that, should not be glossed over. When they are criticized, many readers will want to know for sure, when and where Piaget is wrong. But anyone expecting a definitive answer will be disappointed. I am convinced that one can only give such an answer on the basis of an epistemology and a theory of one's own. When thinking about that, I am often reminded of Piaget's frequent quotations of Gödel's theorem. If one can only evaluate a theory on the basis of the next higher theory, then one would need a theory going beyond Piaget in order to give definitive answers. If I could write such a theory, I would most certainly not have spent my time on this book. What I hope to do, then, is to stimulate a discussion on fundamental issues, not to give the answer.

2 Conservation and Transformation within Piaget's Theory

□As this chapter gives an overview of Volume I the whole of Volume II is a critique of the content of this chapter. Therefore there are no specific references to Volume II.

According to Piaget's theory the organization of any organism is characterized by conservations and transformations. In the same way core-concepts of Piaget's genetic epistemology have remained the same and were conserved during the many years of his scientific career, while other notions were added, differentiated or transformed. A consequence of Piaget's tremendous output is that it is hard not to get lost in all the transformations. Therefore this chapter gives an overview of what will be elaborated in Volume I. Terms are not defined as this is done in later chapters. In this chapter, I follow the chronological development of his theory using prefaces of his books and Piaget's autobiographies (e.g. in **15, 74, 99**) in an effort to trace how he went from one problem to the next. This seemed useful as I tried to organize Volume I in cohesive chapters without adhering to a strictly chronological order. Because Volume I gives an overview of Piaget's work I have not always added his name but "genetic epistemology" means "Piaget's genetic epistemology", "constructivism" means "Piaget's constructivism", etc.

2.1 In Defence of a Constructivist Genetic Epistemology

Piaget's work is largely determined by his efforts to convince others that genetic epistemology—that is, the study of how knowledge develops—is a legitimate subject for scientific research and theorizing. Thus Volume I begins with 1965, the year in which *Insights and Illusions* was published. In this book Piaget defends his approach against the frequent attacks of philosophers (**15**).

However, he does not only have to defend the claims of genetic epistem-ology as a science, but also his constructivist-structuralist-functionalist epistemology itself. His whole work is one long attack against empiricism/positivism and nativism, combined by him into "preformism", while defending constructivism. Because this is the driving force that is still explicitly mentioned in his most recent books, it is wrong to consider him a child psychologist as many simplifying introductions do, or an "educational psychologist" as is fashionable in the United States.

2.2 The Two Phases of Genetic Epistemology

Piaget himself distinguishes two phases in the development of his genetic epistemology. In the first one he concentrated on structures and in the second on functions. Perhaps his most recent work at the Inter-national Centre of Genetic Epistemology is a third phase with a return to logic. But if that impression is correct, it is a more gradual change than that from the first to the second phase.

2.2.1 The Study of Structures

In 1968 Piaget wrote a book on structuralism as an approach which is found in many sciences (**39**). He himself had used the concept of structure since his days as a young biologist. His interest in the structures of the psychogenesis of knowledge was directed at the common characteristics of structures of subjects (i.e. persons) who are at the same developmental level. To indicate this he coined the name "the epistemic subject". For years he studied the logico-mathematical structures as well as children's notions of time, velocity, space, etc. But though he described in detail these structures and their developmental stages, the concept of structures itself was not as clear as one might wish. Thus he described logico-mathematical structures by the properties of groupings and groups. This makes them sound like mathematical structures. But the structures are the structures that underlie the child's behaviour and determine what he can do. It is only the scientist who formalizes them, the child or adolescent having no conscious knowledge of groupings or groups. So there does seem to be a difference between structures as described by mathematical structura-lists and those of the child. As we shall see in Chapter 5, Piaget's concept of structures has become more and more functional in recent years. But that is a development of the second period of his work. As I said, during the first phase he studied structures of intelligence at different age levels.

2.2.2 The Study of Functioning

In 1967 Piaget published *Biology and Knowledge* in which he looked for isomorphisms between biological structures and functions, and cognitive structures and functions. For the biological organism he found that functions and functioning were as important as structures. Furthermore, the process of equilibration was again emphasized. Piaget had published a theory of equilibration in 1957, but a few years later he was already dissatisfied with it. As he never published his critical arguments against his own theory, it is still attacked by his opponents. It took Piaget until 1975 to publish a new theory (**90**) though many aspects of it had been briefly mentioned in *Biology and Knowledge*.

> ☐It is quite fascinating to read Piaget's books in reverse chronological order. There are in every early book short ''indications'' that one does not notice unless one is sensitized to them by the later books. Piaget is so productive and imaginative that he always had far more ideas than he had time to elaborate. So it was often years before he wrote a book on what had been a fleeting notion earlier in his life.

Biology and Knowledge showed that Piaget had not given up his biological interest when turning to psychology as an instrument for answering epistemological questions. In the following years he divided his interest and time between epistemological/psychological research and theorizing—done with the help of the international team of the Centre and his collaborators at the University—and his personal biological interest. The latter led to two books on evolution: *Adaptation vitale et intelligence* (**83**) and *Behavior and Evolution* (**96**). They are both purely speculative, as he recognizes himself. But, though he had hoped that biologists would consider them a challenge and enter the discussion, they never did.

> ☐In Volume I the biological aspect of Piaget's theory has been left to the end, not because I do not think it important, but because it is easier to understand after the overview of the psychogenesis of knowledge.

A look at the publications of the years after *Biology and Knowledge* shows a number of general books (**33, 39, 48, 49, 50, 51, 55**) and some publications on rather specific topics: *Memory and Intelligence*, with Inhelder (**36**) was the sequel to the book entitled *Mental Imagery in the*

Child which had been published in 1966 (**24**). It signified the conclusion of Piaget's research on the figurative aspect of knowledge.

In the same year two volumes of the *Etudes d'épistémologie génétique* summarized the work of the Centre on functions (in the mathematical sense) (**37**) and identity (**38**). It is as though Piaget had not yet found the next fundamental issue when planning the research done on these topics. However, from about 1965 on, the research got under way, full-speed this time, with about 100 experiments on causality.

Piaget had been studying the causal notions of children as early as 1927 (**2**). It is interesting that he then explicitly wanted to limit himself to psychology, studying the relations between the child's thinking and reality such as our present-day science sees it. That reality is taken as an absolute. Not surprisingly he said many years later (**108**, p.93) that the problem had not been well formulated and that he had, therefore, returned to it. In 1971 he published a book *Understanding Causality* (**58**), based on ± 100 experiments of which many have been published in detail (**17-21, 65, 66, 72, 73** and three more volumes yet to be published). His main hypothesis—sometimes called a fact—is that causal explanations of the way objects act on each other, are due to the attribution of the subject's structures to objects. Causal explanations are one type of explanation, the other type consisting in the finding of reasons. A reason is an answer to the question "Why?", where this cannot be answered by a causal explanation.

> **Example:** Piaget often gives the example that $4 - 2 = 2$ if $2 + 2 = 4$. The latter may be considered a "reason" for the former, but it is not a "cause".

Though Piaget had already written about the difference between causes and reasons in 1963 (**14**) his study of causality did not lead right away to that of reasons. Any problem which is temporarily solved, like that of causality, raises many new problems, and so Piaget first followed another path.

The research on causality had shown, once again, the essential role played by actions in the construction of early structures. But it also showed how much later the child can conceptualize than he can act correctly. Though the child's acts are correct and though he can even make many correct predictions, he cannot verbalize what he just did perfectly well. So this problem was taken up in a separate study on consciousness, published in 1974. In the first volume, *The Grasp of Consciousness* (**85**), the tasks were easy for the child and the question studied was when he might be able to verbalize what he had been doing. This does not mean that there is no consciousness at an earlier age than that of the children studied (the youngest being 4 years old). Rather, this earlier consciousness is a sort of awareness, while Piaget is interested in conceptualization which is only found around 7 years old as the experiments showed. In the second volume (86) practical intelligence was studied, the question being what the relation is between finding a solution and conceptualizing it. Though there is always an epistemological aspect in the problems studied by Piaget the research on consciousness and the solution of problems was more psychological than other research. In general, this kind of problem does not concern the epistemic subject, but the psychological subject—that which subjects of the same developmental level have in common in their mechanisms and functioning which lead to the construction of knowledge and the solution of problems.

Solving practical problems implies that reasons are found for what one is doing and so the book entitled *Success and Understanding* (86) formed the starting point for a great deal of research on that topic. But before that, there were more urgent problems.

The time-lag between successful actions and conceptualization, Piaget's thinking about dialectical trends in development, as well as the actuality of dialectics, all contributed to the decision to study contradictions. The research, published in *Recherches sur la contradiction* (84) convinced Piaget that his dialectical thinking and constructivist structuralism might well be combined with a new way of looking at contradictions. Contradictions are neither an internal necessity of thought—as many dialecticists believe—nor a sort of accident, due to poor formalization. They are, in fact, an expression of disequilibrium due to the fact that at the beginning of life our perceptions and notions are directed toward positive aspects of reality. The lack of reciprocal adjustment of positive and negative factors, inevitably, leads to contradictions, even though the young child need not experience them as such.

Contradictions play an important role in equilibration. In *The Development of Thought* (90) Piaget tries to give a causal model for the mechanisms or functions of development. Assimilation and accommodation are still the basis but they work at several levels. The central notion is compensation, and here the link with contradictions becomes evident. A pre-eminence of affirmations must be compensated by the construction of negations.

In general, equilibration is an alternation of periods of relative equilibrium and disequilibrium. The next period of equilibrium is then of a "higher" level than the earlier one and therefore the process is called "équilibration majorante" ("improving equilibration"). The "higher" level is higher because a structure with a greater number of sub-structures is more stable, and because the environment with which the subject interacts extends.

If the process implies a next higher level, this "regulation on regulations" is called "reflective abstraction" ("abstraction réfléchis-sante"). While the book on equilibration is purely theoretical, two volumes on reflective abstraction, *Recherches sur l'abstraction réfléchissante*, published in 1977 (**102**) are based on experiments like most of Piaget's books. Reflective abstraction is a regulation on regulations because it has two components. The first is compared to a projection of what had been constructed or "regulated" at the earlier level, on to the next one. The second component is a reconstruction of what had already been constructed, that is to say a regulation of what was regulated. In another terminology Piaget writes that the lower level is one of differentiations that must then be integrated at the higher level. The differentiations open up new possibilities, while the integration gives us necessities. This topic had to be elaborated, but, once more, there were other urgent topics.

The books on reflective abstraction also take up the aspect of consciousness, now with the question about how far the subject becomes conscious of the structures underlying his actions, though consciousness evidently does not mean formalization. When the subject becomes conscious of the way he acted, Piaget calls this "reflected abstraction" ("abstraction réfléchie"), and when the subject becomes conscious of the operations and structures, he calls it "reflexive abstraction" ("abstraction réflexive") or "metareflexion". But this distinction is not always made. In general, making operations the object of one's conscious thought is called "thematization".

Thematization has become an important concept in recent years because Piaget's interest has turned more and more to the thinking of scientists. This is very clear in *Recherches sur la généralisation* (**110**) which followed in 1978. Reflective abstractions always lead to constructive generalizations and Piaget gives many examples from several sciences, though the experiments were done with children and adolescents. Piaget's interest in scientific thought also led to a book on the common mechanisms of children's thought and scientific thought. This book, which is being written in collaboration with the physicist Garcia, is the only one that could not be included in Volume I as the manuscript was not available on 1 January 1980—the closing date indicated in my title.

When Piaget is working on a "topic of the year" there is usually a paper or article before the book comes out.

☐These publications are often very useful because they contain all the main notions without making the reader lose his way in the abundance of empirical data. Piaget himself regrets it when readers skip them!

This is the case for the topics of recent years though the manuscripts of the books could be used in the overview.

☐From **117** of the list of references on, no page numbers are given, because there is not yet a printed text, at the time of writing.

A new topic was inspired by recent developments in mathematics. In the study of structures, Piaget had found three types of logico-mathematical structures: groupings based on reversibility through inversion (classification), groupings based on reversibility through reciprocity (seriation), and infralogical (logico-geometrical) structures. These structures corresponded closely to the three "mother-structures" elaborated by a group of mathematicians calling them-selves Bourbaki. Their "mother-structures" were "algebraic structures", "structures of order" and "topological structures". The close correspondence was very satisfactory for Piaget, as he had elaborated children's structures independently. But mathematics developed and McLane and Eilenberg and others constructed morphisms. This progress illustrates very well what Piaget means by thematizations of what were used as instruments at lower levels. Bourbaki had used morphisms to find their "mother-structures" but without producing a theory of morphisms. McLane and Eilenberg then used the same morphisms to build the next higher level of theory, that of morphisms and categories. This development also illustrates how structures of a certain level become part of the next higher structure, but without "disappearing". Bourbaki structures are still available, notwithstanding the construction of morphisms. In the same way adolescents can still use groupings though they have integrated them into the INRC-group.

The main characteristic of morphisms is that they are not concerned with transformations but comparisons. The mathematics of morphisms becomes very abstract. There are always "objects" and comparisons between them. But the objects can be anything—objects, sets, groups—and the mathematician is not interested in their nature. What he is interested in are the operations one performs on them and their comparisons (mappings of one set of elements on to another one). Morphisms are represented by arrows: "From where does the arrow go, to where?" "How can these arrows be composed?" etc. Thus there are rules for the compositions of morphisms and these lead to morphisms on morphisms, or categories.

There is, evidently, a tremendous gap between these highly abstract mathematics and any related tasks one might give children. But what interested Piaget was the way children compare objects in contrast to transforming them. Thus a number of experiments were done on comparisons of different levels (120, 121). The final conclusion was that comparing and transforming are the two main functions of reasoning. This sounds very new after Piaget's emphasis on transformations, but in the first place correspondences and transformations become very closely linked during development, and in the second place Piaget had all along written about correspondences and one-to-one correspondence, etc. without producing a theory about them.

Finally, an important development of Piaget's theory links differentiations/integration with success/understanding. As was already mentioned, differentiations lead to new possibilities and integration to necessity. In the solution of practical tasks (86) Piaget had found that children come to understand physical and logico-mathematical reality, but also to solve problems. In other words: there is a close link between the two poles of structures and procedures, tentatively formulated in an article with Inhelder, "Procédures et structures" (116). However, before that, Piaget studied differentiations which open up new possibilities (118) as well as integrations which lead to necessity (119). Integrations were found to be closely linked to "signifying implications" which were introduced earlier in the work on practical intelligence. Signifying implications began to interest Piaget more and more because he had always been opposed to paradoxical conclusions which one might reach through logical implication (material implication). Therefore the most recent topic of the Centre is the natural logic of finding reasons. But there are as yet no results available.

Before this development, a year was spent on the study of dialectics. Just as in his study of the possible and the necessary, the central problem for Piaget is again: "How do we construct new knowledge and how do these constructions develop?" The answer seems to be partly through deductions, as studied in the book on generalizations, but this is not fundamentally new knowledge. A new knowledge cannot be preformed but must be constructed. This construction has to be dialectical, though Piaget's meaning of the concept differs from Hegel's thesis-antithesis-synthesis.

This takes us to the present. It was my intention to show how many differentiations and transformations there were in the 15 years covered by this overview. But the main goal was "conserved": to show that constructivism is the only acceptable epistemology.

B ‖ Genetic Epistemology

3 Piaget's Genetic Epistemology as an Interdisciplinary Science

□In general, a critique of 3.1 and 3.2 is to be found in Chapter 15 and of 1.1 and 3.4 in Chapter 16.

Taking 1965 as the starting point of our overview of Piaget's genetic epistemology plunges us right into the discussions between Piaget and philosophers. *Insights and Illusions of Philosophy* (**15**) was written as an emotional protest against many French and Swiss philosophers. The heart of the matter is Piaget's conviction that philosophies can lead to wisdom while only sciences can give us truth. A further bone of contention is the fact that Piaget's scientific epistemology is a genetic epistemology which is interdisciplinary and closely linked to genetic (= developmental) psychology.

3.1 Scientific Epistemology

3.1.1 The Development of Scientific Epistemologies

Western philosophers have always been interested in the question of how knowledge is possible, but the study of this question has gradually become detached from that of other philosophical problems. Piaget describes this historical development in some detail in *Logique et connaissance scientifique*, a volume of an encyclopedia edited by Piaget and containing a number of contributions by himself (**33**).

Piaget distinguishes three periods in the history of epistemologies: metascientific epistemologies, parascientific epistemologies and scientific epistemologies (for details see Chapter 1 in **33**, and **15**).

Metascientific epistemologies were epistemologies of philosophers who were also scientists or used a contemporary science. The first rational Western thinkers who had freed themselves from the symbolic language of myths approached the problem of what knowledge is or how knowledge is possible from a philosophical as well as a scientific point of view. At first the philosophers themselves were scientists but later generations used discoveries and inventions of their time for the basis of their inquiries. Thus thinking about epistemological problems was done in a "scientific" way, while philosophers whose work was not related to science were interested in other domains of philosophy: metaphysics, ethics, aesthetics.

Parascientific epistemologies developed in the nineteenth century when many philosophers adopted a different attitude towards sciences. Philosophers of this category—which became more important in the beginning of the twentieth century—do accept the existence of sciences in their own right, but consider their results of restricted value. Therefore they try to find other, suprascientific, forms of knowledge. Notwithstanding his original admiration for Bergson, one of the representatives of this category, Piaget later criticized these philosophers very energetically.

Scientific epistemologies have only recently been developed. While "philosophy takes up a rational position to the whole of reality" (**15**, p.57/p.39), scientific epistemologies restrict themselves to problems concerning scientific knowledge, often only in a specific realm of science. Some of them are philosophers but many of them are specialized scientists—mathematicians, physicists, etc.—with an interest in epistemological problems. But notwithstanding the tendency of scientific epistemologists to delimit the problems studied "there is no difference in nature between philosophical and scientific cognitive problems" (**15**, p.65/p.45). Their fundamental difference is to be found in the methods used.

☐The claim that genetic epistemology can be a science is refuted by many authors. See 15.3.

3.1.2 The Main Characteristics of Scientific Epistemologies

Recent scientific epistemologies form the background for Piaget's genetic epistemology and so their main characteristics are important for understanding his theory. Piaget describes two characteristics: an interest in the changes in scientific knowledge, and an effort to arrive at the truth by methods of verification.

Emphasis on the changes in scientific knowledge is a recent development in epistemology. Classical epistemological theories asked how knowledge is possible, what the nature and the conditions are of logico-mathematical knowledge, empirical knowledge in physics, etc. Their common postulate was that knowledge is a fact and not a process. Even though they recognized that knowledge is never complete, epistemologists could study in a static way what had been acquired. But due to the emphasis on change in modern sciences, epistemologists have become more and more interested in changes, that is, in the process of developing knowledge (e.g. **33, 47, 78**). Within Piaget's constructivist theory this process can only be seen as a continuous construction and reorganization (e.g. **52**, p.2) leading from a state of lesser validity to a state of higher validity (e.g. **47**, p.247). Thus the development of sciences goes in a certain direction ("vection"). Even though there may be chance results with unexpected deviations or short-circuits, described as "paradigm-changes" by Kuhn, there must also be general, global directions, in the sense of integrations into more general systems. The latter notion evidently implies a disagreement with Kuhn's notion of arbitrary paradigm "revolutions" (**78**, p.22f). But these reflections have taken us to genetic epistemology to which I return in 3.3, and to constructivism, discussed in 5.1 and many parts of this volume.

Methods of verification are a fundamental requirement for any study which claims to be scientific and are therefore implied in a scientific epistemology. The methods of a scientist either consist of empirical research or of systematic deductions as in logic and mathematics. But whatever method is used, it should be publicly verifiable. This even influences the questions which can be asked by scientists because a question to which the answer cannot be verified by the scientist himself and by other researchers is not a scientific question at all. However, it does not limit sciences indefinitely because what cannot be verified today may well be verifiable in the near future. Verifications must lead to agreement amongst a number of scientists because a truth only exists as a truth "from the moment in which it has been verified (and not simply accepted) by other investigators" (**15**, p.22/p.12). In other words, a science requires objectivity, "all valid knowledge presupposes a decentration" (**15**, p.193/p.142). This decentration can only come about through collaboration with other scientists. Even when a scientist works in personal isolation he needs others to criticize his work, add to his ideas or stimulate him to check them and, perhaps, change them. Only through such cooperation can he arrive at the truth, that is, a truth which is valid at that moment.

☐ For critical arguments see 15.1.1 and 15.1.2.

In Piagetian terminology "the whole of the history of sciences is made up of decentrations" (**15**, p.193/p.143). But decentrations are always temporary, because sciences change. Even Einstein has only rid us of the last centrations—last until the next decentrations occur (**15**, p.194/p.143).

□The French "centration-décentration" has been translated both as centration-decentration, centering-decentering and centring-decentring. I shall mostly use centring-decentring, but also centration-decentration, mainly when quoting or using translations. The term "centring" has replaced Piaget's original "egocentricity" because egocentricity has led to the misunderstanding that Piaget was using a value-laden term in the sense of "egoism".

As often happens, Piaget uses the same term with two slightly different meanings. In writing about methods of verification Piaget uses centration in the sense of paying attention to one's own point of view, excluding that of others. In many other books he uses the same term when the subject pays attention to one aspect of a situation whilst neglecting another one. The best-known example is that of the non-conserver who looks only at the height of the water that has been poured into another glass and neglects to take into account the width of the glass. In Piaget's words: "he centres on the height". The common characteristic of the two ways in which the term is used is, of course, that of looking at the situation or problem in one way while the other possible way is neglected.

3.2 Philosophy and Epistemology

Though a completely autonomous and scientific epistemology would have the foregoing characteristics, Piaget has to admit that this ideal has not yet been reached. All scientists agree that the goal of their science is to attain an objective truth, but when the nature of this objective knowledge has to be specified—i.e. when the "epistemology" of the science must be formalized—the end of agreement is soon reached. For Piaget this means no more than that many epistemologies are still half-way between philosophy and the autonomous, scientific status which other epistemologists think desirable. But Piaget is inclined to gloss over the disagreements between epistemologists because of their common search for objectivity (**78**, p.14).

Comparing this situation with that of philosophy, one finds a very different picture in the latter. Even when writing in a less emotional vein than in *Insights and Illusions*, Piaget emphasizes the fundamental discord amongst philosophers concerning the goals and tasks of philosophy. This discord is not astonishing in view of the methods they use.

In contrast to the verifiable methods of scientists, philosophers use reflection, intuition, and sometimes introspection. Their most valuable method is "reflexive analysis" which allows the philosopher to discover and formulate new important problems, and is therefore indispensable for any modern scientist. As Piaget himself explicitly says, all the problems he has studied experimentally have been inspired by philosophy (**78**, p.18n). But, on the other hand, the results of philosophical reflection cannot be verified and so they can be no more than a coordination of values or wisdom. In attaining such wisdom, there is no need to decentre, and thus many different wisdoms can thrive at the same time, all being of equal value and being considered as absolute truth by philosophers. In contrast, in a science only one "true" knowledge is possible at a certain time, however approximate and restricted it may be in its level of elaboration. Though one might want to make a clear delineation between the wisdom of philosophy and the knowledge of sciences, there are, in fact, all sorts of mixtures between the two (**15**, p.291/p.219). Even Piaget's emphasis on the need for verification does not prevent him from speculating. However, he acknowledges it when doing so, e.g. in *Biology and Knowledge* (**32**), *Behavior and Evolution* (**96**), and *Procédures et structures* (**116**). In such cases his goal is not to get at scientific truth, but to stimulate discussions amongst scientists as a basis for future research.

□The relationship between philosophy and science is criticized in 15.1.2 and 15.1.3.

The conviction of having found absolute truth causes many philosophers to prescribe norms of what scientists should do and how they should do it, often criticizing the work of scientists without a close study of its factual subject-matter. Others consider the scientific facts and theories irrelevant, because the theory of knowledge studies the question of the validity of science, the criteria of this validity and its justification, independently of the sciences themselves (**52**, p.4). Piaget calls such an attitude "imperialistic", giving positivists like Comte and dialectical philosophers as examples. While Piaget is very much opposed to any form of positivism, he is far more tolerant towards dialecticians, but only as far as dialectical methods and notions of dialectical development are concerned (see 10.3), and as long as this does not imply an "imperialistic" dialectical philosophy (see 17.2.4).

3.3 Genetic Epistemology and its Methods

If an epistemologist emphasizes that the change of knowledge from states of lesser validity to states of greater validity is the subject of a scientific epistemology, his next step may well be to become a *"genetic epistemologist"*. *The goal of genetic epistemology is to link the validity of knowledge to the model of its construction.* Piaget's genetic epistemology has three aspects which are closely related to his methods of research.

3.3.1 The Historico-Critical Approach

One of the aspects of genetic epistemology is the study of the development of scientific knowledge using the historico-critical method. This is the popular method of French-speaking epistemologists which Piaget learned from Reymond and Brunschvicg (**15**, p.14/p.7; **33**, p.111ff).

The historico-critical method is more than a history of science enumerating the succession of discoveries through the ages. It requires a "critical" analysis—e.g. in order to dissociate the role played by deduction and by experience in the construction of a principle such as the physical principle of conservation. This analysis means more than deciding in general what can be deduced and found by experimental research. The historico-critical method consists of finding out how the inventor of a principle, or those who had prepared its discovery, actually worked. What sort of experiences (experiments or "mental experiences") did they use, what were their deductions, by which deductive or interpretative system did they find these experiences, etc.? It is not because of the "psychological" aspect of the scientists' work that these questions are important. Their answers throw light on all the problems concerning the relations between subject and object, and between mathematical deduction and physical experience, as well as those concerning the specific nature of these deductions and experiences and the processes of invention and discovery. Thus the historico-critical method is that method of epistemological analysis that uses the history of a science for the discussion of such problems (**33**, p.106).

Piaget gives numerous examples of this approach in several publications. A single one must suffice to give an impression of Piaget's reasoning.

> **Example of the historico-critical method:** Piaget uses a "free" summary of Boutroux's description of the development of mathematics as a starting point. The first level is called the "contemplative" period of Greek mathematics. In Piagetian terms, this period is characterized by the fact that mathematicians do not yet become conscious of the operations as activities of the subject (e.g. refusal of algebra). The second level is called "synthetic":

operations become conscious (algebra, analytic geometry, etc.). The third level is characterized by the construction of structures (from "groups" to the present synthesis). What is important is that this is not a chance succession but a kind of centripetal total direction, going from static mathematics projected on to objects (figures and numbers) to operational transformations executed by the subject, and ending in their present coordinations (**78**).

3.3.2 The Psychogenetic Approach

Though the historico-critical approach is essential, there are four reasons for adding the psychogenetic approach.

In the first place, an experimental verification is impossible in the historico-critical approach—interpretations of the facts therefore remaining speculative.

In the second place, one finds less and less data on man's thinking the further back one goes in history. Though prehistoric man must have had some kind of epistemology containing a view of reality and man's way of interacting with it, we just do not know anything about it.

In the third place, Piaget is convinced that we cannot understand adult natural and scientific cognitive structures unless we know how they have developed, that is, how they have been constructed. In Piaget's words,

"the child explains the man as well as and often better than the man explains the child...every adult, even if he is a creative genius, nevertheless began as a child, in pre-historic times as well as today."   (**23**, p.6ff/p.IX)

In the fourth place, a link between biological development and epistemology is required.

For all these reasons the psychogenetic approach is included by the genetic epistemologist who is looking for an answer to the epistemological question concerning how the essential notions or categories of thought develop. Originally Piaget wanted to study their development from birth to adulthood. In more recent work the psychogenetic approach has been extended to scientific thought, though not to that of the non-scientific adult. For Piaget the line of development goes from the child to the scientist. The average adult does not interest Piaget because his thinking has been influenced too much by the learning of scientific knowledge and technologies. Secondary-school curricula (at least in Switzerland, Piaget adds) teach so many facts that adults are no longer spontaneous in their thinking, and—what is worse—they lose the scientific way of thinking shown in adolescence unless the university teaches it anew (**15**, p.227/p.168). And, above all, the average adult is not creative or inventive. This does not mean that present-day children are not being influenced by the knowledge and technologies of their surroundings. It is just that, notwithstanding this influence, each of them has to construct his own cognitive instruments for solving the problems offered by the social and material surroundings (**112**, p.73), and it is this development that is studied by the psychogenetic aspect of genetic psychology.

☐The critique of the methods of psychogenetic research can be found in Chapter 22.

3.3.3 Common Mechanisms in the Development of Sciences and of Cognitive Psychogenesis

The two approaches mentioned so far can be profitably combined in the comparison of the development of a concept or theory in the history of science with that of the same concept or theory in the ontogenesis of present-day children. Such comparisons show that sometimes the sequence of the child's physical or physico-mathematical ideas does not correspond to the historical sequence of thought from the Greeks to the present, but to "the logical order that links the fundamental to the derived" (**71**, p.23). An example can be found in the development of the notions of space and geometry. More often, however, one does find a parallel between the individual and the historical development of a physical or physico-mathematical idea. Looking for such parallels certainly does not imply a revival of Haeckel's principle that onto-genesis repeats phylogenesis. There are three reasons why this would not make sense: in the first place, "notions" are not transmitted hereditarily; in the second place, there are no hereditary links between Aristotle and present-day subjects in Piagetian experiments; and in the third place, children's experiences come before those of adults (**112**, p.64).

When the genetic epistemologist compares "theories" from the past of a science with psychogenetic constructions, he uses cognitive achieve-ments of two different levels. The scientist reflects on his problem and consciously builds a theory, while the child has probably never reflected on the problem given in an experiment. Notwithstanding such differences the comparison shows that neither development is a linear sequence: both consist of a sequence of reconstructions of fore-going structures with an integration into later ones (**112**, p.65).

> □Piaget repeatedly gives such comparisons and often causes his readers serious difficulties due to their lack of knowledge of the history of mathematics or physics.

The combination of the historico-critical and the psychogenetic approach is not only of value for genetic epistemology itself, but also for other sciences. Taking mathematics as an example, it is evident that mathematicians all agree on the truth or correctness of operations and theorems. But they most certainly do not agree on such problems as the nature of number, structures, etc. With problems such as these genetic epistemology can help in finding the most acceptable answer (e.g. **29**, p.244).

3.4 Genetic Epistemology and other Sciences

For genetic epistemology interdisciplinary cooperation is absolutely indispensable.

In the first place, the historico-critical approach—either by itself or in combination with the psychogenetic approach—requires the cooperation of specialists in many realms of science: mathematics, physics, biology, etc.

In the second place, every scientist is influenced by his own epistemology when choosing his problems, methodology, etc. This influence is probably of little importance in sciences like mathematics but of far greater importance in all the "sciences of man".

> □ "Les sciences de l'homme" include psychology, sociology, history, linguistics, economics and law.

To study the relationship between the scientist's epistemology and the content of his science, knowledge of epistemology and of the science concerned is required.

In the third place, genetic epistemology needs the help of many sciences in studying the psychogenesis and sociogenesis of knowledge. This may imply a multidisciplinary cooperation in which scientists from different domains of science contribute to the understanding of a phenomenon without, however, influencing each other's work. A higher level of cooperation is reached in interdisciplinary work where scientists from different disciplines actively interact and influence each other's theories. For all the sciences mentioned in what follows, Piaget indicates such two-way interactions, but for reasons of space only the importance of other sciences for genetic epistemology will be summarized.

☐ Piaget sometimes writes on the relationship between genetic epistemology and other sciences, and sometimes on that between psychology and other sciences. As psychology has a central place in genetic epistemology there is no essential difference between the two approaches—the choice depending on the context. In what follows the relation between genetic epistemology and psychology is summarized first and then the two are taken together where the relationship with other sciences is concerned.

3.4.1 Genetic Epistemology and the Sciences giving Data and Theories about Man ("les sciences de l'homme")

There are close relationships between all the sciences of man. Man is a biological organism and therefore biology is of prime importance. But man is also a thinking and talking individual within social groups and hence psychology, linguistics and sociology are also relevant. Further, as man and society change continually, history also enters the picture. Our "centring" on Piaget's own work allows us to limit ourselves to psychology, biology and sociology in summarizing their relations with epistemology.

3.4.1.1 Genetic epistemology and psychology

Epistemologies of psychologists
Every psychologist has an implicit or explicit epistemology that influences his psychological theorizing and experimentation. In the next chapter some of these epistemologies will be mentioned with Piaget's critical arguments against them. Their full importance will be better seen in Volume II.

Genetic epistemology and psychological research
All epistemologies lead to factual questions concerning the knowing subject and his relation with reality, but in anti-empirical epistemologies such psychological questions remain implicit and are answered by intuition or reflection. However, Piaget wants to take psychology seriously because empirical (not empiricist!) psychology can give scientific verifications of epistemological questions which cannot be given by philosophical reflection (e.g. **47**, p.247; **52**, p.9; **49**, p.103/p.68). Such questions have to be considered within the context of the development of sciences and also within the psychogenetic development of the child, and whenever possible in a comparison of the two.

But, even considering genetic psychology as the main science for the verification of epistemological questions and hypotheses, the help of other sciences is required as well.

□The relationship between genetic epistemology and psychology is discussed in 15.2.

3.4.1.2 Genetic epistemology, psychology and biology

As already mentioned in Chapter 1, Piaget looked from the very beginning of his epistemological interest for a link between problems concerning the adaptation of the biological organism to its environment and epistemological questions concerning relations between the subject and the object. Psychology formed this link and, as Piaget summarized his position in 1976, his theoretical reflections have always consisted of efforts to translate what he says psychologically into a biological language and, reciprocally, to translate biological models into cognitive ones. Such a translation should be very profitable for psychology (**103**, p.105). This topic will be elaborated in Section D. We shall then see in more detail that the relations between the biological organism and cognition can be studied at different levels. On the one hand, the study of cognitive structures leads us back to infancy and hence to biological problems—because the general coordinations of actions must have organic sources. And at the other end of development, scientific thought is also tied to the functioning of the brain so that physiology becomes more important for the psychological study of knowledge the further physiology and psycho-physiology themselves advance. On the other hand, there are the problems of evolution which have interested Piaget from his first research on pond snails to the present day, and which lead to comparisons between mechanisms of evolution and cognitive development.

However, there should not only be a link between biology and psychology, but also between biology, psychology and sociology. In contemporary biology the unit is no longer the individual but the entire population as a source of genetic recombinations. In an analogous way human thought, which is no longer based on instincts, cannot conserve its acquisitions by way of internal transmissions, but has to use external transmissions (linguistic or educational). Thus the new unit is not the population or the gene pool, but the social group of which the individual is a structured element, taking part in multiple interactions going beyond the individual (**29**, p.248). Reasoning in this way, one would expect a close link between psychology studying the individual and sociology studying the social group. But as is well-known, there is in fact a gap between the two.

☐ Critical arguments against the integration of biology with epistemology are given in 16.2.1.

3.4.1.3 Genetic epistemology, psychology and sociology

Piaget claims that the gap between psychology and sociology is "due to the sterile disputes aimed at determining to what extent the action and thought of people are based on social factors and to what extent they are due to individual initiative" (**115**, p.6). The fact that Piaget considers them sterile is not due to a notion that social influences on the individual are unimportant. In addition to this, we can add that he wrote as early as 1928 that the development of the child is adaptation of his mind to the social environment as much as to the physical environment (**3**). French sociologists even went so far as to conclude that his research on intellectual development and moral judgement studied no more than the results of the educational influences the group has on the individual, without ever showing the more or less spontaneous development of the child's intelligence. Looking back on this discussion in 1966 (**29**), Piaget wrote that, being a biologist, he evidently did not believe in the existence of isolated individuals. No individual ever "invented" that $2 + 3 = 5$ or that $A < C$ when $A < B$ and $B < C$. But Piaget's problem was that he did believe in the importance of the nervous system and he remained troubled by the question of what its role might be in inventions if development is only due to social transmission. During some twenty years Piaget kept worrying about the problem of whether the operations he was studying in children were the products of social life or the result of nervous or organic activity used in the coordination of actions. Finally, he understood that the question itself was wrong. It is not "either...or", but "and...and". In fact, the operations which regulate intellectual interchanges between individuals are the same as those functioning within the individual. Seen this way, society is not completely independent of the biological organization of the individuals. The child's development is the result of continual interactions and not simply of educational influences (**29**, p.249). Or, as Piaget writes in other passages, social life is a necessary but not a sufficient condition for cognitive development.

As the comparisons by means of the historico-critical and the psychogenetic methods show, modern young children have the same notions of movement and force as Greek scientists had, notions no contemporary adult has. But the child then, more or less rapidly, catches up with contemporary adults. This can only be explained by the adult social environment which constantly offers the child new problems, thus stimulating his development. This leads the child to new questions for which he must then construct his own solutions (**112**, p.73). From this point of view discussions about "competences" of psychology and sociology can indeed be considered sterile.

□ See 16.2.2 for critical arguments.

3.4.2 Genetic Epistemology and Sciences offering Models

As we shall see in more detail in Chapter 6, scientific explanations require models. A constructivist theory in which structures and the processes of their development are basic requires two types of models: one for the structures and one for processes. The first can be found in mathematics and logic, the second in cybernetics and artificial intelligence.

3.4.2.1 Genetic epistemology, psychology, mathematics and logic

Logicians do not agree on the nature of logic. Simplifying the differences of opinion one may distinguish two types of solution. Some logicians consider logic a well-made general language. Piaget is not interested in this approach. Others consider logic an absolute which is the starting point of all sciences including mathematics (**29**, p.252). However, the latter does not mean that there is only one kind of modern logic, and therefore there are still many disagreements on the nature of logic, and the use of different kinds of logic. In fact, Piaget started his own "intuitive logic", developing the notion of groupings from the classification system of zoology. Groupings were then formalized by logicians.

For Piaget logic and mathematics are so closely related that he writes about "logico-mathematical" structures. Mathematics only come into the picture when he analyses them in their historical or individual development. Where models are used they are based on logic.

In general, logic is a formal, deductive and normative science— symbolic logic often being called "a logic without subject". From this point of view there is no relationship between logic and psychology. But, on the other hand, "every subject has a logic". As early as the sensorimotor stage there is a "logic of actions" which can be seen when one action includes another, succeeds another in a necessary order, or when there is a one-to-one correspondence between one set of actions and another set of actions (**88**, p.90). Later on, the "natural logic" of the child leads him to make inferences, to construct groupings, etc. while the logico-mathematical structures of the adolescent include groups as well. This does not mean that the child is a scientific logician. As Piaget repeated for many years, the way children and adolescents reason and solve problems can only be understood if the genetic epistemologist formalizes the structures of which psychological research has shown the development. In Piaget's words,

> "every time that we come upon some completed structure in the course of the development of thought, we make an effort, with the collaboration of logicians or of specialists within the field that we are considering, to formalize this structure."
>
> (**52**, p.10, and see also **50**, p.222/p.52).

Logic is a normative science determining the norms of truth and validity in reasoning. Using logic in the study of children's cognitive development does not mean that these norms are imposed on the child's thinking. Genetic epistemology studies the way in which the child develops his own norms for what is true and valid at different levels. What the child does not consider necessarily true at a certain level, is seen as "necessarily" true at the next, e.g. conservation and transitivity. Genetic epistemology studies this development of the subject's norms together with the development of structures, as there is a close link between necessity and the "closure" of structures, a theme to which I shall return later.

The fact that natural thinking has to be formalized does not mean that this formalization is used as a causal explanation of natural thinking. If this were done it would be a highly undesirable use of logic, called "logicism". Piaget's hypothesis is that there is a close correspondence between the psychological formation of thinking and the logical formalization, though the one cannot be explained by the other (**52**).

The foregoing shows that logic is used by Piaget as an instrument and he defends himself against the accusation of "dabbling in logic" by saying that no experimentalist would be accused of "dabbling in mathematics" when resorting to mathematical methods or models (**50**, p.222/p.52).

Notwithstanding the necessity of logical formalization there are limits to the possibilities it offers. In the first place, there exist many different logics, each one being coherent in itself but too weak to serve as the foundation for human knowledge. In the second place, Gödel (also spelt Goedel) has shown in his theorems that one cannot prove the consistency or non-contradiction of a system by logical arguments of the same level as that system. Only when a system of a higher level has been constructed can the consistency of the lower level be proved.

> **Example**: Gödel's example, often quoted by Piaget, is that one can only prove the consistency of elementary arithmetic by the use of transfinite arithmetic (e.g. **51**, p.294/p.29)

The importance of Gödel's theorems for Piaget's argumentation is that they lead to the question of what the basis of the axioms and undefinable notions of any system of logic is. If the correctness of a formalization can only be proved by the higher system, what is it that has been formalized? In other words, formalization must have a more fundamental basis. At the beginning there was natural thinking. Then some people began to think about their way of thinking and this gradually led to a formalization of thought. Therefore one must conclude that formal logic has formalized natural thinking by way of thinking. So, formal logic is not only a useful instrument of formalization but also shows how closely psychology and logic must be linked for an understanding of the development of thought. In the third place, genetic epistemology wants to explain knowledge as it exists within the different areas of science and this kind of knowledge contains more than a formal aspect alone, thereby limiting the usefulness of logic (e.g. **52**, p.11ff; **51**, p.294ff/p.29ff).

While logic must be included in the interdisciplinary approach, the problem of the nature of natural logic and its relationship with the different formal logics was far from solved at the time of the publications quoted so far.

> □In fact, these publications only form useful summaries, written during the period of Piaget's work covered by this book. However, they also express Piaget's notions dating from a much earlier period.

After paying much more attention to conscious thought than he did in his earlier work, Piaget turned once more to the problems of logic, making this the theme for the Centre during 1978/79 and 1979/80.

> □Piaget's use of mathematics and logic led to many critical arguments, given in 16.2.3 and 16.2.4.

3.4.2.2 Genetic epistemology, cybernetics and artificial intelligence

Piaget's notions of autoregulations were developed long before cybernetics became a new science and he has therefore been called "a cybernetician before cybernetics". Piaget has been interested in cybernetics from its beginning, because cybernetics "lies exactly half-way between physics and living phenomena" ("le vital") (**15**, p.129/p.93).

One of the great advantages of cybernetics is the possibility to replace any "mystic" idea of finality or teleology by a causal determination in the form of teleonomy—i.e. in a direction towards the future instead of a direction determined by the future.

Writing about cybernetics in the early stages of its development, Piaget could still claim that there is, however, a fundamental difference between human thought and computers. The computer is capable of solving complex problems and even of finding new solutions. But its functioning is strictly limited to causality while the mathematician or other scientist using the computer judges the value of the results by implication. It is he who works scientifically due to the validity of his implications while the machine can do no more than produce causally "with the same detachment as a stone that takes the form of a beautiful crystal when the circumstances force it to do so" (**14**).

☐ For the difference between implication and causality see Chapter 7.

Piaget writes every now and then about artificial intelligence, without, however, making a clear distinction between artificial intelligence and cybernetics. In a recent publication Piaget wrote more carefully about cybernetics, saying that problems of the origins and especially the modifications of programs have not yet been entirely solved (**115**, p.6).

☐ A critical reaction to this can be found in 17.1.2.

3.5 A Summarizing Description of Genetic Epistemology

Following Piaget's example I did not begin with a definition. However, it may be useful to end with a description of genetic epistemology, based on the many, slightly different, definitions given by Piaget.

Genetic epistemology is an interdisciplinary science studying the necessary and sufficient conditions that make knowledge—including animal and human knowledge (the latter from that of the new-born child to that of the scientist)—possible, as well as the historical development of knowledge from states of lesser validity to those of higher validity.

4 Piaget and Other Epistemologies

☐There is no corresponding chapter in Volume II.

The driving force of Piaget's tremendous output has been his desire to show that constructivism is the only possible epistemology and to convince others that he is right. This does not mean that he is uncritical of his own work; he often admits that a problem was put in the wrong way (e.g. causality), or that his answer to a question was wrong (e.g. concerning equilibration). But notwithstanding the changes and elaborations in his theory, of which Chapter 2 gives an overview for the period covered by this book, he has always remained a constructivist. His efforts to "prove" the correctness of this epistemology consist of elaborating his own theory and of showing how others are wrong. The latter is stimulated by the fact that his critics have repeatedly labelled him an empiricist, positivist, Kantian, nativist and maturationist— always in a pejorative sense. As he complains, it is very difficult for him to make himself understood (**60**, p.192) or to have discussions beyond a dialogue of the deaf (**15**, p.28/p.17).

In this chapter a summary of his characterization of other epistemologies will be given, followed by a few remarks on his own theory. The latter gives no more than an impression of his counter-arguments because they will be elaborated in later chapters.

☐The reader who wants to know more about Piaget's views before going into his fight against others, can read later chapters first, without a loss of coherence.

My confrontation of Piaget's epistemology with that of others is not written from an objective point of view but on the basis of Piaget's writings. His interpretation of and his selections from other theories influence his arguments and are therefore taken as a background (**15**, **30**, **33**, **44**, **46** and **49** are the main publications used).

4.1 Piaget's Classification of Epistemologies

Epistemologies can be classified in a number of different ways, depending on the criteria used. In his early publications Piaget uses a two-by-three matrix. One dimension indicates whether an epistemology is non-genetic or genetic, the other indicates whether the object or subject dominates, or whether there is an indissociable link between the two. The essential advantage of this classification is that the same matrix can be used for any science—the psychology of intelligence and biology being the most important in Piaget's theory. This enables him to find isomorphisms between psychology and biology.

An epistemology which is genetic and in which the object dominates is empiricism. This has its parallel in associationism in psychology and Lamarckism in biology. An epistemology which is also genetic but in which the subject dominates is conventionalism. In psychology this is found in Claparède's trial-and-error psychology of intelligence and in biology in Darwinism and Neo-Darwinism. The third epistemology is relativism, or as Piaget now calls it, his "constructivism". In psychology there is Piaget's theory of cognitive development and in biology Waddington's *"tertium quid"*.

☐The biological aspect of Piaget's theory will be elaborated in Section D.

There are also three non-genetic forms, but apart from apriorism, including Kant's, they are not important in our context, because the equivalents in psychology became part of the history of psychology quite a while ago.

☐Piaget's arguments against Gestaltpsychology are often repeated by him, but are left out by me because Gestaltpsychology has lost its relevance in many branches of modern psychology.

In more recent work Piaget uses a classification with three classes: metascientific, parascientific and scientific epistemologies. Though the fact that there are so many intermediate epistemologies reduces its scientific value practical usefulness makes me employ this classification in the following summary.

4.2 Piaget's Overview of Other Epistemologies and his Arguments against them

4.2.1 Metascientific Epistemologies

The main epistemologies of this type are Hume's empiricism and

Kant's apriorism. Though Kant came after Hume in history, I begin with Kant because he influenced Piaget so much in a positive sense while Hume's empiricism only stimulated him as an object of criticism.

4.2.1.1 Apriorism (Kant)

Kant asked himself how science is possible. On the one hand, there are deductive processes and, on the other hand, there is the experience we get through our senses. How can we reconcile the two?

In order to do this, Kant definitely gave up the "realism" of what we perceive. For him the subject is not only the source of deductive necessity in reasoning, but also of the categories or structures such as space, time, causality, etc. that make objectivity and thereby experience possible. In other words: Kant discovered the role of the *a priori* adding synthetic *a priori* judgements to analytical *a priori* judgements. Logical structures, like syllogisms, are analytical in the sense that the conclusion is contained in advance in the premises and only has to be detached from them. At the same time these structures are *a priori* due to the fact that they belong to the internal necessity of our mind, without the need for experience. Most synthetic judgements, on the other hand, are *a posteriori*. We experience "reality", find relationships and synthesize them afterwards (*a posteriori*) into knowledge. Now Kant's originality consisted in considering mathematical truths synthetic but at the same time *a priori*. In a judgement like $7 + 5 = 12$, there is a synthesis as 12 has characteristics that are not included in 7 and 5. By adding these, a new and specific totality has been constructed. On the other hand, this judgement is *a priori* as it is not founded on experience, but results from the categories of our mind. For Kant the *a priori* comprises universality and necessity, but also priority in relation to experience. This priority is a logical one insofar as the *a priori* is a necessary condition; it is a chronological one insofar as the *a priori* can never manifest itself after the experience and it is a priority of level insofar as the subject already has an underlying structure determining his activities and experiences.

The second important aspect of Kant's epistemology that has to be considered in relation to Piaget's theory is that of the "Ding an sich" or "noumenon".

Piaget feels nearer to Kant's theory than to other epistemologies. The idea that we construct our experiences on the basis of structures of space, time, quantity, etc. as well as the idea of universality of such structures are, of course purely Kantian aspects of Piaget's theory. However, there is an important difference in the *a priori* character of these structures. Kant does write that they are prior to experience without going into the question of their genesis, while for Piaget the genetic aspect is fundamental in any epistemological question. Piaget's genetic research has shown that these structures themselves are constructed. It takes a long time for the infant to construct "a permanent object", the group of displacements, etc. It takes about seven years before the first structures of concrete operations are achieved and "necessity" is only felt when actions are interiorized into concrete operations. In general, as Piaget often summarizes the argument: "necessity" comes at the end of a long period of construction in which experience plays a part, and not at the beginning as Kant wrote. In other words, Kant's concept of the *a priori* is too rich, as it should only contain universality and necessity, but no priority in relation to experience.

The difference between Kant's "noumenon" and Piaget's ideas on the "reality" of objects was recently formulated by Piaget (**119**). As this is closely linked to his realism, a summary of this has been post-poned to the next chapter.

4.2.1.2 Empiricism (Hume)

While Kant's epistemology is important because of its fundamental influence on Piaget, notwithstanding the essential differences, empiricism is important because Piaget has spent so much time and energy in refuting it. Furthermore, empiricism is still very influential in England and the United States in the epistemological background of psychological theories. Piaget emphasizes that empiricism has led to many different ideas, from knowledge as a copy of reality to logical positivism which aims at reducing scientific knowledge exclusively to physical experience and to language (**46**).

Leaving logical positivism aside for the time being, we see that the original empiricists turned to sciences to verify their main idea that knowledge comes from experience. This experience is based on percep-tion and tries to copy reality as closely as possible. Empiricists look for verification in facts. Classical empiricists tried to look for "psycho-logical" facts, but psychology had not yet become a science. They (therefore?) invoked the influence of experience in already existing sciences like physics (*33*, p.25).

Piaget uses many arguments against the possibility of a copy of reality to which I turn in 4.2.3. For the time being, one important critical remark concerning experience in physics needs to be made here. Experimentation in physics implies a dissociation of factors, and their interpretation in the context of a logico-mathematical framework. It is doubtful whether such a complicated experience can be reduced "to simple experiences in perception", or whether one would not find already in the analysis of simple experiences elements announcing the structuration and active organization characterizing experimentation (**33**, p.25).

4.2.2 Parascientific Epistemology (Husserl)

In the second half of the nineteenth century and above all in the twentieth century, irrationalism (as a reaction against Kant, etc.) in conjunction with the resistance against scientistic metaphysics led to theories of knowledge that form really parascientific epistemologies. In France the development went from Ravaisson, Lachelier and Boutroux to Bergson.

    □The interested reader can find Piaget's summary and criticism of this in Chapter 1 of **15**, and in **33**, p.26ff.

As for phenomenology, which was developing at the same time, Piaget has been not so much interested in its purely philosophical aspects as in its epistemology. This is truly parascientific as it not only wants to go beyond science but also wants to duplicate it by adding a "phenomenological" psychology to scientific psychology, as well as an extratemporal, ideal genesis to real genesis. Originally Husserl was not opposed to empirical psychology, but under the influence of Frege's accusation that Husserl was guilty of psychologism (1894), he turned more and more away from empirical psychology in his efforts to go beyond it.

Piaget summarizes a phenomenological epistemology as follows. Its central idea is that there exists an intuition of "essences" but that these cannot be separated from phenomena or facts. The phenomena bring us to "intentions" which reach—at all levels—"significations". The passage from the fact to the essence is said to take place thanks to a process of "reduction" or conversion consisting in liberating the subject of his "natural" limitations, with the result that the subject comes to understand himself as a basis of the natural world instead of a part of it. Phenomenological reduction would thus consist in a sort of liberation from nature and one's own body (**33**, p.34).

Phenomenology has been very influential in psychology. On the one hand there is Gestaltpsychology which was inspired by the very valuable idea of going beyond idealism and realism in accepting an interactionism in which subject and object are indissociably linked. However, Gestaltpsychology also took its anti-geneticism from Husserl. On the other hand there have been several efforts to found a psychology of consciousness based on intentionalism and the experience of the subject, for example, those of Sartre, Merleau-Ponty, Jaspers, etc.

Piaget appreciates Husserlian intuitions in so far as they are directed at phenomena without a separation of the subject from the object. Husserl is rightly opposed to idealism and Kantian apriorism, which attributes everything to the subject as well as to empiricism or positivism, which neglects the subject in favour of the object. But there Piaget's appreciation nearly ends. While he is quite willing to join Husserl in his critique of empiricist psychology, he does not want to conclude that this must lead to a rejection of empirical or experimental psychology in general. One can very well be an empirical psychologist without being an empiricist. Husserl's methods do not lead to the verification Piaget considers essential and therefore he is convinced that a suprascientific psychology is no science. Furthermore Husserl, too, neglected the genetic aspect, just as the idealism and apriorism he criticized did.

☐It would take us too far to go into details of Husserl's epistemology and Piaget's criticism. The interested reader can find them in Chapter 3 of **15**, and in Chapter 1 of **33**, with many quotations of the relevant passages of Husserl's work.

4.2.3 Scientific Epistemologies

When sciences began to change more and more rapidly, philosophers and scientists became interested in the foundations of sciences. This led to different types of scientific epistemologies.

4.2.3.1 Positivism

The most important positivist was Comte, but there are also contemporary forms of positivism. Comte's essential premise was that there is a stable barrier between metaphysical philosophy and the sciences, due to the nature of their problems. This is still accepted by contemporary forms of logical positivism. There are scientific problems which can be solved by appropriate methods and metaphysical problems which cannot be solved (Comte) or are simply devoid of any significance (contemporary logical positivism) (**33**, p.44).

Comte thought that sciences should study phenomena without looking at "the nature of things", and that science only knows laws and ignores "the way in which phenomena are produced". Comte counters the emphasis given to deduction by Descartes, Leibniz and Kant by saying that one should limit the role of deduction, and certainly not deduce laws across the fixed boundaries between sciences (*33*, p.44).

Contemporary neo-positivism stemming from the Vienna Circle (Mach, Schlick, and the young Wittgenstein) is called "empiricism" or "logical positivism" in Anglo-Saxon countries. It is an important advance in comparison with Comte. Here two distinct and hetero-geneous sources of knowledge are recognized, the experimental source based on perception, and a logico-mathematical source based on a syntax and semantics common to all languages. Modern positivism maintains the notion of strict barriers between sciences and restricts scientific problems. There is a fundamental difference between the problems of sciences and metaphysics, the latter being considered "without signification" ("sinnlose Sätze") because they cannot be phrased in terms of logical formalizations nor in terms of strict experience. This implies that synthetic judgements (Kant) are unnecessary, all logico-mathematical judgements being tautological or analytic (*33*, p.48).

We have already seen in Chapter 3 that Piaget will not accept differences between the type of problems of metaphysics and sciences and, if possible, will allow even less any barrier between sciences. Recent developments of sciences seen to bear this out as they go more and more towards an integration—even if we look at sciences other than Piaget's interdisciplinary genetic epistemology.

The other central idea of empiricism or logical positivism is that cognitive mechanisms have to submit to reality in order to reproduce a copy of reality. This reduction of reality to observable features is evidently just as unacceptable to Piaget. If we knew reality as it is he says, the "associations" on which learning is based would show a one-to-one correspondence with a series of relationships already existing in the external world (*44*, p.140). However, knowledge cannot be a copy of reality because one can only make a copy of something one knows. So one would have to know reality in order to copy it and this is evidently impossible (*52*). Other arguments are based on Piaget's own theory: knowledge can never be a copy because there are always factors of adaptation, organization and regulation at work due to the fact that all knowledge is related to actions and the coordination of actions (e.g. **32**, p.20/p.4; p.51/p.28). A copy would be pure accommodation, thereby contradicting Piaget's theory which says that we must transform reality in order to know it (e.g. **44**, p.141).

Another type of argument against empiricism is found in biology. Biologists have amply shown that biological organisms and their environment always interact (see Section D).

According to Piaget, sciences ·should not limit themselves to "observables" nor to laws and predictions, but should look for explanations. It is in the nature of humans to be dissatisfied with contemplation and prediction because humans always act and produce. Therefore, in the sciences of man and in all other sciences, the need to understand and explain cannot be ignored.

Finally, it is impossible to reduce logico-mathematical knowledge to a language, as these structures are formed at a deeper level than language, i.e. at the level of the general coordination of actions.

4.2.3.2 Epistemologies within sciences

Comte and philosophers of science like Cournot, Brunschvicg and Cassirer were, of course, philosophers. However, recently scientists with an epistemological interest have developed epistemologies within their science. There are many nuances in this field but there is no need to go into them.

□They can be found in Piaget's summary in **33**, p.52ff.

4.2.4 Nativism and Maturationism

In his older matrix Piaget combined nativism with idealism and apriorism, as the subject dominates while it is a non-genetic epistemology. Though nativism as such is rarely mentioned in modern epistemologies or psychologies, many authors emphasize the importance of maturation (see 17.2.1 and 21.1.2). But, according to Piaget, a strictly maturationist view implies nativism or preformism. If maturation were the only influence, the structures which mature would have to be preformed in the hereditary program. Such a program excludes any novelty and the notion of novelty or "new" knowledge is essential. How does the child construct new structures, how did Cantor come to create set theory? Though evolutionary novelties are of great interest to Piaget (**83, 96**) they do not suffice as explanations of individual novelties.

The fact that maturation is not a sufficient condition for biological and cognitive development, does not imply that it is not a necessary condition. Maturation determines whether constructions are possible or not (e.g. **60**, p.193).

5 The Core-Concepts of Piaget's Epistemology

☐The critique of the core-concepts is given in Chapter 17. But, as the theoretical background of the critics is considered important, the text is organized by author and not by topic. In this chapter cross-references will be added under each topic for the convenience of the reader who wants to look up the critique of some specific core-concept.

Every psychology is based on an implicit or explicit epistemology and this is certainly true for Piaget's genetic psychology. In this chapter the core-concepts of his epistemology will be briefly summarized, most of which will turn up again in later chapters. However, some concepts of a more psychological nature have also found their way into this chapter. This was unavoidable because Piaget's epistemology and his genetic psychology go together, the latter being the method or instrument for answering questions raised by the former.

☐The main problem raised by this organization is where to discuss Piaget's recent theory of equilibration. Equilibration is a fundamentally biological concept and as such it belongs to Section D. On the other hand it is the basic model of psychogenetic development, and would thereby belong in Section C. Also one cannot imagine Piaget's epistemology without equilibration, because of its genetic aspect. The problem has been solved by briefly mentioning equilibration in this chapter and discussing it in detail in Section C. In Section D the reader is then referred back to Section C.

5.1 Constructivism, Realism and Interactionism

5.1.1 Constructivism

The very foundation of genetic epistemology is constructivism. But notwithstanding its essential importance there is relatively little to be said about constructivism as such. Piaget wrote no special book on the topic, though it turns up in many of his publications.

□Piaget's "constructivisme" is usually translated as "constructivism", but occasionally also as "constructionism". As far as I can see there is no difference between the two.

5.1.1.1 Arguments in favour of constructivism

The central issue of a constructivist epistemology is the question of how the construction or creation of what did not exist before this construction is possible. Piaget's empirical work tries to demonstrate that the next level is always a reorganization of the foregoing one (**102**).

An argument of a different nature is given by Gödel's theorems. If there must always be a next higher level to formalize the foregoing one, this implies a restructuring at the higher level.

Finally, constructivism must be the "correct" solution if Piaget is right in his arguments against other epistemologies, which were mentioned in Chapter 4. There is only one specific argument to add. Both innatism (nativism) and empiricism accept a form of reductionism. If a reductionist hypothesis were well-founded, this would then invalidate constructivism, while a refutation of reductionism would strengthen the hypothesis of constructivism. In this context the term "reductionism" is used for the scientific effort to either reduce higher levels of knowledge to lower ones, or—on the contrary—to reduce lower levels to higher ones. Reductionism in this sense is based upon the fact that, in all fields of knowledge, concepts in use are divided periodically into two levels. One of them is more complex than the other and is therefore considered "higher". There is then a tendency to reduce the higher to the lower, in the way behaviourism does in psychology, to give but one example. As a reaction to an excessive reductionism of the higher to the lower, there follows an opposite tendency to subordinate the lower to the higher, e.g. in biological vitalism. Both views imply that every "new" structure is preformed, either within the simplest elements or within a complex one. Novelty would therefore be no more than a successful explanation of pre-existing relationships. In the *Principles of Genetic Epistemology* (**48**) in which Piaget summarizes this view, he then continues by giving a number of examples of different sciences, all illustrating the impossibility of a one-way reduction of two structures of different levels (p.122/p.93).

The autoregulation which plays a fundamental role in Piaget's theory is not a form of reductionism. As the creativity of such a regulation cannot consist of productions *ex nihilo*, the process must correct what was wrong at the foregoing level of knowledge, as well as add to this knowledge. Such a reconstruction at the higher level of what was present or possible at the foregoing level does not imply reductionism in the above-mentioned sense. In reductionism a higher level is reduced to a lower one by considering it an additive result of lower-level elements. However, a reconstruction means far more than an addition of a greater number of elements of the lower type in order to get the higher level. As we shall see in detail in Chapters 9 and 10, such reconstructions require a correction or a differentiation and integration. The reconstructive process is often summarily called "the dialectic nature of the advances of constructive thought". However, Piaget prefers to detail the steps of such a process of reconstruction or auto-regulation, and to call it "constructivism" (**103**, p.139).

5.1.1.2 Consequences of constructivism

One of the direct consequences of constructivism is that the epistemologist studying any level of development, let us say X, will ask what came before this level, that is at level $X-1$. If X is indeed a construction based on $X-1$, or a reconstruction of $X-1$, then one can only understand X through the knowledge of $X-1$, or in Piaget's words, "there is no absolute beginning." Having gone back to the neonate one could go further back to embryology, but Piaget does not do so. Instead he goes back to "knowledge" in organisms of the sub-human level and this is very important for Piaget's wish to link biology to epistemology.

Another consequence of constructivism is that the development towards higher levels is stressed. Any level of individual or scientific knowledge is no more than a temporary equilibrium opening up new possibilities, "le développement mental est indéfini, toujours ouvert vers le haut" (mental development is unlimited, always open to higher levels) (**33**, p.393; also **106**, p.35). But Piaget adds immediately that the higher levels become ever less general and more differentiated, and are therefore only to be found in the minds of specialized scientists (**33**).

5.1.1.3 Development of modern epistemologies in the direction of constructivism

In a discussion on scientific knowledge and philosophy (**78**) Piaget tried to show that contemporary epistemologies, which detach themselves from philosophy, develop in the direction of constructivism. The short summary given below will not make this completely clear, but is only meant to indicate the direction of Piaget's thinking.

☐The interesting aspect is Piaget's effort to convince others of the importance and even the necessity of a constructivist approach, whether the authors mentioned would have agreed or not.

a) *Logical positivism* (or *analytic philosophy*) has been obliged to give up the static character of its original notions and to develop in the direction of a very hesitating or implicit, but nevertheless discernable, constructivism (Popper, Quine, Apostel).

b) Originally *methods of logico-mathematical formalizations* were far removed from constructivism (Russell, Hilbert), but the limits of formalization as clarified by Gödel and others and later work of a related nature (Feferman, Schutte) have shown that there seem to be levels of construction. The operations that served as instruments at a lower level become thematized as new objects of thought at a higher level.

c) In the analysis of theoretical *"models"* used by physicists, causality is seen more and more as an operational reconstruction of the phenomenon that is to be explained and of its laws, instead of a simple sequence of the type: *p* leads to *q*.

d) An analogous tendency is seen in biology, psychology and sociology with the use of *dialectical methods*, in the sense of an immanent dialectic that tries to find the epistemological aspects that are present, implicitly or explicitly, in scientific work.

e) While dialectics describe the general changes in historical development, the *historico-critical method* is required for any epistemology which tries to grasp the construction of scientific knowledge. In the way Piaget interprets this approach, it must be constructivist.

f) The same is true for the last approach mentioned: *genetic epistemology*.

☐For a critique of constructivism see 17.2.3.1, 17.2.3.4 and 17.2.5. An extreme position is described in 17.1.1.1.

5.1.2 Realism

Constructivism immediately raises the question whether the subject is the only one responsible for what is constructed or whether the subject is influenced by "reality". As a biologist, Piaget studied the adaptation of organisms to their environment and this convinced him that there must be an organism (subject) and an environment (object) with an interaction between the two. This explains why Piaget says, "I am a realist as biologist." His early studies in psychology formed the continuation of his biological approach, intelligence being defined as adaptation to the environment. Thus, again, there is a (mental) subject adapting to an object, or as Piaget says, "I am a realist as psychologist." But, gradually,

Piaget's interest returned more and more from this adaptational intelligence to epistemological issues concerning knowledge. While in his earlier work he writes about "intelligence" we rarely find this word in the books of the period covered by this overview. It has been replaced by "knowledge" or "understanding" ("connaissance", "comprendre"). But his return to epistemology did not change his conviction that there is a subject and an object, the full quotation being, "I am a realist as biologist, as psychologist and as epistemologist" (**103**, p.65).

There are, however, different brands of realism and Piaget certainly does not mean the realism of empiricists or, as it has been called, "naïve realism". He does accept that reality exists or rather "the object as such", where "object" means material objects and persons. His arguments are twofold. In the first place, there is an intersubjective consensus about objects: if one person does not perceive an object any longer, another one may verify that it is still there. In the second place, empirical abstraction gives us knowledge about the physical world and in this there may be intersubjective consensus as well. But though these are arguments in favour of realism, they do not imply that we know the world as it is. Even in the case of physical knowledge arrived at by empirical abstraction, objects are no more than "observables" which only get a meaning or signification for the subject by being assimilated into his schemes. In other words, Piaget goes so far as to agree with what the physicist Foerster said in a lecture at Geneva: "the environment contains no information. It is what it is, period." (**103**, p.59). Thus, Piaget is not interested in the ontological question concerning what reality "is". He is only interested in what we get from reality by directing our schemes on to the object in order to give it meaning. This fundamental theme will be elaborated in later chapters. For the moment it is enough to emphasize that for Piaget reality does exist but cannot be known as such by the subject.

This notion has often been identified with Kant's "Ding an Sich" or "noumenon". However, Piaget sees a fundamental difference between Kant's theory and his own. According to Kant the thing is not only unknowable, but it is also unchanging. In contrast, Piaget sees reality as forever moving away from the subject. That is to say, due to his cognitive progress the subject gets to know the object better and better, but every step of this progress leads to new problems because the object becomes more and more complex. Thus one might say that the object moves away whenever the subject comes closer. Though the absolute distance between object and subject diminishes, it can never be reduced to zero. In this sense the object remains "a limit" and the change of the object implied in this notion is seen by Piaget as fundamentally different from Kant's theory (**119**).

The opposite misinterpretation to seeing Piaget as a naïve realist would be to see him as an idealist, on the basis of his subordination of reality to the cognitive instruments of the subject. This is certainly not his intention, as he repeatedly stresses that the subject as organism and source of material actions is itself an object and therefore is in this respect a part of reality. This is also Piaget's explanation of the close fit between mathematics and physics, a fact that has worried many epistemologists. According to Piaget, mathematics are neither an invention—because the subject is not completely free in his mathematical constructions—nor a discovery—because mathematics are not "out there" waiting for us to discover them. Mathematical constructions are ultimately based on the actions and coordinations of actions of the subject. These actions are determined by the nervous system and the regulations of the organism, this organism itself being an object among other objects in the physical world. And so we end up with a close fit between mathematical constructions and reality (e.g. **76**, p.17; **115**, p.4).

In summary, Piaget's constructivism is also a type of realism but not naïve realism.

◻Critical arguments are given in 17.2.2 and 17.2.4. An extreme position is found in 17.1.1.1 and 17.1.1.6.

5.1.3 Interactionism

The foregoing has already shown us that Piaget's epistemology combines constructivism with a type of realism in which the subject and the object constantly interact. Therefore, not much has to be added on the topic of interactionism.

The essential aspect of interaction in Piaget's theory is its dialectical movement : $S \rightleftharpoons O$. In other words, the subject influences the object at the same time as the object influences the subject. We shall see many examples of such dialectical interactions. For the moment, assimilation and accommodation might be mentioned as an illustration : assimilation is often supposed to take place before accommodation, but according to many passages in Piaget's work the two take place at the same time.

◻A more extreme position is described in 17.1.1.6.

5.2 Structures and Procedures

As a young biologist Piaget came to the conclusion that every organism
has a permanent structure and that logic would correspond in the
subject to a process of equilibration. These ideas have remained core-
concepts in his theory ever since (e.g. **15**, p.16/p.8). In what follows I
shall concentrate first on structures and then on the main aspects of
equilibration.

In Piaget's constructivist epistemology the idea of structure is as
necessary as that of construction—constructivism and structuralism
being indissolubly linked in such a way that Piaget sometimes describes
his theory as "structuralist constructivism" and sometimes "constructivist structuralism". But nothing is static in his theory, and the
character of "his" structures has changed in recent years, coming ever
closer to a new concept in his theory, that of procedures. In the development of knowledge there are two aspects "savoir faire", that is
"know-how", and "dégager des raisons", that is "know-why".
Procedures lead to the solution of problems—to knowing how to do
something. Their end result is (or should be) success. Such procedures
can be studied in general or in the way individuals solve problems.
Though Piaget is—as usual—interested in the general aspects of
procedures, Inhelder and her team have recently turned to the study of
individual strategies. Nevertheless Inhelder also published a general
article on procedures and structures in association with Piaget (**116**).

The study of procedures is much more a part of psychology than the
study of structures is, and hence the subject who develops and uses
procedures is called *the psychological subject.*

 ☐Inhelder gives the clearest description of the psychological subject:
 "The child, in his progressive discoveries of means meant to solve problems which are
 indissociably linked to concrete and specific contents. " (**297**, p.100).

Strictly speaking, procedures of the psychological subject should not be
included in this chapter but as they are always linked to structures of
the epistemic subject their general characteristics are included (5.2.2
and 5.2.3).

In contrast to the psychological subject, *the epistemic subject is that*
which structures of all subjects of the same developmental level have in common.

 ☐This is a recent definition. Comparing it with earlier definitions one
 sees that the earlier ones included more, e.g. "the epistemic subject, i.e.
 the mechanisms common to all individual subjects of the same level, or
 in other words, the subject 'whoever he is' ['le sujet quelconque']"(**39**,

p.58/p.68). My translation, the official one using "the average subject" is very "un-Piagetian".

In **15** Piaget said explicitly that one only becomes an epistemic subject at the level of concrete operations. However, when asked how a pre-operational subject should be described, he said that there is an epistemic subject as soon as there are structures, that is at the sensorimotor level (**114**).

Piaget's phrase "sujet épistémique" has been translated as "epistemological" and as "epistemic" subject. I use the latter as it is closer to the original and, probably, more correct.

Just as procedures can never be isolated from structures, structures can never be isolated from procedures.

When a structuralist approach became fashionable Piaget was invited to write a booklet on the subject in the series "Que-sais-je?". This booklet (**39**) soon became a bestseller with 107 000 French copies sold (1974) and translations into many languages (**99**, p.37).

☐ It is worthwhile mentioning this series because "Que-sais-je" booklets are limited to a maximum of 120 small pages and are written for a lay-readership. Though Piaget resorted to small print, wherever at all possible, he had to limit his topic to structuralism in a number of sciences and some philosophical movements inspired by structuralism in the sciences of man (**39**, p.8/p.6). These imposed limitations have seldom been recognized by critics.

Piaget's own structuralism is restricted to dynamic structures and it is from this point of view that the booklet is written. I shall not go into structuralism in other sciences, but concentrate on structures in Piaget's own theory. As I said at the beginning, Piaget's structuralism dates from his training as a biologist, but since he began to use the concept it has lost any static characteristics it may have had and a structure now comes close to being a process. In his most recent article structures are called "mechanisms" (**116**, p.165).

5.2.1 Structures

5.2.1.1 Characteristics of structures

☐ Piaget uses the terms "structure" and "system" without distinguishing them.

In *Structuralism* (**39**) Piaget characterizes *a structure as a system of transformations, which*—as a system (in contrast to the properties of its elements)—*includes laws and is conserved or enriched by the very interplay of its transformations* (p.6ff/p.5). These transformations take place within the system.

☐This text differs slightly from the official translation, keeping closer to the original which stresses that the system has laws, though this may be an irrelevant detail ("un système de transformations, qui comporte des lois").

In summary, Piaget concludes that a structure, as used by him, is a totality with transformations, and self-regulation.

As a totality or whole any structure contains elements and relations between them.

In cognitive structures the elements forming the content of the structure are perceptions, memories, concepts, operations, structures, or "an object whatsoever" in mathematics and logic. The relations between the elements giving the form to the structure can be spatio-temporal, causal, implicative, etc.

Though the distinction between content and form seems to be rather simple and straightforward, this impression is misleading, especially in logico-mathematical structures. Confusions are mainly due to the fact that what was form at an early stage of development may become content at the next stage. The earliest logico-mathematical structures are seen at the sensorimotor stage when observables give the content and the coordination of actions give the form.

☐The distinction is evidently made by the observer and not by the infant! The infant is "acting on objects".

Many years later, at the stage of concrete operations, objects still contribute the content. This is true for the groupings as well as for the facts and laws which the child can find. These facts and laws are found by empirical abstraction and inductive generalization in which the subject contributes the instruments for reading off the facts and for their structuration. Thus the relation between the observables—that is the form—is given by the subject.

☐In a structure like conservation the operations of identity, reciprocity and reversibility are the form while the "observables" (quantity of water, weight, number of objects, etc.) are the content.

At the next stage, that of formal operations, the operations of reciprocity and reversibility become integrated into the INRC group. In this sense formal structures become independent of extralogical content. In general one may say that at the higher logico-mathematical levels the structure from a former level becomes a sub-structure (i.e. content!) in the higher-level structure.

This elaboration, which is to be found in many of Piaget's books, clarifies how perceptions, operations and sub-structures can all be called "content" in the passage quoted from *Structuralism*.

The next characteristic of structures is their transformational aspect. The difficulty in understanding what this means is that "transformation" is one of those words Piaget uses with different meanings, never giving a clear definition. Perhaps the clearest "definition" can be found in his interviews with Bringuier, though even this looks simpler than it is. Asked what he calls a transformation, Piaget answered: "I call transformation an operation which transforms one state into another" (**108**, p.148). He then illustrated this by referring to the group of displacements where returning from B to A is "the transformation of the direct operation". Reversibility, composition and addition are transformations because the operations of negating, composing and adding transform the original state. So, on the one hand, we have a "transformation as the operation transforming a state", but also "transformation as transforming an operation"—i.e. as "an operation on operations". Thus "transformation" is used for changes of different levels.

The characterization of transformation given above is illustrated by operations within a group, but at the same time these transformations change reality. If objects are counted, their "state" for the counting subject changes; if they are classified they are changed as well. This takes us back to what I said concerning "reality". By using his structures to assimilate reality—that is to say, to give significations to reality—the subject changes the latter. So there are really transformations within structures as well as transformations by structures. And, to make matters worse, structures in Piaget's sense are not static but are reconstructed, or "transformed" by differentiation and integration. This shows again the close link between structures and construction.

To turn once more to the assumption that every structure is a system of transformations, we can distinguish mathematical structures in which transformations are by definition non-temporal from structures in which transformations are temporal. Before elaborating this difference, which is an important one in distinguishing "closed" and "open" structures, we must turn to the transformation of structures. These transformations take place through autoregulation (= self-regulation) or equilibration. As the process of self-regulation is different in open and closed structures the main aspects of equilibration will be mentioned in the next paragraph.

5.2.1.2 Closed and open structures

Originally Piaget took the notion of structures from biology, where structures are "open". Then when he tried to formalize mental structures he became interested in mathematics and logico-mathematical structures which are "closed". But under the influence of (von) Bertalanffy Piaget came to consider structures again as "open", though with modifications of Bertalanffy's concepts. The result is his distinction between closed and open structures which is described in detail in *Biology and Knowledge* (**32**) and briefly in *Structuralism* (**39**).

Closed structures, or logico-mathematical structures, are characterized by non-temporal transformations, closure and "perfect" regulations.

Logico-mathematical structures are by definition non-temporal in consequence of their reversibility. If $2 + 3 = 5$, then $5 - 3 = 2$ follows by immediate necessity, even though an actual person would need time to give the answer. Closure means that the transformations within a structure do not go beyond the boundary of the system but always lead to another element of the structure. However, this limitation does not fix the structure once and for all as a structure may become a sub-structure in a larger structure. In this case the laws of the original structure remain valid (there is no annexation but a confederation as the Swiss Piaget writes!), so that the change involves an enrichment of the larger structure. Logico-mathematical structures are complete and closed because they have been produced through deductive invention or axiomatic decision. Psychologically, the closure is important because it is experienced as "necessity", though this need not be conscious or expressed verbally.

If a structure is to become a sub-structure of a higher-level structure this presupposes an autoregulation of the structures. There are several levels of complexity of autoregulations. At the top they will proceed by well-determined operations which are none other than the laws determining the totality of the structure (**39**, p.14/p.15). One might begin to wonder—Piaget writes—whether there is any need to introduce a concept of autoregulation. Either one is talking about the laws of the structure which regulate the structure by definition, or about the mathematician or logician who is at work, in which case there is no autoregulation. But granting that the laws of the structure are laws of transformation and that the operations of the scientist are well regulated, the question remains as to what an operation is as seen from a structuralist perspective. This takes us to the peculiar characteristics of the "perfect" regulation, a concept taken from Ashby's cybernetics. In a "perfect" regulation there is not only a correction of errors due to the results of the actions, but also a pre-correction thanks to internal methods of control such as reversibility. Reversibility means that $+n-n = 0$. This is, in its turn, a source of the principle of contradiction: if $+n-n \neq 0$, then $n \neq n$ (**39**, p.15/p.15).

> ☐ This passage was summarized in detail because I wanted to make clear that any difficulties are due to Piaget and not to my summary. The point is that Piaget's logico-mathematical structures are inspired by mathematics but differ from structures as seen by a structuralist mathematician. For a mathematician an operation is just a mapping or correspondence between sets, not something one does. In contrast, an operation within a Piagetian structure is an interiorized action, something that a subject knows how to do. Even in the case of a non-temporal structure there is always a formalization of this type of "structure-of-the-subject" (see also 5.2.4).

Apart from closed logico-mathematical structures there are unlimited numbers of linguistic, sociological, psychological, etc. structures which are open.

Open structures or systems *are characterized by* the opposites of closed structures: *temporal transformations, openness towards the environment, and autoregulations by anticipation and feedback.*

The temporal aspect has already been mentioned: the transformations in these structures take time—e.g. to become a married couple, to cite Piaget's example.

The aspect of openness requires more elaboration. Openness of systems was a fundamental notion in Bertalanffy's systems theory. Though Piaget came to agree with Bertalanffy that every structure of this type is open to the environment with interactions between the two, he did add an important restriction. According to Piaget the system always strives for closure. This is due to the fact that an open system is threatened by the environment: lack of food, sex, cognitive stimulation, etc. Therefore the organism tries to extend its mastery of the environment, biologically by, for example, the extension of its territory, and cognitively by extending its knowledge of the environment. This is true at all levels: the individual extends his cognitive structures, sciences expand their knowledge and behaviour is the driving force of evolution (**96**). If the organism could succeed in closing the system this would mean a restriction of the organism's action to a circumscribed field in such a way that the exchanges would guarantee the conservation of the system. Seen in this way the closure of the system is no more than a limit that is never attained.

Describing the mechanisms of autoregulation in such an open system in cybernetic terms comparable to those used for the closed system, it is clear that there are no "perfect" regulations based on reversible operations but that one will find instead a sequence of antici-pations and retroactions (feedback).

☐In reading this passage one should remember that the cybernetics mentioned (e.g. Ashby's "perfect" regulations) date from the first stage in the science of cybernetics. As we shall see in Volume II cybernetics have developed so rapidly that Piaget's text of 1968 is already out of date.

Transformations by autoregulations lead to qualitative changes and if such changes follow a universal sequence one can think of them in terms of "stages". As psychogenetic development is discussed in Section B the concept of stages has been postponed to 11.1. Though many psychologists first think of "stages" whenever Piaget is men-tioned, it is not one of the core-concepts of his epistemology.

☐Many authors criticize structuralism or Piaget's version of it (see 17.1.1.4, 17.2.2, 17.2.3.3, 17.2.3.4 and 17.2.4).

5.2.2 Procedures

Procedures have only been described in the more recent publications of Piaget. Their general characteristics, which are the only ones relevant for this chapter, will be summarized from an article published in 1979 (**116**) and then compared with Piaget's views on structures in the same article.

Procedures are the mechanisms used, step by step, by the subject in order to attain a specific cognitive goal. There are unlimited numbers of procedures because they are multiplied and diversified according to the unlimited number of different goals the subject wants to attain and the different paths by which a goal can be attained. During a specific effort pro-cedures follow one after the other, the one replacing the other until sub-goals and, finally, the goals themselves are reached. Old "means" are often used in this process though they may be adjusted, while new ones are also searched for. The multiplication of procedures enlarges the power of the subject as does their diversity. Being able to reach the same goal by different roads evidently leads to enrichment for the subject.

5.2.3 Structures and Procedures

In Piaget's theory new aspects are always integrated with old ones and this is also true of procedures which are closely linked to logico-mathematical structures. In fact, Inhelder and Piaget suggest in their tentative article on the subject (**116**) that structures and procedures are two mechanisms which form the opposite poles of an indissociably linked couple. Piaget has come to look more and more for such dialectical couples and in the following chapters we shall encounter several of them.

Before comparing structures and procedures I would like to repeat what has already been indicated about the changing character of logico-mathematical structures within Piaget's theory. Originally Piaget had stressed the state of equilibrium to which the autoregulation of structures tended, thereby giving many readers the impression that a final equilibrium had been reached with formal operations. But even if this impression ever was correct, it is definitely incorrect now. The transformation of structures certainly continues, especially in scientific thought—the process of improving equilibration ("équilibration majorante") being far more important than the temporary states of relative equilibrium which may be reached on the way. Development is a spiral in which the well-known stages form no more than a detour (see 13.2.2.2). At the same time, the fact that structures transform reality has become so important that structures are being called "mechanisms" (e.g. **116**, p.165). Structures come close to what are now called "procedures". Distinguishing the two clarifies the issue of structures and at the same time introduces procedures—two opposite poles of the same dimension.

☐The differences between structures and procedures mentioned in the foregoing are summarized in Table 5.1.

Notwithstanding these fundamental differences there is a constant and fruitful interaction between the two. In fact, every structure is the result of procedural constructions and every procedure uses certain aspects of structures. This is as true for the very young child as it is for the scientist trying to solve a problem. Furthermore there is a continuity due to these interactions. Early and primitive structures are used in procedures and reconstructed at later stages: the primitive groupings of classification are the fundamental basis of systematic zoology and biology. Without structural instruments which characterize the psychogenesis of knowledge from early childhood on, science itself would be

Table 5.1 Differences between structures and procedures

Structures	Procedures
Nontemporal (French "intemporel").	Temporal.
Directed toward understanding reasons, "know-why" ("comprendre").	Directed toward reaching a goal, "know-how" ("savoir faire").
Manifesting themselves in inferences.	Manifesting themselves in more empirical behaviour.
Conscious understanding ("compréhension") is required from the operational level on (e.g. looking for similarities in categorizing).	Conscious comprehension may be helpful but is not necessary.
Developing through inclusion ("emboîtement"); the "over-taken" ("dépassé") structure is integrated in the "overtaking" one ("dépassant").	Developing through a sequential chain ("enchaînement"), one link at least partially replacing the former.
As structures consist in finding the internal laws relating elements they are limited in number: progress consists in linking them together (e.g. classification and seriation in number).	Enrichment through variety: reaching the goal by different roads.

impossible. But at the same time procedures are the starting point for technical developments, and everyone knows nowadays that science and techniques form a very closely linked couple in which one cannot call techniques simply applications of scientific knowledge.

5.2.4 The Final Question: "Do Structures Exist?"

Though Piaget has spent little time in answering criticisms, he is very well aware of the objection which is raised so often: structures do not exist, or (in mitigated form), structures are constructed by the logician and are irrelevant for the child. His answer can be found in numerous writings, especially published discussions after lectures. The most recent formulations were given in the discussion in honour of his eightieth birthday (**103**) and in the article mentioned in 5.2.3 (**116**).

Structures certainly are not "observables", but what is observable is what the child does and knows how to do when given a problem ("sait faire"). Sometimes this is an incidental success but usually the subject becomes very consistent using the same procedures which allow a semi-formalization. The adult may then translate them into operations and construct the structure. In other words

"the structure is indeed constructed by the observer, but it is
not at all a product of the observer's thought; it is the description of the actions which the subject is capable of executing
['sait faire'] independently of what he thinks or says about it"

(**103**, p.73)

What the child says and gives as intentional justifications are no longer abstract structures but a set of rules and intellectual norms accompanied by a feeling of logical "necessity" (**51**, p.274/p.19). In the article (**116**) the same idea about structures is repeated in slightly different words and a comparison is added: saying that structures only exist in the mind of the psychologist "would be like saying that the child can eat and breathe but that his stomach and lungs only exist in the mind of the physiologist" (**116**, p.169). Comparing structures and procedures we find a comparable situation in so far as the child is, at first, only conscious of his goal and not of the procedures used. But at a later stage both may become conscious though it is far easier to become conscious of procedures than of structures because it is simpler to follow in one's mind a succession of steps than to unite the different parts connected into a simultaneous whole (**116**, p.169).

☐The close connection between structures and procedures is seen again in the use of "sait faire" (can-do) in describing structures and "savoir faire" (know-how) in describing procedures. I think that this rather confusing use of the same term is due to the close interaction between the two. In any experiment the child is given a task and questioned about what he is doing and observing. This means that a problem has to be solved whether the experimenter wants to know how the child "understands" his world, i.e. structures his world, or how he succeeds in solving the problem. The child uses certain procedures to solve the problem but to what extent he is successful in terms of the criteria used by the adult (e.g. conserves in a conservation task) will depend on his structures; hence the term "operational behaviour" used by Piaget and often considered a contradiction. In other tasks the influence of the empirical situation is more important, having been made so by the experimenter who studies the child's procedures. More critical readers probably only see a confusion or a circular reasoning instead of a continuous dialectical interaction between opposite poles.

5.3 Action, Functions, Equilibration

Accepting that the individual constructs his structured world, the question now arises about how he does so. We saw that his procedures to solve problems are closely linked to his structures. But this is not yet very explicit and furthermore the notion of procedures was only recently introduced into Piaget's theory. So there still remains the question of how the construction of structures can be explained.

Constructing is an activity, whether physical or mental, so action will be the core-concept. But action cannot be random, later becoming shaped by operational conditioning, if one accepts that structures are more than aggregates of elements. This takes us to the relation between actions of the subject and the reality on which he acts: assimilation and accommodation. But if assimilation dominated, the subject would hardly progress, while a domination of accommodation would lead to a copy of reality. Therefore the two must be in equilibrium. Yet if equilibrium were a return to the former state this could never lead to development, and thus the process of equilibration must be improving ("majorante"). Finally, as the subject himself is a structure of the whole (totality), and disruption of this whole would be fatal, development must be organized by an equilibrium between transformation and conservation and between differentiation and integration. Through this process of equilibration the subject adapts to his environment.

The main aspects of the concepts integrated in this very concise bird's-eye view of Piaget's theory will be elucidated in what follows and elaborated in detail in later chapters.

5.3.1 Action, Action Schemes and Operations

Action is indispensable for biological survival as well as for cognitive development. It is therefore doubtful whether a person living in a state of complete immobility from birth on would survive, and if this were possible one would wonder if such a person would ever become capable of mental actions like adding or subtracting (**58**, p.40/p.31). In making such an assumption *it is necessary to take action in a very wide sense, including material actions as well as interiorized actions*. But though taken in a wide sense, *action as behaviour must be clearly distinguished from physiological activities. An action is directed towards specific and modifiable objects with differentiated goals for the use of each object which remains exterior to the body as long as the action takes place* (**96**, p.184ff/p.153). This implies that physiological activities are not actions, the same being true of random movements.

    Examples: In eating, the search for food and the intake of food are actions, while the rest of the digestive process is no longer an action. Directed eye-movements are actions, but the accommodation of the eye is not.

Part of an action can be transposed, generalized or differentiated from one situation to the next. *The part that is common to applications or repetitions of the same action is called a "scheme" or an "action scheme".*

    □Originally Piaget used the term "schéma", translated as "schema" (pl. schemata or schemas). As early as 1936 he switched to "schème". This should be translated as "scheme" (pl. schemes) as Piaget now uses the word "schéma" in a different sense, that is, within the figurative aspect of knowledge (**55**, p.705n and see Chapter 7). According to Flavell: "*Schema* is a mistranslation of the Piagetian French original, *schème*, perpetrated by writers (the present writer prominently among them) insufficiently versed in French, Piaget or both." (**244**, p.17n, italics in original). An additional problem is caused by the fact that in some languages it is impossible to find two different words for "schème" and "schéma". In quotations "schema" and "schemata" will be changed into "scheme" and "schemes" to avoid confusion.

Actions do not remain isolated but become coordinated, such coordinations of actions forming the earliest logico-mathematical structures (permanent object, group of displacements). At a later stage, towards the age of 6 or 7, actions which have become interiorized become reversible and are integrated into structures. These are the well-known *operations* defined as *"interiorized, reversible actions grouped into overall systems having their laws of composition as systems or totalities."* (e.g. **106**, p.33, italics added)

    □A detail that often confuses the reader is that operations as interiorized actions and "concrete operations" characterize the child from the age of 6 or 7 on. Nevertheless, Piaget often illustrates "operations" with examples from the sensorimotor stage. Taxed with this discrepancy he admitted that it is just a case of sloppy writing, as he meant "coordinations of actions" rather than "operations".

The importance of actions is exaggerated according to many critics (see 17.1.1.2 and 17.2.1).

5.3.2 The Functions of Assimilation and Accommodation

The kind of structures in which Piaget is interested are always linked to "functioning". Every introduction to Piaget tells the reader that there are two invariant functions: adaptation, consisting in assimilation and accommodation, and organization. However, the preliminary question of what functions are is usually skipped, possibly because of its biological origin.

□My efforts at clarification may not be helpful enough. The interested reader is advised to turn to the relevant passages in *Biology and Knowledge* where Piaget gives more details.

□Criticisms of assimilation and accommodation have been put off till Chapter 23.

5.3.2.1 The nature of functions

There are mathematical functions and biological functions—the latter being meant in this context.

In general, dynamic structures are considered to be active and this activity is called their "functioning". Within this *very general approach* the term *"function"* is used in the sense of *a totality of structures including their functioning:* the cognitive function, the symbolic function, etc.

There is, however, a more *restricted sense in which structure and function are opposed*, though remaining closely linked in the same way as structure and procedure are linked together though opposed to each other. In this restricted sense

"function is the action exerted by the functioning of a sub-structure on that of a total structure, whether the latter be itself a substructure containing the former or the structure of the entire organism."   (32, p.200/p.141)

An example of a function in this sense would be that of respiration or, a still wider one, that of assimilation.

In order to be complete, this definition has to be qualified by adding three aspects of functions. In the first place, the functioning action of a sub-structure is only considered a function as long as the activity remains within the limits of what is "normal", i.e. useful in conserving the structure of which it is a part. In the second place, if we speak of a function like "the function of respiration", this term refers to a whole class of analogous actions, each of them being normal and useful. In the third place, the notion of a function considered as normal and useful only makes sense in the context of organization. We then speak of organization as a function in contrast to its structure. This function of organization is defined as the action (or class of actions) exerted by the functioning of the total structure on the sub-structures it includes (32, p.201/p.142).

One of the essential characteristics of functions is that they are invariant during the lifetime of an organism. While structures are repeatedly reconstructed, thereby changing qualitatively, functions do not change.

☐This is a fundamental difference and neglecting it leads to a lot of misunderstandings about the differences in the nature of development in empiricist theories (especially behaviourism) and Piaget's constructivism.

5.3.2.2 Assimilation and accommodation

Assimilation and accommodation are basic functions that owe their importance to the fact that adaptation of the organism to its environment consists of different levels of assimilation and accommodation. *In general, assimilation means incorporation into an existing system* (e.g. 96, p.28/p.7). The system may vary from an organ to a biological organism, or from a simple sensorimotor scheme to the highest cognitive structures. This definition holds true for all kinds of assimilations and it served for a long time, leading to the use of "food for assimilation" even where cognitive schemes were concerned. More recently, however, Piaget explicitly distinguishes *two types of assimilation.* At *the physiological level assimilation consists of the organism's intake of substances or energies from the environment with the "goal" of conserving the system.* If the metabolism of the organism then leads to conservation of the system, there is no need for change. This assimilation must be opposed to *behavioural assimilation which consists of the integration of objects into schemes of action.* The two are often combined, e.g. in looking for food and digesting it—to take the example used in illustrating actions. Behavioural assimilations are aimed at an extension of the environment and of the organism's power over the environment. A further, very important, difference between the two types of assimilation is that physiological assimilation proceeds by simple repetitions while behavioural assimilations lead to memories, thus multiplying relations and contributing to the extension of their number (96, p.172/p.141).

The importance of assimilation is clearly seen in what Piaget calls the first postulate: *"every assimilatory scheme tends to feed itself, that is, to incorporate elements that are exterior to the scheme and compatible with its nature"* (**90**, p.13/p.7 italics added. My translation). Piaget defines a "postulate" as a general hypothesis derived from an examination of the facts.

The postulate shows that assimilation does not only depend on the subject because objects have to be compatible with the scheme in order to be assimilated. This implies that the subject must be capable of distinguishing what is compatible and what is not at a very early age. Piaget calls this activity "classification".

☐In general Piaget makes no distinction between what is usually called "discrimination" and what is usually called "classification".

If an object cannot be assimilated there are two possibilities. Either it is too far outside the range of what is "assimilable" and is therefore just left aside by the subject. Or it is close enough to assimilable objects for the scheme to be changed so that, ultimately, assimilation becomes possible. This change is called "accommodation" of the scheme to the object. Again there is *physiological accommodation* and *behavioural accommodation*. When accommodation is necessary because the environment is unusual, the physiological organism accepts it, resulting in an assimilatory cycle differing as little as possible from the original one. But, in contrast, accommodation of an action scheme means an enrichment that does not abolish the earlier scheme but leads to new sub-structures by differentiation.

The relationship between assimilation and accommodation is expressed in a second postulate:

"every assimilatory scheme has to accommodate to the elements it assimilates, that is, to change as a function of their characteristics, but without losing its continuity [i.e. its closure as a cycle of independent processes] *nor its former powers of assimilation".*

(**90**, p.13/p.7. Italics added. My translation)

In the general definition of assimilation as "incorporation into a scheme" nothing is said about the nature of what is assimilated. However, one can distinguish objects (in a large sense: a theory as well as a material·body are both objects!) from other schemes. Thus there are *several levels of assimilation* depending on the nature of what is assimilated and, automatically, of what the scheme accommodates to.

The *first level* is that of *the assimilation of an exogenous object and the accommodation of the scheme to this object*—e.g. when an infant grasps an object or when a theorist assimilates a notion from another theory and accommodates his own theory in consequence. In this interaction between subject and object, the object changes through assimilation and the subject through accommodation. Assimilating something into a scheme implies that the subject gives a signification (or meaning) to the object, and in a constructivist theory this means that the object is changed for the subject. Something that had no meaning for the infant becomes "something to suck", "something to grasp" and is changed. In the same way, assimilation of a notion into the theorist's theory gives a new meaning to that notion. When accommodation follows, this evidently implies a change of the infant's scheme or the theorist's theory.

At the second level, schemes are assimilated reciprocally, if necessary with accommodation; eye-hand coordination is the best-known example.

The *third and highest level* is far more complex. A given structure of actions or operations is first *differentiated* into sub-systems as a result of accommodation. These new sub-systems are then *integrated* into a new totality of a higher level—this integration being due to assimilation. At the higher levels of cognitive development this complex level is much more important than the simple assimilation/accommodation of objects which is already being seen in the very earliest days of sensorimotor assimilation/accommodation. Piaget's recent work on reflective abstraction, generalization, the possible and the necessary is an elaboration of this level and will be discussed in later chapters.

5.3.3 Equilibration

From assimilation and accommodation to equilibration is but one step, as the former have always been the basis in Piaget's descriptions of the latter. The notion of equilibrium itself has been central in Piaget's theory from the very first, but even he found it a puzzling concept, as can be seen from the different versions of his theory of equilibrium and equilibration. The first version, published in 1957, only satisfied him for a very short period—though he never said so explicitly in his writings, thus giving his readers the impression that it was still the theory to criticize! But as he said (**114**), there is no need for this because he himself took care of the criticism. Finally, in 1975, he wrote a new book in which the whole process of "improving" equilibration is analysed in detail.

◻Piaget does admit that he is rather careless in his use of "equilibrium" and "equilibration", but his intention is to use the first for the state and the second for the related process.

Piaget loves to invent new names e.g.: "équilibration majorante".

This has the unpleasant consequence that every translator makes his own "English" word. "Majorante" is derived from the Latin "major", meaning more, higher, better. Thus "équilibration majorante" has been translated as "heightening equilibration", "augmentative equilibration", "incremental equilibration", "improving equilibration" and "improved equilibration". The last term is definitely wrong, because it is not the equilibration which is improved but the structure due to the equilibration. I think that "improving" is the least unharmonious word and have therefore chosen it as it also expresses Piaget's intention.

"Improving equilibration" serves as a general model for the causal explanation of what the subject does in the constructions of his progressive cognitive development, as well as showing how the scientist proceeds from one theory to the next. In this sense equilibration is a theory of the psychological subject and of the scientist, in contrast to the logical analysis of the epistemic subject and the "content" of scientific theories. As the psychological subject and its development are discussed in Section C, a more detailed summary of Piaget's recent theory on the subject will be postponed. However, a few general remarks here will show how assimilation and accommodation are related to equilibration.

At each of the three levels of assimilation and accommodation an equilibrium must be established between these two functions and their results. But as every state of equilibrium is only temporary, the question arises as to what the causes are of the disturbance of the equilibrium, in other words, of disequilibrium. Equilibration is in fact a continuous sequence of equilibrium-disequilibrium-equilibrium, etc. and it is the nature of this process which is so difficult to explain in a satisfactory way.

☐ Equilibration is criticized in 17.1.1.3, 20.1 and 23.2.2.

5.3.4 Organization

When defining functions (5.3.2.1) I followed Piaget in saying that a function is the action exerted by the functioning of a sub-structure on that of a total structure. But there is also, reciprocally, an action exerted by the totality on its sub-structures. *This very general function of the totality, characterizing all living organisms of whatever level, is called "organization".* Speaking of biological organization in the sense of such a general function one risks confusing it with life itself (**32**, p.209/p.148). However, one has to postulate such a general function because otherwise all the transformations mentioned so far would lead to incoherence, in the biological as well as cognitive senses. Thus organization is essential for any kind of continuity. It is even so fundamental that it is not transmitted by the genome but is a necessary condition for any hereditary transmission.

☐In *Biologie et Connaissance* the French text reads: "à titre de *condition nécessaire de toute transmission et non pas à titre de contenu transmis*" (p.210, italics in original). In the official translation the *"non pas"* (= not) has slipped out though the foregoing text clearly shows the error (p.148).

As far as cognitive organization is concerned three characteristics are essential. The first characteristic is that of conservation. From the inborn reactions on, intelligence develops step-by-step with a partial conservation of what has been achieved. The conservation is no more than partial because functioning modifies the structures by using them, but the continuity clearly indicates a tendency to conserve. Concrete examples of conservation are seen in the construction of invariants at all levels of development. Its earliest forms are action schemes that are relatively invariant notwithstanding their use in different situations with different contents. The importance of these invariants is so great that they are projected by the subject on to reality in the form of the notion of conservation applied to objects. At a still higher level the principle of identity constitutes an invariant though reality constantly denies it. At the scientific level "principles of conservation" become elaborated, reappearing in new forms at all levels whenever their preceding form does not suffice to organize the facts.

☐This passage puts the well-known experiments on conservation in an epistemological context instead of reducing them to an ability to give the correct "yes" or "no" answer to the experimenter's question in a con-servation test, or—still worse in Piaget's eyes—to teaching the correct answer as an isolated skill.

The second characteristic of cognitive organization is a constant tendency towards differentiation and its complementary integration. Without such integrations in which relationships are still of funda-mental importance, there would be no more than a reunion of atomistic elements—a notion contrary to structuralist constructivism.

The third characteristic of cognitive organization is its dynamic nature, that is, its integration of a continuous stream of changing content into permanent forms. This is true of sensorimotor schemes that tend to generalize to new situations by generalizing assimilation, as well as being the case at all higher levels of conceptual structures. The latter only function effectively when new circumstances or new problems assure a continual circulation in the content of ideas.

□Relating these notions from *Biology and Knowledge* (published in 1967) to more recent publications one sees in the last characteristic a forerunner of the more recent couple of structures and procedures. New structures develop by way of procedures as was mentioned earlier.

Though adaptation and organization are the most important functions mentioned in Piaget's earlier works, they certainly are not the only functions. In *Biology and Knowledge* "anticipation" is described, while in recent publications Piaget says that the two main functions of creative reason are "comparing" and "transforming". As the term suggests, "transforming" changes the content. The fundamental difference between these two functions is that in comparing, the content of the comparison is not changed. Though comparing has only been elaborated in recent years (**101** and books in press), it is perhaps as important epistemologically as transforming—though again the two go together (see Chapter 8).

5.4 The Driving Forces of Development

If one accepts a constructivist epistemology with successive levels of higher equilibrium, the final question must be why this equilibration takes place. Why does the subject go to the trouble of looking for new knowledge, either his individual knowledge or scientific knowledge? This question is easily answered by any kind of preformism because the individual is seen as either hereditarily programmed or as conditioned by his environment. It is more difficult to find a constructivist answer.

Many readers interpret Piaget's theory, especially his earlier writings, as though he considered the final mature equilibrium as being the force of development. But this would be a pure form of a final cause and— unless one accepts a hereditary program—a very mysterious one, because it can never be the subject's goal.

□In the publications of other authors one finds two different descriptions of the "telos", or end state, in Aristotle's work. One maintains that the observer sees a "telos" in the development taking place. In this sense cognitive maturity might well be the end state. The other maintains that this "telos" determines the development or, in other words, is the cause of development. The latter is unacceptable, not only for critics of Piaget, but for Piaget as well.

In fact, every action of whatever kind contains a finality, in the cybernetic sense of a program. Psychologically speaking, this finality is given by a goal or a representation available in the present of what the subject wants to achieve in the future. Though this teleonomy has replaced teleology, it does not give an answer to the original question. Why then, does the subject have these goals of wanting-to-know?

One of the answers given by Piaget is that "affects" are the driving force of development, "affect" being used in the sense of interest or need (e.g. **108**, p.131). However, many critical readers still find this answer unsatisfactory: at the colloquium in honour of his eightieth birthday one of his "opponents" asked him to elaborate on the "why" of development. Piaget's answer is partly to be found in his theory of the possible (see Chapter 10) and partly in his theory of behaviour as the driving force of evolution (**96**).

In the first place, the subject is active and never limits himself to registering what can be observed, but tries to coordinate, assimilate, reconstruct—in short to find the "reasons" for the laws that have been derived from observables. Even when the subject does not yet have a procedure for actualizing something that has become "a possibility" ("une possibilité"), he is certain that he can "overtake" the structure he has already achieved and that this structure must be merged as a sub-structure into a larger one. As was already mentioned, this internal dynamism of the structures is to be found at all levels from the most elementary need to "feed" a scheme to mathematical generalizations (**103**, p.54).

In the second place, there is a general tendency in every organism to enlarge its environment and to conquer new parts of it, due to the fact that the organism as an open system is always threatened by the environment. In so far as the organism succeeds in doing this, it is more powerful. But in his efforts to expand the environment the subject is constantly faced by problems the environment poses. These perturbations lead to compensations (see Chapter 9). Thus the need for coherence and consistency driving the subject on implies a continuous sequence of reorganizations.

This consistency also explains the universality of structures. They have to be as they are in order to become closed structures with their necessity. In contrast to procedures, which show an endless variety, consistency and closure explain the universality of the answers to the epistemic questions asked by Piaget concerning space, time, causality, etc.

> ☐The universality of notions, structures, etc. is an important point of discussion. See 17.1.1.1, 17.2.3.2 and 17.2.4.
>
> Many authors emphasize the influence of society (17.2.3), or of history and society (17.2.4). One might say that the social position of the child is also a "driving force" for his cognitive development.

C

The Psychogenetic Construction of Knowledge

6 Piaget's Way of Tackling Problems of Cognitive Development

☐The fundamental difference between Piagetian and non-Piagetian methodology is mentioned in 14.3 and elaborated in Chapter 22. In general, Chapter 22 closely follows the organization of this chapter. The only exception is that training experiments are discussed in 20.2.

In his early works (**1, 4**) Piaget carefully explained his clinical method and its pitfalls. Later on, though his experiments became less verbal he saw no need for explaining the new procedure in detail. In his more recent work we find two sources of information on his methodology. On the one hand Piaget writes about general problems of research in the sciences of man (e.g. in **49** and **76**) while on the other hand we find interesting incidental remarks in many volumes in which experiments are described and interpreted. Using these two sources of information I shall first turn to the general aspects of ''verification'' and then to the research.

☐The following is as much based upon Piaget's writings as other chapters but the details of 6.2 are combined by me.

6.1 General Aspects of Research

6.1.1 Verification and Experimentation in Psychology

As was already mentioned, verification is the essential criterion distinguishing a science from philosophy or metaphysics. Scientists are united in their common wish to look for verification and this leads to progress by mutual control and criticism. Verification can take place through any form of experimentation where facts are concerned, or through algorithms or formalizations in the case of a deductive science like logic.

Verification encounters many problems which are partly shared by all experimental sciences and are partly exclusive to sciences of man.

The history of sciences shows that, in general, experimental sciences develop later than deductive ones. There are three reasons for this phenomenon. In the first place, it is much easier for human intelligence to know reality intuitively or deductively than experimentally, because of the far greater freedom of the former. In the second place, in deductive reasoning the most elementary operations are at the same time the simplest ones: uniting or dissociating, ordering, etc. In experimentation a complex situation has to be analysed first in order to dissociate factors that may then be varied. In the third place, the so-called "reading-off" of facts is never as simple as it sounds, because factors have to be isolated and this in turn requires a logico-mathematical frame.

The specific difficulty of the sciences of man is that they concern the very complex activities of man yet are, at the same time, elaborated by man. In other words, man is at the same time both object and subject of these sciences. This leads to practical as well as to epistemological problems. On the practical side there is the danger that the experimenting subject might be changed himself by the observed phenomena or that his activity might influence the phenomena he wishes to study. Generally the experimenter is personally engaged in the objects that he should study from the outside and this engagement makes him attribute values to the facts which interest him. The risk is that he might begin to trust his intuition instead of using objective techniques. Thus the de-centring required for objectivity is much more difficult here than it is in other sciences. Many psychologists, fearing the influence of their intuition and engagement, do try to be objective by an excessive use of measurement. But Piaget sees many problems for the sciences of man when they try to measure phenomena. In order to experiment one has to isolate one factor or a single group of factors, the others being more or less neutralized. But maintaining a situation of "all other things being equal" is very difficult in the sciences of man in general, and particularly in psychology. In the first place organisms are entities in which the elements are interdependent, and in the second place moral restraints often limit the possibilities of experimentation. However, these difficulties are partly compensated for by the fact that humans are capable of describing verbally a part of their reactions. But, even when a factor or group of factors has been isolated, its measurement is often impossible because there are no equal units. Knowing that a subject remembered eight words out of sixteen in one memory test and four out of six sectors of a journey in another test, does not allow any conclusion because we cannot compare the words amongst themselves nor the sectors of the journey with the words. The only solution for Piaget was to make use of broader and more flexible logico-mathematical instruments and structures.

As I have already mentioned, not only do problems as these have to be solved, but there are also epistemological difficulties. The fact that in this field man is subject and object at the same time, while the object is a conscious person capable of words and other symbolizations complicates the research situation. The object of the psychologist may differ from one culture or subculture to another, thus causing many problems which would be unknown to a physicist (**49**, Chapters 3 and 4).

However, though these difficulties encountered by a scientific psychologist should be fully realized, they certainly do not give him an excuse for giving up his efforts at verification.

6.1.2 Explanation

Positivism insisted that science should limit itself to laws and the predictions derived from them. But even in the "sciences of nature" many scientists do no more than write their preface in this manner and then introduce explanatory hypotheses and reasons behind the laws. In the sciences of man the influence of positivism is still less, in the first place because these sciences are young and modest, in the second place because "positivists" differ so much from each other, and in the third place—and this is the most important reason—because man wants to act and to produce and not only to contemplate and to predict. Thus the wish to understand and to explain is more explicit and more conscious in the sciences of man (**49**, p.110/p.74).

Stressing the importance of explanation leads to two questions: "What is an explanation?" and "What are the necessary steps for finding explanations?"

6.1.2.1 What is an explanation?

To explain is to give an answer to the question "Why?", that is to say, it is to find the "reason" in deductive sciences and the "cause"—though that is a dangerous word—in physical sciences (**76**, p.7).

In deductive sciences one cannot speak of "causes" but only of "reasons". Piaget generally illustrates this with the example that $2 + 2 = 4$ leads to $4 - 2 = 2$, though $2 + 2 = 4$ cannot be said to be the cause of $4 - 2 = 2$ in the same sense as a cause can be said to lead to an effect in reality. As we shall see in detail later, "reasons" are found by "signifying implication" ("implication signifiante"), originally called "implication in the broader sense". Causes are due to attributions of our logico-mathematical structures to objects. Notwithstanding this difference, reasons and causes have two important characteristics in common: they should have an intrinsic necessity and find something new.

The latter is essential because it means an implicit admission that an explanation cannot be found by any form of simple reductionism. This holds true for what Piaget calls "external reductions" as well as for "internal" ones. In external reductionism one claims to explain a law by seeing it as a specific form of a more general law. In fact this explains nothing because it only leads to the question of how to explain the more general law. Furthermore, it teaches nothing new, as the general law is a known one. In internal reductionism one looks for the reason for a new reality in a reality that already exists, and therefore could have predetermined the new one.

The notion that an explanation must have the characteristic of necessity and yet be at the same time saying something new, looks paradoxical. Piaget's main problem is therefore to understand how something new can at the same time be necessary. The explanation cannot be preformed because then it would not be new, but at the same time it cannot be due to contingencies because that excludes necessity. In deductive sciences structures are closed and thereby possess an intrinsic necessity. But structures are also systems of transformations, thus leading to new constructions. Because there are laws for these transformations the constructions are rational. Therefore structures lead to new constructions that are necessary, thus solving the formal problem of finding adequate reasons. As Piaget considers causes as being attributions of logico-mathematical structures of the subject to reality, they satisfy the requirements of being new and necessary.

6.1.2.2 What are the steps leading to explanations?

Three steps lead to explanations, the first of which is not yet explanatory (**49**, p.111ff/p.74ff; **50**, p.150ff/p.17ff and p.212ff/p.47ff).

□The translation in **49** of "étappes" as "stages" is misleading because the next step is not a reconstruction of the former one, which is a requirement of stages.

a) *The first step: collecting facts and finding laws*
Laws derived from facts add nothing new to the facts themselves as they are limited to establishing the generality of the facts. This is done by the process of inductive generalization that increases the extension

of facts, leading from "some" to "all" (or to a certain proportion of "all" in a statistically determined law).

Such a generality, found by inductive generalization, allows predictions of future facts, without, however, explaining them, because the criterion of causality—the presence of necessary and sufficient conditions—is lacking. There is only one intermediate step which leads to necessary relations and this can be seen in functional dependences of the form: $y = f(x)$. In the case of multiple variants of this kind one can acknowledge a certain degree of causality in the role ascribed to the determining factors (**49**, p.112/p.75).

◻The last sentence will be far from clear for many readers, but Piaget does not elaborate this statement.

b) *The second step: coordination of laws by deduction*
The difference between the generality of laws and the necessity of explanations is that the former are only derived from the facts, while necessity is a characteristic of logical or mathematical relations. The form of deduction used is called "constructive deduction" and it adds the necessity of transformations to the generality of laws, thus coming close to explanations. In other words: laws are inserted into mathematical structures with their own norms of composition (e.g. lattices, groups, etc.).

However, even a logico-mathematical deduction due to such constructive generalizations is no more than logic or mathematics. In order to find a true explanation these deductions must be related to the facts, and this is done in the third step.

c) *The third step: construction of an abstract model of a mathematical, logical or cybernetic nature*
Any model must be adapted to reality in such a way that deductive transformations correspond to real transformations. In other words, for Piaget a model is the projection of a logico-mathematical structure on to reality, or—as he also says—logico-mathematical structures are "attributed to" reality.

6.1.2.3 Description or explanation?

Piaget has often been accused of giving descriptions instead of explanations, e.g. in his theories of equilibration, reflective abstraction and assimilation/accommodation.

In the Appendix to his book on equilibration (**90**), he goes into this problem.

> "Description ascertains a certain number of general facts...but
> without exceeding the level of 'reading off' [constatation] and
> of determining their level of generality."
>
> (p.179/p.190, my more literal translation)

Explanation looks for the reasons for these facts, linking them to each other or to others which are not yet known. An explanation contains a deductive necessity and is "orientated towards a theoretical construction" (p.179/p.191). However, there are many levels of necessity, from links that are no more than probable to a completely formalized theory. As for experimental results we also find many levels, from a global agreement with the facts to a detailed verification.

Piaget says that his own theory can

> "boast neither of an advanced deductive theory nor of an
> agreement with the verified facts except when cross-checking
> between the results of varied research has been possible."
>
> (p.179/p.191)

On the other hand, Piaget is convinced that he has gone beyond descriptions by finding reasons. Some of these are functional, that is to say "they limit themselves to indicating the necessity of an observed function" (p.180/p.191), while others are structural. In the chapters on equilibration I shall return to the structural reasons he summarizes. For the time being, the fact that he goes beyond pure description is the essential point.

6.2 Piaget's Research on Cognitive Development

6.2.1 The Usual Type of Experimentation

6.2.1.1 The steps in experimentation

a) *The first step: a general question*

Every piece of research begins with a question that must be formulated in such a way that verification and agreement are possible. Piaget's questions are very general ones and this is true for epistemological issues ("How do notions of time, speed, etc. develop?") as well as for more psychological ones ("How does consciousness develop?"). Such general questions and Piaget's notions about their answers form guiding hypotheses.

b) *The second step: translating the guiding hypothesis into experiments*

This is a difficult issue because Piaget's theorizing is on a high level of abstraction, while the experimental tasks must be concrete enough for children from 4 to 12 years (the usual age-range) to perform. In his recent research on "the possible" Piaget explicitly admitted this difficulty, though he finally found solutions that satisfied him.

The same general question is always translated into a number of experiments—on causality there were a hundred of them!

c) *The third step: finding facts*

The task of finding facts leads to the problem as to what facts are. A "fact" has three characteristics. In the first place it is an answer to a question. In the second place it involves a "reading off". This "reading off" or the establishment of a fact, contains far more than empiricists believe because it is always bound up with a system of interpretations. This is true for the very young child who assimilates something into an action scheme as well as for the scientist who establishes the fact that young children do not conserve. In the third place such "facts" only become scientific facts when the scientist explicitly interprets the facts in order to understand or explain them (**15**, p.170ff/p.125ff).

    ☐ In the original Piaget distinguishes the French "constatation ou lecture" from "vérification". The former is the establishment of the fact, the "reading off" from the observable. A later step of interpretation, control by others, etc. is the verification. It is confusing that both terms have been translated as "verification".

d) *The fourth step: linking the interpretations of separate experiments to the original question*

Piaget's experiments are never constructed in such a way that a hypothesis can be falsified. The results always confirm his guiding hypothesis, in so far as the original question was formulated in such a way that it could be confirmed. In rare cases Piaget was surprised by the new insights experiments gave him, e.g. in the experiments on contradiction.

e) *The fifth step: verification by replication*

Piaget never does systematic replications. Some of the experiments on conservation and classification are used in other experiments to determine the operational level of the child. As the results correspond to what was originally found, this is—in a sense—a replication. Piaget is very happy when replications by other investigators confirm his

interpretations, as has happened again and again with conservation, etc.
☐If somebody could show the opposite by methods acceptable to Piaget,
he would regret having been wrong, but he would take it seriously. It is
only impossible to convince him of being wrong when his opponent philo-
sophizes, starts from an empiricist epistemology or changes the task so
much that it no longer corresponds to what Piaget did.

f) *The sixth step: reporting the results*

Piaget repeatedly emphasizes that experiments and their results must
be published in such a way that others can check his work. Anyone who
has read one of his books on experiments knows the general lay-out: a
long introduction, then a rather inexact description of the experiment,
followed by some examples of the reactions of each level with a very
detailed interpretation. As this is repeated for each experiment redundances are unavoidable. Finally there is a conclusion, which links up
more or less with the introduction.

g) *The seventh step: the next question*

Every answer to one of his questions leads Piaget to a new question.
Sometimes this is taken up right away but sometimes many years go by
before he returns to a topic. When reading his recent books, e.g. on
"the possible" (see 10.2), one could easily believe that this was a
totally new topic. In fact, it was prepared by foregoing work and one
can find allusions to the topic many years before Piaget finally concentrated on it.

6.2.1.2 Details of the experimental procedure

a) *The material and instruction*

Piaget always wants to make a child think about a problem, either to let
him understand what is happening or to make him look for a solution
to the problem. His thinking is provoked by the material, the instruction and then by the questions of the interviewer.

The experimental material is usually very simple. It is rarely completely standardized, sometimes being adjusted to the age of the subject
and sometimes varying without any apparent reason.

The instruction is simple and adjusted as much as possible to the
child's language. Where necessary it is repeated by the experimenter,
and Piaget often emphasizes that the instruction is not too difficult for
the child (e.g. **84b**, p.41). However, this does not necessarily imply
that the child always interprets the question in the same way as an
adult would. Piaget quotes a remark by Papert who said, "the child

always gives a correct answer to the question he puts to himself". Such a "misinterpretation" of the question does not lead Piaget to change the question, but rather to an effort to find out why the child does not see the difference between the question as intended by the experimenter and his own interpretation. As this interpretation is due to an assimilation into the child's own schemes it is comparable to the fact that the child only reacts to that aspect of the material he can assimilate to his schemes. All this teaches us a lot about the schemes he uses (85, p.98/p.120).

In some rare cases Piaget tells us that the material is graded in difficulty and that the early tasks might have had a "learning effect" on the later ones (86, p.111/p.99; p.212/p.195). Though he says that it might be advantageous to present the more difficult tasks in the middle and at the end of the interview to check for such a learning effect, he does not seem to have done so.

b) *The interview*

The child's mind functions best in a relaxed atmosphere. Therefore the interview is a clinical one, questions being adjusted according to the answers of the child. This is not at all easy, and in an early book Piaget suggested that a year of intensive training was required. This was evidently shortened, but Piaget is convinced that one psychologist may only get a minimum reaction from a child, while another may well stimulate him and even make him cross the threshold to the next stage when he is close to it. There are often time-lags between the results of rigorously standardized interrogations and free ones, which explains the differences in the results of tasks given in different settings (45, p.8).

For many years Piaget interviewed most of his subjects himself and he was certainly good at it. He also realized the difficulties of his interviewing technique

> "it is rather disturbing to find that the children one interviews oneself answer more often in conformity with one's own theory than do the children interviewed by other people."
>
> (4, p.240/p.208)

Piaget's remark was made in connection with the difficulty of using statistics. His conclusion characterizes him extremely well: he did not change his method but discarded statistics.

c) *The interpretation of the data*

In all the experiments from the 1940s on, a child is given some material to manipulate while he is questioned about what he does and why. These data must be interpreted, the main problem being how much value the verbal utterances of the child have. Though the tasks are quite simple, most children have never thought about them in the way they are being offered in the experimental situation. To take the famous conservation tasks: all children in our culture have poured water, seen others pour water, etc. But it is highly improbable that anyone has ever asked them questions about it or "taught" them to conserve. Thus the answers are rarely "spontaneous" if we mean by this that the children were already conscious of it before the experiment. But the acts or thoughts that are provoked by the experimenter tell us as much about the level of the child's structures as his spontaneous thinking. Only if he has reversible operations available can their use be provoked by the experimental situation.

Though talking is a necessary aspect of the situation, it is not so much what the subject consciously believes or says that is important, as is the way in which he solves a specific problem. His structures are shown in his behaviour and in his way of tackling problems (e.g. **62**, p.547), as has already been emphasized. Whenever possible Piaget tries to check verbal reactions by the child's behaviour. For instance, the concrete operational child may say, "it has to be...", or "of course..." when given a transitivity problem. But though such expressions indicate a feeling of necessity, and are therefore important, it is dangerous to trust such verbal expressions too much. One's interpretation is safer when the child uses this feeling of necessity in his behaviour—in this case in the systematic way in which he constructs a seriation. If he does this correctly, it shows that transitivity has been understood as "necessary" because the system is closed (**34**, p.271).

Though sometimes, e.g. in seriation, the child's behaviour as well as what he says change from one stage to the next, there are also tasks in which the child's behaviour changes much less, but where the interpretation of observables changes, even without leading questions from the experimenter (**85**, p.160, p.205).

It is important to stress passages where Piaget is wary about the value of what the child says because at other moments he gives the impression of believing whatever the child says, even after his actions. Thus in *The Grasp of Consciousness* he writes that the young children only describe their actions, but that the older ones say, "I saw that...", "Then I said to myself..." (**85**, p.265/p.337). Many, many years ago Piaget wrote somewhere (!) that the young child cannot recount correctly what he has just done. So it is astonishing that he seems to accept such sentences here as being true presentations of what the child has really thought. However, when asked about this, he said, with a twinkle in his eye, "Mais je ne suis pas si naïf que ça!" (But I am not so naïve) (**114**).

So the problem remains as to what to take from the protocols. Piaget attaches much importance to the similarities of the answers within a certain level, whether they are right or wrong. Furthermore, the changes from one level to the next—and, above all, the many reactions that are intermediate between levels or sub-levels—give a consistent picture.

Thus Piaget is quite critical in his analysis of the data and he is sure that he does not just find in the protocols what he expects to be there. One of the advantages of studying children is that the psychologist is much less tempted to find a structure that exists only in his own mind in the behaviour of a child than he would do if he were dealing with an adult subject (**49**, p.60/p.36). Piaget himself never compares the actions of young children with his own notions, but only with the foregoing and the following level and this gives a sufficient guarantee for objectivity (**103**, p 66).

d) *The final conclusion*

As was already mentioned, Piaget's conclusions generally confirm his guiding hypotheses, and thus bring him one step further in the elaboration of his theory.

6.2.2 Training Experiments

In Volume II I shall pay far more attention to training experiments than in this volume. There is only one training experiment, on commutability, of which Piaget is coauthor (**93**). Furthermore, he also wrote an enthusiastic Preface in the Genevan book on learning experiments (**300**). There are several reasons for using training experiments but for Piaget only one of them is important: to test whether a hypothesis about the process of thinking or the process of intellectual development is confirmed by a training experiment based on this hypothesis.

Though the results of the Genevan experiments have been favourable, Piaget has his doubts about the value of training experiments for theoretical purposes. He raises three questions about them:

—"Is the progress obtained stable or only temporary?"
—"Is the acceleration achieved accompanied by unfavourable deviations from the general developmental trend?"

—''Is the progress achieved a basis for new spontaneous constructions?'' (**300**, p.10/p.XIII).

At the moment there are no answers to these questions which would
require a very careful longitudinal study with all its inherent difficulties.

7 The Object in the Subject-Object Interaction

□There is no general critique of Piaget's view of the figurative aspect of knowledge and hence the numbers are not exactly the same. Otherwise this chapter is organized in the same way as Chapter 18. Perception: 18.1.1.1; imitation: 18.1.1.2, etc. Causality is criticized in 18.1.2, though critics have said little on this topic. The critique of 7.2.2 is found in 18.2.2 with identical headings.

In trying to understand Piaget's interactionist constructivism one is always struck by the fact that the subject dominates within the interaction. Evidently it is the subject who constructs, the subject whose actions transform the world in this process of construction, etc. But as I said in Chapter 5 (5.1.2), Piaget is a realist as well, and reality out there is essential for the constructing subject, though he can never copy it. This reality consists of the material world and of other subjects. Though Piaget has done far more of his research on the knowledge of physical reality and though his frequent use of the term "object" makes one think of physical reality rather than persons, he does consider other people important for cognitive development, as I mentioned in Chapter 3 (3.4.1.3). Starting our overview of cognitive development with the object's part in it we must therefore think of persons as well as physical objects.

7.1 Physical Reality and Knowledge

Piaget's conviction that knowledge is never due to reality alone led him to research in those domains of cognition where other theories see the greatest influence of reality: perception, imagery, memory or—as Piaget calls them collectively—the figurative aspect of knowledge. All the research in this field is directed by the guiding hypothesis that "intelligence" co-determines the results of perception, imagery and memory.

However, objects are not only perceived, represented and remembered. They are also seen as interacting with each other. One object causes another to fall, etc. The physical world is full of causal relationships and our knowledge of the world must include an understanding of these relationships as well as an understanding of our way of understanding them. Here again, the subject must construct his knowledge, but also take reality into account. Thus the second aspect of knowledge in which the importance of objects is stressed is that of causality.

7.1.1 The Figurative Aspect of Knowledge

In Piaget's theory there are rarely isolated processes or functions. Far more often there are couples which show similarities in some aspects and yet are opposites in others. We have already seen the examples of structures-functions, assimilation-accommodation and structures-procedures. In studying one aspect of the theory one must therefore often take the complementary aspect into account for the sake of a full understanding. Thus the figurative aspect of knowledge cannot be isolated from the operative aspect of knowledge, nor from the semiotic function and empirical abstraction.

7.1.1.1 The system of cognitive functions

a) *The figurative and the operative aspects of knowledge*
The simplest way to distinguish these aspects is by saying that the figurative aspect gives us knowledge of "states" while the operative aspect leads to knowledge of "transformations". A better understanding of this distinction requires a closer look at "states" and "transformations".

"The physical, mathematical, and other realities which the mind strives to know appear in two forms: as states or as transformations" (**106**, p.18). From the logical point of view, "descriptors" are the instruments required for knowing characteristics of states or transformations, while "operators" enable us to reproduce or manipulate transformations, including their initial and final states. But as descriptors are not sufficient for comprehension, knowledge of states is subordinate to that of transformations.

From a psychological point of view a similar distinction between descriptors and operators can be made. Cognitive functions, or aspects of these functions, that are descriptors are: perception, imitation, mental imagery and memory.

   □Memory is sometimes included (e.g. **55**, p.717), and sometimes not (**106**, p.18). Its position will be clarified in 7.1.1.2.

Cognitive aspects of functions that deal with transformations are actions (sensorimotor schemes including the dynamic instinctual mechanisms) and operations, as well as their coordinations in structures.

We can now say more precisely that the knowledge given by descriptors is called the "figurative aspect" of knowledge and that due to operators is the "operative aspect" of knowledge.

□The French "opératif" is translated as "operative", while "opératoir" (the adjective of "opération") is translated by some as "operational" and by others as "operatory". Because there is less risk of confusing "operational" and "operative" than of confusing "operatory" and "operative", the former translation has been used throughout this book. "Operativity" is generally used as the substantive for "having reached the stage of operations".

In logic and mathematics the operative aspect of knowledge can be seen without the figurative aspect. In all other cases the operative aspect subsumes the figurative aspect. On the other hand, the figurative aspect can never do without the operative.

b) *The figurative aspect of knowledge and the semiotic function*

While the figurative and operative aspects of knowledge generally go together, though one or the other may dominate, the figurative aspect of knowledge and the semiotic function are two classes with an intersection.

Piaget prefers to use "semiotic function" instead of "symbolic function" because of its broader scope. *The semiotic function includes language, symbolic games, mental and graphic images* (the latter being drawings) *and deferred imitation.* It consists of symbols and signs. In symbols as well as signs there is a differentiation between the "signifier" which represents objects, events, etc. and that which is represented, called the "signified" or "significant". This differentiation only takes place in the course of the second year of life. Before that moment there are already signifiers, called "indexes", but they are not yet differentiated from the signified.

We thus have the following concepts:

"Indexes are signifiers that are not differentiated from their significants since they are part of them or a causal result" (**55**, p.717, italics added).

Examples: Examples of indexes are: whiteness, indicating milk (part-whole relation); the door being opened, indicating mother's arrival (temporal antecedent); a stain, indicating spilt food (causal result), etc.

In perception the signifier is the perceptual index while the signified consists of schemes going beyond what is given by the senses (schemes of identification, seeing relations, etc.), though the two are not yet differentiated from each other (**36**, p.14/p.11).

☐ Piaget's "signifiant" and "signifié" are sometimes used without translation. When translated, the "signifiant" becomes the signifier and the "signifié" the signified or significant. Piaget's "indice" has been translated both as "index" and as "indicator".

Symbols are signifiers that retain a measure of similarity with their significants (**55**, p.717, italics added).

Example: Examples are easily found in symbolic play when a white stone represents bread and green grass represents green vegetables. The language of deaf-mutes is full of symbols.

Symbols are individual or shared by a relatively small group of people.

Signs are conventional and more or less "arbitrary". They are always social and, as every social group has a language, signs act on the internal cognitive structures of the individuals (**36**, p.14/p.11).

☐ Piaget followed de Saussure and other linguists in his choice of the terms "symbol" and "sign". In *Mental Imagery in the Child* he mentions in a footnote that it is unnecessary to specify that what mathematicians call "symbols" has nothing to do with images and constitute "signs" in his terms (**24**, p.447n/p.382n). Psychologists are often irritated by Piaget's use of "symbol" and "sign" and consider it one more idiosyncratic use of terms, not knowing that he took them from de Saussure.

In turning to the relation between the figurative aspect of knowledge and the semiotic function, we find an intersection between the two. On the one hand, the class of perceptions is purely figurative, as indexes do not yet belong to the semiotic function. On the other hand, most of adult language is purely nonfigurative though sometimes figurative elements enter, e.g. through the use of metaphors. In young children this figurative element probably plays a more important role, though even then the purely semiotic dominates. The intersection consists of the mental image, symbolic play, deferred imitation, language by gestures, etc.

c) *The figurative aspect of knowledge and empirical abstraction*

Piaget distinguishes empirical abstraction—originally called "simple abstraction"—which gives us knowledge of physical characteristics of objects, from reflective abstraction, which is related to schemes and operations with their coordination into structures. Just as the figurative aspect of knowledge cannot do without the operative aspect, so empirical abstraction is impossible without the cooperation of reflective abstraction. One cannot decide whether an object is heavy or light unless one can see it as a member of the class of heavy objects or that of light objects. The classes (even when they are not yet quantified at the level of concrete operations) are due to reflective abstraction while empirical abstraction gives us such characteristics as heavy or light of a specific object.

Empirical and reflective abstraction are discussed in detail in Chapter 8. For the moment, only the relationship between the figurative aspect of knowledge and empirical abstraction is relevant. The figurative aspect of knowledge is, in general, more or less oriented toward a total ''picture'', either in perception or in imagery. Empirical abstraction, on the other hand, ''abstracts'' a physical characteristic of an object or situation, thereby being less directed at the totality. However, the two will often go together, figurative knowledge being necessary in order to use empirical abstraction.

Piaget repeatedly writes that empirical abstraction is ''what is usually called abstraction''. This does not mean, however, that it is the same as abstraction within an empiricist framework. Empirical abstraction always requires a mental activity of actively directing the subject's attention to the specific aspect of an object or situation. Often it also requires a physical activity, e.g. when weighing an object in one's hand to feel its heaviness or lightness. Furthermore, empirical abstraction gives us new knowledge of physical characteristics while abstraction in the usual sense means no more than directing our attention to the specific characteristic, ''abstracting'' from the rest.

Empirical abstraction is as important for our knowledge of reality as the figurative aspect of knowledge, the more so because a repetition of the same abstractions can lead by inductive generalization to rules or laws concerning facts or reality (see Chapter 8).

7.1.1.2 Types of figurative knowledge

a) *Perception*

In 1961 Piaget summed up many years of research by himself and his collaborators in a book on mechanisms of perception. Epistemologically seen the experiments were important because they clearly showed that perception itself is influenced by action and, what is more important, that concepts of intelligent thought are not derived from perception as empiricists claim. Perceptual adaptations are adaptations to specific situations and are irreversible while operational concepts are general and reversible.

Piaget wrote several short summaries of the research on perception which had consisted mainly in a very careful analysis of different types of visual illusions (e.g. **23, 44, 55**). Illusions were exceptionally suitable for his purpose because they so clearly show that perception cannot be based on sensations or impressions of the senses alone.

☐ See **294** for a critical summary of Piaget's theory followed by a detailed critique by Hotopf.

The specific theory about the influence of eye-movements need not be summarized here. A short overview of different forms of action that play a role in perception shows that the figurative aspect of knowledge, even where "states" are concerned, is always indissociably linked to the operative aspect of knowledge, that is to say, to action.

Examples: Eye-movements are necessary for seeing an object of some size. Already in his early work Piaget had written about "looking schemes". Eye-movements are also required for taking in a "structure" demonstrated by someone else, e.g. the early group of displacements or, at a later stage, classifications or seriations (**32**, p.27/p.9). Another type of action required in many perceptions is that of moving around, thus getting to know an object by seeing it in different perspectives or from different distances (**106**, p.20).

In such cases, especially the last two, one might say that action makes perception possible, but that the "act of perceiving" is not an action. However, it is only through action schemes that sensations, the impact of light-waves—or whatever one wants to call the physiological aspect of perceptions—become meaningful or get their signification. As I quoted in a more general context, reality gives us no information. Only through the assimilation of reality to action schemes does the subject attach meaning or signification to reality. Objects thus become the "indexes" mentioned above.

If every meaningful perception requires an assimilation into an action scheme the question arises of how these early action schemes develop. The very first actions of the new-born are the few genetically pre-programmed reflexes (e.g. sucking). In recent publications (e.g. **90**) Piaget also calls them "innate schemes". After the research by Bower and others showing that new-borns are already very "competent", Piaget is now willing to accept that there are more innate schemes. However, most of them disappear after a short period while only a few rapidly extend into action schemes by different types of assimilation: reproductive or functional assimilation, generalizing assimilation and recognitive assimilation (e.g. **23**, p.10/p.7). Once habits and then action schemes have been developed, assimilation into an action scheme gives signification to the object. An object that at first cannot be assimilated into any action scheme has no signification for the child, even though it may be present in what the observer would call the "visual field" of the child. After a shorter or longer time the same object becomes "something to be sucked" or "something to hit", or just "something to look at" or an index for "something to be searched for" (seeing part of an object) or "something to be listened to" (seeing mother as index for "hearing her sing a lullaby").

As I said at the beginning, empiricists suppose that concepts are derived from perception. If perceptions are not a copy of what reality gives us but are also based on actions, the question remains whether these perceptions lead to concepts. According to Piaget this is impossible. To begin with, even the earliest sensorimotor schemes are not perceptible. Therefore, as we just saw, perceptions themselves require non-perceptible aspects of knowledge. A further analysis of the relation between perceptions and analogous concepts confirms that concepts cannot be derived from percepts:

The perception of projective or apparent size is better in 6- and 7-year-old children than it is in adults. In contrast, the concepts of perspective only develop from the age of 7 years on. Now if perception deteriorates while concepts in the same domain improve, the latter cannot be built on the former.

Another important indication is the time-lag between early constancies and operational conservations. The latter require the construction of a system of transformations while in the case of the former the object does not really change. This system of transformations is derived from actions and their coordination, and therefore there can be no linear relationship between the two.

In general, concepts are more complex than perceptual data because they incorporate specific constructions. Concepts, especially the logico-mathematical ones in which Piaget is interested, always presuppose operations that are abstracted from actions and their coordinations— as we shall see in more detail in later chapters. For the time being, it is sufficient to conclude that the figurative aspect of knowledge (consisting of perceptions) cannot do without the operative aspect, and that perceptions cannot lead to concepts in the way empiricists believe.

b) *Imitation*

Imitation is very important in the transition from the sensorimotor level to that of representations, but Piaget has written very little about this topic recently because there has been nothing new to add. Looking for a suitable topic in a book in honour of Wallon, he chose imitation (95) in order to illustrate similarities and differences between Wallon's theory and his own. Without going into Wallon's theory, a short summary of the importance of imitation is given, using Piaget's article and other overviews (23, 55, 95).

During the sensorimotor period the child progresses in a number of steps from echopraxis or contagion to the imitation of facial movements. At this stage "Imitation is first of all a prefiguration of representation" (23, p.44/p.55). The next important development is seen in so-called "deferred imitation", the imitation of an action when the model is no longer present. In deferred imitation the action is detached from its context and, thus becoming a differentiated signifier, already constitutes a representation in thought. Deferred imitation therefore leads to mental imagery and representation.

Imitation also plays an important role in symbolic play, drawing and language—though the latter is only acquired in a context of imitation and is not due exclusively to imitation.

In summary, imitation, though only studied in detail during the observation of his children and therefore often neglected in summaries of Piaget's theory, is very important in the transition from the sensori-motor stage to the next stage in which the semiotic function begins to play the fundamental role.

c) *The mental image*

The study of the mental image is a continuation of that of perception, and raises the same type of problems. The first essential question is whether the image simply copies what was perceived or experienced by the child. The answer to this psychological question then takes us to the next, epistemological, question: "What is the relationship between the mental images of the subject and reality?"

Piaget and Inhelder (24) did a number of experiments on mental images. (For summaries see 23 and 44.) Studying the two questions mentioned, they were not interested in all types of images (including creative fantasy, dreams, etc.) but only in the more limited class of mental images that are closely related to perception and thought.

□This is one of the many examples of titles that are more general than the material covered. As a result critics, especially book-reviewers, often complain that the author did not include such-and-such, etc. Nobody can be expected to cover all aspects of such general issues as Piaget studies but, admittedly, the titles are misleading.

The experimental study of mental images is complicated by the fact that images cannot be observed directly in the behaviour of the child nor can verbal introspection be trusted, because the child can have an image without being able to verbalize it. Piaget and Inhelder therefore used drawing, choices between ready-made drawings, gestures and, whenever possible, verbal descriptions of these.

A mental image can be a reproduction of an object or situation that was experienced at an earlier moment or an anticipation of what is going to happen. Theoretically a reproduction can be of a static object, a movement or a transformation. As the child is as much surrounded by objects that move or are transformed as by static objects, one might expect that all three kinds of reproductive images would cause no problems for 4- or 5-year-olds provided that the tasks are simple. The results however, have been very different. Simple static reproductions, also called "copy-images", are indeed easy, but reproductions of movements and transformations cause many difficulties for children up to 7 or 8 years of age.

Example: A simple task to show a reproductive image of a movement is to get the child to draw a stick after he has imagined that it has turned 90° around one fixed end (like the hand of a clock). This is a reproduction because such movements are well-known to the child. A reproductive image of a transformation can be shown by getting the child to draw a wire which has been changed from a straight line into an arc or the other way round (without seeing the transformation). Here it is the form that changes while in the first task it is the position that changes.

Reproductions of movements and transformations require anticipations or re-anticipations of actions and are therefore closely related to anticipatory images.

Anticipations of movements are as difficult as those of transformations, but there is a difference between the younger children and those of about 7 or 8 years old. The younger children can only anticipate the end result without being able to ancitipate the road that led to this result. In contrast 7- or 8-year-olds can anticipate the road as well.

It is thus clear that there is a development in the images. If one looks at each task separately one finds several levels of achievement for each task, as indicated by the percentage of children giving a more or less advanced solution. However, the ages at which about 75% find the correct solution varies from one task to another. If one tries to reduce those partial stages and to find general developmental stages, one only finds two decisive moments of change. The first is situated around the ages of 1 ½ to 2 years when the first images appear, i.e. the first time images are clearly seen in symbolic play, while earlier behaviour could be explained without images. The second is the only change within the development of images and can be located at the ages of 7 or 8 years when anticipatory images take their full flight, though anticipations of end results come somewhat earlier.

In summary, the conclusion that there are two levels in the development of images corresponding to the pre-operational and operational stages of logico-mathematical structures is justified. In order to understand anticipatory images of movements and transformations we must therefore invoke operations.

The first reason why operations are important is that pre-operational children still centre on states and, in the case of a transformation, on the end state, while operational children centre on the transformations themselves.

□This theme of looking at the end result and not at the transformation by which it was reached, has been repeatedly taken up by Piaget in recent work. In *The Grasp of Consciousness* (**85**) he confirmed the notion that the pre-operational child centres on the results of his actions and not on the actions themselves. The same is then seen in experiments on reflective abstraction (**102**). In the book on morphisms (in press at the time of writing) he found that comparing and transforming are at first separated and are combined at the age of concrete operations. All these results will be taken up in detail in later chapters.

The second reason why operations and anticipatory images are related is that operations, which lead to deductions and anticipations, do not remain abstract but are accompanied by representations. The third reason for their close relationship is that movements and transformations consist of successive images in a temporal or spatial sequence and thus require a seriation. Finally, many anticipatory images require conservations, e.g. the length of wire transformed from a line into an arc can only be represented successfully when the length of the wire is conserved. Thus we see that operations are a requirement for images of movements and transformations. This leads to the question whether ''pre-operational'' images might help in the development of operations. There are two aspects to this question: ''Do images give useful information about 'states' that can then be useful for knowledge of transformations?'' and ''What is their role in the discovery and representation of transformations?''

In answer to the first question, pre-operational images certainly favour the acquisition or consolidation of information and this is useful for development in general.

> **Example:** One of the anticipating tasks consists of predicting the height the water will reach after pouring in the traditional conservation task. There were two types of pre-operational answers. Children of the first type said that the level and the quantity would be the same before and after pouring. The latter is a pseudo-conservation that disappears when they see the difference in height. Children of the second type predicted correctly but without conservation. The correct prediction was due to earlier experiences which were fixated in their memory, the image of which gave a correct knowledge of the "states" that would have to be explained. It was therefore a step in the direction of conservation and as such a help in its construction.

But, useful as correct pre-operational images are, they do not lead to insight into the transformation, as the example shows.

While pre-operational images contribute very slightly to the development of operations, anticipatory images that become possible thanks to operations, are in their turn a necessary help for the functioning of operations. Images give the knowledge of beginning and end states and—even though they are no more than partial images of transformations—help the full development of operations. In many cases one sees that images that became anticipatory through operations then form a stepping stone for the operations, leading to a better understanding of the transformations themselves.

> □This influence of operations on images and of images on operations is one more example of the kind of dialectical interaction that characterizes development in Piaget's theory. For an empiricist critic it is easy to see this as reasoning in circles though that is not at all what it is.

The mental image has been described as belonging to the intersection of the figurative aspect of knowledge and the semiotic function. The semiotic function is absolutely essential for thought because, without it, thought could not be put in an intelligible form either for others or for oneself. One might think that language would be enough, but Piaget sees two reasons why the extension to the figurative aspect is necessary. In the first place, language is always social and the same for everybody but this common language is unsuitable for the expression of individual experiences that are then expressed in images. In the second place, language only expresses concepts (classes, relations, etc.)

or individuals (classes with one member). There are, however, enormous numbers of individual experiences that one does not want to lose which are retained in memory as images. The image is then a symbol because it stands for what was experienced.

Finally, the epistemological question about the contribution of the subject and the object to mental imagery has to be considered.

If one supposes that images are a copy of reality, there are, as it were, two steps in this process: perception is a copy of reality and images are a copy of perception. To take the latter aspect first: visual images are a figurative evocation of objects, etc. Compared with the perception of the object the image is a mere "schéma" (not a scheme!)— i.e. it is schematized and poorer in detail than the perception. This is even true of the reproductive images that are therefore not true reproductions of what was perceived. A closer look at reproductions, especially of movements and transformations, allows us to see that they always presuppose an effort to anticipate the movement. This anticipation of the execution of the movement prepares the gesture meant to imitate the movement. *This aspect of imitation makes the image into an interiorized imitation* which shows again that it cannot be the result of a "perception" taken in the empiricist sense of a copy of reality.

Once again Piaget thus fights the notion of classical empiricism that the image is a continuation of perception, copying reality and being the source of concepts.

If the image is not a copy of perception neither can it be a copy of reality. If it were a copy it would be a global and schematized picture and therefore not a real copy, or it would analyse the details, but such an analysis goes beyond the image.

In conclusion, Piaget and Inhelder's very detailed study of mental images (**24**) of which the final chapter was summarized in the foregoing, gives one more argument for the importance of action and mental activity.

d) *Memory*

The reproductive image is based on what has been perceived and experienced before the construction of the image, and the study of memory has been, therefore, the natural successor to that of images. Once again Piaget and Inhelder showed the influence of the subject's activity and intelligence, now on memory.

□ Their book (**36**) gives all the details while the main points are summarized in **23**. A summary by Piaget can be found in a paper (**40**) and a few notes in another discussion (56). A summary by Inhelder is given in Elkind & Flavell (295).

The first question concerns what memory is, and how it is related to the figurative aspect of knowledge and the semiotic function.

"Memory" is used in two senses: what Piaget calls "the broad sense" and "the strict sense". *Memory in the broad sense is the residue of all foregoing experiences.* This type of memory is shared by animals, even of a very low level, and man. It is most simply illustrated by the scheme. Repetitions of specific behaviour lead to schemes that continue their existence in the individual's system as long as they are exercised. The individual using a scheme does not remember how and when it was built up even though this did take place in his past experience. Therefore Piaget writes that "the memory of a scheme is the scheme itself" (23, p.64/p.81). Though memory in this broad sense plays an important role in development it is not studied in this research.

☐Many remarks on memory in the broad sense can be found in *Biology and Knowledge* (32).

In contrast to memory in the broad sense, *memory in the strict sense is individualized and located in the past.* One can recognize something as having being experienced there and then (or if one forgot where and when, one has the feeling that one should remember this). One can also evoke the past in a more active type of recall than in simple recognition. Finally there is a third type of memory, situated between recognition and evocation and called "reconstitution" or "reconstruction" by Piaget. This is in part deductive and closely linked to language. Recognition is based on the figurative aspect of knowledge and is found in animals and in man from the first days of life on. Evocation is not only closely linked to the figurative aspect of knowledge but also to the semiotic function, and is therefore only found in man after the development of images and language. There is thus a close relation between memory in the strict sense and the figurative and semiotic functions. And again this relation is not a one-sided one. All the semiotic mechanisms depend on memory. Especially in the case of a reproductive image and a memory-image the figurative aspect and the memory aspect are very closely linked. The only difference between the two is, in fact, that the memory-image is located in the past while the reproductive image is not. But as the reproductive image is due to perceptions in the past, which it tries to imitate or copy, it implies the use of evocative memory.

Memory is often described in terms of encoding and decoding. If one uses this terminology Piaget and Inhelder can be said to be interested in the code itself. If the code remains the same during storage the memory should remain the same or deteriorate. But if the structure of the code changes during the course of the development of operations, one can hypothesize that memories not only remain the same but even improve. The research was directed at this problem.

> **Examples:** Several types of tasks were given, all of them being related to cognitive structures. As these develop between the ages of 3 and 8 years subjects of this age-range were used. The child was told to look carefully at the model and after a week, and once more after a number of months, he was asked to reproduce by gestures and drawings what he had seen.
>
> As tasks a simple seriation and an M-shaped seriation were given. There were also tasks concerning the horizontality of the water level in a bottle (a drawing of a tilted bottle partly filled with a coloured liquid on top of a horizontal table), numerical and spatial correspondences and situations involving causal relationships and arbitrary arrangements.

In summary, the reproductions improved after a longer period of time instead of showing the deterioration that a theory of "engrams" would make one expect. The changes observed were generally in the direction of the development of the operational structures. The memory code is determined by the construction of operational structures. Piaget and Inhelder's research on memory showed once more the importance of "intelligence", though there are still many details in need of elaboration.

> ☐Inhelder warns in her summary that one should not expect any encoding to lead to progress even though the situation be related to operativity. There may be far more complex situations, and different schemes might well conflict with each other. Hence deformations and simplifications may also be due to the influence of schemes. However, the essential point is that memory is not independent of operational schemes.

7.1.2 Causality

Piaget's interest in causality dates from the earliest years of his psychological research. His first experiment on causality was published in 1925. In 1927 a book on the subject followed, which he later called "antique and far outdistanced" ("ancien et bien dépassé", **99**, p.35). In an interview he made clear why he had gone beyond it, saying that the problem had been put in the wrong way (108, p.93). What was wrong was that he had started from the point of view of the subject (how the child explains the movement of clouds, etc.) instead of the point of view of the object (99, p.35). As a result he returned to the problem at the beginning of the 1960s, with a formulation of his basic hypothesis in 1963 (14) and a number of experiments in 1965 (17, 18, 19, 20, 21). These experiments only form a small part of all the experiments on causality done under his direction. Because there were so many (about 100!) Piaget gave up his usual procedure of describing and analysing the experiments, followed by a general conclusion. In 1971 he first published the conclusions in one general book, summarizing each experiment (58). Within the next two years four books with details of the experiments followed (65, 66, 72, 73) while three more are still in press at the time of writing. There are also two useful summaries (71, 89).

7.1.2.1 Philosophical solutions of the problem of physical causality

Reality around us is full of objects acting one upon the other, each "causing" whatever the other does. But while we have no difficulties with such notions in our everyday life, philosophers have had problems in trying to interpret our notion of physical causality. Piaget reduces their interpretations to three general types.

The first type, represented by Hume and logical positivists, recognizes no "results" and no inherent connection between what we consider cause and effect. There are only sequences of events and the "process" we see is due to our associations between events. Hence the necessity of causal links remains purely subjective.

The second type, represented by Maine de Biran, looks for a situation in which causality is experienced directly and intuitively. Such a situation can be found in our own actions and thus physical causality is considered a generalization of these actions to those of objects on each other.

The third type, represented by many philosophers since Descartes and Leibniz, is the solution of rationalism. A direct connection between physical cause and effect is granted though it is not observed but deduced. According to Piaget all solutions can be reduced to these three types (71, 89).

Piaget's question asks what the study of the development of the child's notions of physical causality can contribute to a choice between

these interpretations. In a nutshell the conclusion is that the development of the child's notions is in agreement with the rationalist hypothesis (**71**, p.26).

7.1.2.2 Stages of development

a) *Causality: the sensorimotor stage*

At the beginning of life there is as yet no differentiation between the
subject and the object as far as the infant's point of view is concerned.
This lack of differentiation, called "adualism" after J.M. Baldwin's
use of this term, makes it impossible to distinguish causal actions from
other actions of the infant.

The first beginnings of causality are therefore seen when the infant
is about 4 or 5 months old. As Piaget's observations have shown, this
early causality is of a magico-phenomenistic type—i.e. the subject relies
on his actions when wanting to influence objects (magic), accepting the
fact that two things happen at the same time as a sufficient reason for
a "causal" link (phenomenism).

> **Example:** Piaget suspended a new and interesting object over the
> child's crib and attached a string to it in such a way that the object
> moved and made a noise when the infant pulled the string. This
> action of pulling the string was soon learned. Then Piaget attached
> a new object to a long pole so that it could be seen several metres
> in front of the crib. The infant again pulled the string. Later on a
> whistle was blown behind a screen and again the string was pulled.
> This behaviour can be interpreted as an effort to use an action that
> was successful in order to repeat an interesting experience inde-
> pendently of any perceived connection between the action (or
> object on which the infant acted) and the desired effect.

During the rest of the sensorimotor stage actions remain central in
development, being as important for the future development of physical causality as of logico-mathematical schemes and structures. Every
action of the child has, in fact, a causal effect, but this effect is a specific
one: making an object move, producing a noise, etc. However, many
of these actions are repeated, becoming generalized into schemes (a
scheme for pulling objects, etc.). Then the schemes become coordinated and these coordinations form the basis for future operations and
structures. Thus there is, from the beginning, a close connection
between causal actions and the beginning of logic, but also a difference
between the specific and the general. Yet this is not a strict frontier

because there are many transitions. Furthermore the complementarity in functioning—actions and schemes both being actions—is evidently not to be considered as a confusion in the child's mind between a specific causal action and the use of a scheme. Such differentiations between the specific and the general, between physical causality and "logic" only develop very gradually.

At the end of the sensorimotor period the child constructs the permanent object while causality includes the notion of spatial context (spatialization) and the notion that objects act upon each other as well as being acted upon by the subject (objectivization). Though this may lead to perceptual causality (i.e. perceiving objects as pushing each other, resisting each other, etc.), it does not imply that perceptual causality is the earliest form of causality and the basis of causal thinking. Piaget fundamentally disagrees with Michotte's claim that perceptual causality is the earliest form of causality and the basis for future causality. For Piaget, perceptual causality is based upon tactilo-kinaesthetic causality originating in the actions of the child (65, p.19). In general, Michotte's theory is not a fourth type of interpretation according to Piaget (71, 89).

□Michotte was an influential psychologist whose work on causality in Louvain (Belgium) is well-known in Europe. There was an intense discussion between Piaget and Michotte that is well summarized in 65. In *The Psychology of the Child* there are some pages on the subject where the interested reader can get an impression of what it is about. For a good understanding I would like to remark here that the translation should read: "Michotte tried to explain our interpretation of sensorimotor causality by way of his perceptual causality". The official translation is confusing, giving the impression that Michotte accepted sensorimotor causality (23 p.29/p.34).

b) *Causality: stage IA* (± 2 to ± 5 years old)
At the end of the sensorimotor stage representational intelligence develops, but the child is still for a long time in the pre-operational stage. The youngest children in the experiments on causality were 4 years old, but stage IA could cover the whole period from sensorimotor stage to the second half of the pre-operational stage when "constituent functions" are constructed.

Though the child's constructions improve considerably with the achievement of representation there is still a lack of differentiation between causal and logical structures which slows down the development of both. A look at non-conservers, for instance, shows that the causal aspect of their actions prevents the development of operations. The child is still convinced that his actions in pouring water, changing the spatial arrangement of objects, etc. cause a change and there is as yet no reason why this change should not include a change of quantity. Furthermore such causal actions are irreversible. Thus, in order to interiorize actions into operations, which are reversible, actions must lose their causal aspect. As long as this dissociation does not take place the development of logico-mathematical structures is prevented.

At the same time pre-operational logic limits the development of causal thinking. In general, pre-operational thinking is characterized by a lack of understanding of "all" and "some" (no groupings of classes), and of reciprocal relations (no groupings of relations). The pre-logical considerations resulting from these "shortcomings" directly influence causal thinking.

The poor insight in "all" and "some" is clearly demonstrated by the fact that the child has as yet no complete concepts but only pre-concepts that are half-way between the individual case and the collection or class to which the individual belongs. In the observation of his children Piaget found many examples of pre-concepts.

> **Example:** At 3;2(23) (= 3 years, 2 months, 23 days) J. cannot understand that all the houses together form Lausanne, as she has been used to calling her grandmother's house "the Lausanne house". When walking in the garden (2;7) she wonders whether a second snail on the garden path is the same snail or another individual of the same kind.

In the same way as the child cannot decide between "one snail" and "the snail", he does not differentiate a specific shadow from shadows in general.

> **Example:** Asked to explain the shadow thrown by a screen on to the table, the child will say that it is the shadow from under the trees.

Such analogical thinking leads to "transductive thought", i.e. concluding from the specific to the specific. This type of causal reasoning, so frequent at stage IA, clearly results from the use of pre-operational logic.

Thus, in general, there is still a lack of differentiation between causal or pre-causal and logical or pre-logical connections leading to continuous influences of the one on the other in both directions. This can also be seen in the experiments on causality (**58**).

Example of an experiment on causality (see R_2 in **58**, p.22/p.12 and the detailed description in **65**):
There are several techniques of which the results converge. The main point is that a marble rolls down an incline and hits an obstacle. On the other side of the obstacle there is a row of four or more marbles of which the last one will roll off. In a variation of the experiment the same marbles are used without the obstacle. The subject has to predict what will happen when the top marble rol _ down (released by a spring to avoid human actions) and explain after the event what he saw. At level IA (68% of 4- to 6-year-old children) the child does understand a direct transmission of movement but not mediate transmission. The child either expects that all the marbles will roll off or none of them. When he sees the last one go off the child gives very ingeneous explanations, e.g. A (the rolling one) was very quick to make that one (the last one) roll, or A passed under (or over) the others in order to get to the front one and push it off.

c) *Causality: stage IB* (± 5 to ± 7 years old)

The main progress of this period, just before the construction of concrete operations, is that the child begins to understand so-called *"constituent functions"*. That is to say, in a function like $y = f(x)$, the child sees the dependency of x and y, but does not conserve the total of $x + y$ (e.g. when a string is being pulled over a pulley, one part being called y and the other x).

☐ Piaget uses "fonction constituante" which has been translated both as "constituent function" and as "constituting function".

In 1968 a book on functions was published in which constituent functions formed the most important topic (see Chapter 11). In that book, Piaget supposed that such pre-operational functions formed the basis for the construction of both logical structures and causal explanations (**37**). As we shall see in Chapter 8, later research convinced Piaget that this supposition was incorrect, because functions are due to comparing, whilst operative structures are the result of transforming. Hence stage IB is no longer as important for Piaget as it seemed to be at the time of writing his book on causality.

Example: In the same experiment the children of level IB (28% of 4- to 6-year-olds and 35% of 7- and 8-year-olds) find an external mediate transmission. The push goes from the active A to the last C by way of a displacement of the marbles or block in between.

The child insists that he felt the marbles or block move "a little" when holding his hand on them.

d) Causality: stage II (7-8 to 10-12 years old)

In this stage of concrete operations, operations can now be applied and sometimes even attributed to objects. In order to understand the differentiation and mutual influence of logico-mathematical structures and causality, we must consider what Piaget means by "application" and "attribution".

In an "application" of structures the subject uses and acts on objects without changing the objects as such. A simple example is counting.

> **Example:** When counting ten pebbles the subject "applies" his notions of number to the pebbles, but the number is not a characteristic of the pebbles. The pebbles allow themselves to be counted, but that is all. Any other ten objects might provoke the same action and structure.

The fact that the young child himself believes that in counting the number is a characteristic of the pebbles is interesting from the developmental point of view, but it is an error that will be corrected without changing the structure or its application. *In an "attribution" of a structure the object is seen or interpreted as being the actor (operator).* A rolling marble makes the other roll off. But in order to explain the influence of one marble on the other we have to use our own structures and we come to think that the marble "behaves" as if it had these structures. This sounds like magic, as Bringuier remarked in his conversation with Piaget (**108**, p.94). But Piaget does not see it as magic. We do not attribute our virtues to objects but we do think that they behave rationally and act upon each other with structures isomorphic to our mathematical structures. Without such isomorphisms we would not understand anything. "That is no magic, but the general conviction of occidental science" (**108**, p.94).

> ☐Piaget is very fond of the term "isomorphism". He uses it with different nuances of meaning. In Chapter 8 we shall see him using it in the exact mathematical sense of one-to-one correspondence. In Chapter 12 we find his arguments for speaking of "partial isomorphisms", a concept unknown in mathematics (**32**). Very often he uses it in the sense of more or less exact analogies.
>
> The passage quoted is one of the few where Piaget explicitly writes about occidental science. In other writings the "attribution" is considered a general tendency, occurring from the end of the concrete operational period on.

Returning to the characteristics of stage II we find a progressive differentiation of structures and causality. However, there are limits to this differentiation due to the "concreteness" of the concrete operational structures. This characteristic means that the form of the structures has not yet become completely independent of the content, as can be seen in the well-known time-lags, e.g. of substance, weight and volume. Such a gradual construction of the structures must impose limits on causal explanations even though the child can already apply and, toward the end of stage II, even attribute those structures that have been constructed so far. There is, however, a second reason for the limitations of the child's progress. Even when completely developed, concrete structures are no more than groupings. This implies that thought proceeds by contiguities and therefore causality, due to the attribution of such structures, must itself be unilinear in time and space.

☐Piaget talks of "'contiguités', c'est-à-dire de proche en proche" (58, p.119/p.119). Translating "de proche en proche" is difficult because "step by step", which is the usual translation, suggests a succession while "de proche en proche" applies just as well to space and other contiguities.

While the limitations of concrete operations prevent a full development of causality, causality in its turn handicaps the progress of operative structures. As concrete operations are directed at objects, their characteristics influence the structurization. This is clearly seen in the difficulties encountered in understanding transitivity, conservation, etc. of weight. Weight causes things to fall, but it also holds things up, prevents their falling sideways, etc. and all these partly contradictory experiences and interpretations must be taken into account before a structure can be fully developed.

So, notwithstanding the progress seen right from the beginning of stage II, a complete differentiation of structures and causality, required for a full attribution as opposed to application, is not yet reached at this stage.

Example: In the experiment with the marbles, stage II is called the stage of "semi-internal mediate transmission" (31% at 7 years, 72% at 8 years, 100% at 9 years, 81% at 10 years and 37% at 11-12 years of age). At this stage a notion of "force", "strength", etc. is invented and its transmission differs from the foregoing because it cannot be observed ("it passes through the marbles" as several subjects say). However, this force is still combined with supposed movements of the marbles. The most interesting aspect of the experiment is that children of this age have constructed transitivity (if $A < B$ and $B < C$, then $A < C$). In a causal, internal mediate transmission (i.e. transmission of the impulse without external movements of the marbles in the middle) the child has to discover as well that the relation between A (the first active marble) and C (the last one going off) is the same as that between A and B (B being the collection of marbles in between) and B and C. The difference is that in the logical composition the components are usually given and it is the end result that has to be found, while the opposite is true in the case of transmission. But this is more a heuristic difference than a structural one.

e) *Causality: stage III* (from 10-12 years on)

At this stage, operations become more and more detached from their content and considerable progress is possible when such formal structures can be attributed to objects. At this stage the child's thought functionally resembles scientific thought, which is characterized by a permanent harmony between deductive instruments and experience, and by an uninterrupted sequence of mutual services by which experiences necessarily lead to new formalized constructions and the most abstract theories lead to new verifications with unforeseen results.

> **Example:** In the experiment with the marbles this is the stage of "internal mediate transmission" (10% at age 10, 62% at age 11-13). The children no longer invoke movements of B but only talk about forces passing through the marbles. This can partly be explained by general aspects of development.

Many other experiments showed that the notion of force itself becomes vectorial. In the first place, forces may be composed according to their directions in such a way that the observable direction of a force R is conceived as the resultant of two unobservable forces F^1 and F^2 coming from different directions. In the second place, unobservable forces may continue to act while remaining immobile, in intensity as well as direction, e.g. in systems of equilibrium.

In addition to these general factors there is a fundamental change in the understanding of the resistance of objects. The resistance of objects is discovered at a very early age as an observable fact because the child has already experienced at the sensorimotor stage that objects resist his actions. This experience continues and even at stage II of the present experiment the child says that objects brake the movement. It is only at stage III that the resistance is no longer reduced to such a braking and there is an intuition of "reactions" opposed to the "actions". This is seen at the very moment that vectorial compositions become available to the child. The most important aspect of stage III, seen from the point of view of "reactions", is that the child no longer believes that the force increases during transmission.

However fragmentary such intuitions still are, they are coherent and show the development of a new system of explanations based upon vectorial compositions and thereby going beyond a force in a unilateral direction. Thus mediate transmission finally becomes purely internal.

7.1.2.3 The development of causality in general

A description of successive stages illustrated by one experiment gives a rather simplified picture of a process that is, in fact, very complicated. A more general overview of Piaget's theory of causality will show how complicated the issue of causality is, and will also make clear how Piaget's next topics of research (the grasp of consciousness, contradictions, equilibration, the possible and the necessary) all followed from his research on causality (see also Chapter 2).

a) *The central hypothesis*

Piaget's *central hypothesis*—sometimes called a "fact"—*is that our adult explanations of causal relationships between objects are the result of attributing our own operations and structures to objects.*

> □The word "adult" has been inserted by me because the study of development summarized in the foregoing clearly shows that a complete attribution is only reached at the formal stage.

This central hypothesis is not the result of Piaget's research, as is shown by the fact that it was already published at least as early as 1963.

The notion of attribution, which remains within the rationalist tradition, explains the parallelism between causality and operational compositions. But this raises the question of what is parallel to what. All operational compositions are characterized by production or transformations, and conservation or coherence. In looking for attributions we should therefore not concentrate on parallelisms or isomorphisms between causal explanations which are specific and operational compositions of transitivity, reversibility, etc. which are very general, but on the characteristics of transformation and coherence. Then a closer look at development will give us a better picture of the similarities and differences between causality and operations, as well as the dialectical process of undifferentiation, oppositions, and mutual deformations finally leading to the differentiation of the two. The steps leading from their common source in actions—though from the very beginning causal actions are more specific and action schemes more general—has been summarily described in the previous paragraph.

□The reader with an interest in details is referred to the book (**58**) and the far more detailed interpretation of experimental results in the books on the experiments (**65, 66, 72, 73**). However, only the general book was translated into English.

b) *The contribution of reality*

In causality, objects are far more important than in the construction of logico-mathematical structures on the basis of the coordinations of actions. This influence of the object was clearly seen in the experiments which constantly showed unexpected and, at first sight, contradictory results. Hence the number of experiments. But Piagetian experiments closely reflect problems encountered in real life, and there too, we see that reality constantly challenges the functioning of intelligence by its many varied and interesting causal problems. From the sensorimotor level on, objects are of the greatest interest when they produce causal effects either by themselves or as instruments of the child's actions (banging a spoon on a metal surface!). These causal effects then stimulate the development of schemes and their coordinations.

Another influence of objects is seen in the experience of contradictions between observed facts and inferences, which eventually leads to new inferences. In general, objects show the child when his anticipations are wrong (hopefully banging the spoon on a soft surface) sooner than representation or thought. This then is, again, a contribution of objects to the development of causal thinking.

But, if the influence of objects can thus be stressed it must not be overlooked that there is at the same time a contribution from the subject. The characteristics of objects themselves are seen by empirical abstraction, but—as was already mentioned—this type of abstraction always requires reflective abstractions and their results. Furthermore, a causal effect of one object on another is itself never observable but is an inference, and the inference is made by the subject. So, even where objects contribute as much as in causality, the causal relation would not exist without the subject.

When the subject looks for causal explanations the objects sometimes "cooperate" and sometimes "refuse" to do so. This is true at the sensorimotor stage as the example of the spoon-banging infant showed. But it is still true at the scientific level. One cannot attribute whatever one likes to objects. Every attribution has to be verified and this leads to new experiences with objects. This means a return to empirical abstraction, but now guided by a more limited system of attributable operations.

In summary, one can say that causality is the principal partner in the exchanges between the subject and reality. These form a complex pattern of interactions in which at one moment the objects lead development while at another the subject leads, though at any moment the two are active and in interaction.

c) *Causality defined*

As no definition of causality was given to begin with, it is important to end with the question of what exactly Piaget means by "causality". Following Piaget this question has been put off until the end because the foregoing is needed for understanding why Piaget wants to distinguish between lawfulness and causality.

□In his review of Piaget's book on causality Mischel (**361**) writes that Piaget's "légalité" should be translated as "lawfulness" and not as "legality".

There are four reasons for distinguishing the two. In the first place, laws are due to observable relations between objects while causal connections cannot be observed. In the second place, laws only find general relations while causality contains necessary relations. In the third place, even general laws can remain isolated while causal explanations coordinate several relations into a system, and it is to this system that necessity is due. In the fourth place, lawfulness does not go beyond the application of operations while causality requires an attribution with objects becoming operators. But such attributions are not simply added to the foregoing applications. The same operations are first applied and then attributed, so—as far as operations are concerned—nothing new is added. What is new in the attribution is that the objects as operators are seen as necessarily "acting" the way they do, and such a necessity can only be due to deductions. *Causality is therefore always characterized by a system of transformations that cannot be reduced to a simple relation of cause and effect.*

7.2 Other Subjects and Knowledge

Though Piaget considers social life a necessary condition for cognitive development, there has been no research on this topic during the period covered by my book, and only a few publications. One gets the impression that Piaget wants to consider this aspect but that he is fundamentally less interested in the interaction between the subject and other subjects than in that between the subject and other "objects". Characteristically one of the first topics that made Piaget famous was "egocentricity", that is to say, a handicap for communication and cooperation.

□Social development being the fashionable topic of our time Piagetians and anti-Piagetians alike dug up his early work on moral development. But this was a side-issue for him, taken up when he was challenged with neglecting the aspect of values. Though Piaget and Inhelder summarized the results in *Psychology of the Child* (**23**), in another context (**74**, p.37 (English)/p.86 (French)) Piaget rejects the book as an early and immature part of his work.

7.2.1 Egocentrism

Piaget started his work on egocentrism in the context of language development and later replaced the term by "centring" or "centration". He claimed that he did this because of the tendency of many readers to attach an evaluative and pejorative connotation to the word "egocentrism". He might have added that "centring" has the advantage of having an opposite—"decentring"—that egocentrism lacks. But the change goes much deeper, because Piaget switched his attention from "social centring" to "cognitive centring" (two terms introduced by me).

□In the three-mountain experiment—mentioned in 1.4.1, and often used as a sort of "test" for egocentricity—Piaget and Inhelder were primarily interested in the child's conception of space. Whether the child can understand a situation seen from different perspectives, and not whether he can see them from the perspectives of different persons, is the fundamental issue.

In the conservation task of pouring water, the pre-operational child centres on the height or width instead of their relationship. Here no other person enters the picture at all.

Piaget's only recent remarks on egocentrism also concern the cognitive aspect of development. He reminds us that egocentrism not only has a negative influence but a very positive one as well. The negative one is seen in what I have called "social egocentrism". The child encounters systematic difficulties in liberating himself from his own point of view and coordinating it with that of others. And—one might add—the child is not alone in this respect. Even scientists have to decentre in order to reach objectivity and they are certainly not free from problems in doing so. But there is another side of the coin, as far as ''cognitive egocentrism'' is concerned. The child tries to assimilate everything he encounters to what he already knows and can do. The child's action in pushing an object by way of a stick, illustrates this very well. The object is immediately seen as something to be assimilated into the action with the stick. But what the child then learns is an early form of transitivity: he moves the stick, the stick moves the object, hence he moves the object. The activity, starting by centring on his own perceptions and actions, thus forms an invaluable step in his cognitive development, even though the decentring to transitivity of movements between objects comes much later, as we saw in the research on causality. In general: the child must first explore his actions before he can place them in a complex system of images and perspectives. This assimilation of reality to action is very ''rational'' and useful for the child's cognitive development, even if the dominance of material actions and one's own perspective are ''irrational'' (**45**, p.7).

In social situations decentring is required for cooperation. Here the same difficulties in decentring were found as in Piaget's observations of the spontaneous talk of the child and the child's efforts to explain something to another child. Only when children reach the stage of concrete operations do they cease to speak from their own point of view. In quoting this early view, Piaget and Inhelder add that this does not imply that the child has the impression that he speaks for himself and not for the other. This is only the observer's interpretation (**23**, p.96/p.122).

> □I think that this addition is very important because it clearly shows that the inability of the child to cooperate and communicate is not due to a lack of intention to do so, but to his level of cognitive development. In consequence the child might well be able to communicate successfully in tasks and situations that do not require operations. This is confirmed by observations of spontaneous talk in different situations where the percentage of egocentric talk is always smaller than that of social talk.

7.2.2 Social Transmission

Though the child's social interactions may be limited from our point of view because of his centring, this does not alter the fact that he is a social being from the beginning of life. In every culture we find social exchanges between children and children and between children and adults, though their specific forms can vary. ''In all environments individuals ask questions, work together, discuss, oppose things, and so on" (**27**, p.65/p.35). The process of socialization this entails lasts throughout life. Three aspects deserve closer consideration, though, again, Piaget did no research on them in the period covered.

7.2.2.1 Language

Piaget's fight against the theory that logic depends on language and the importance he attaches to actions and progressive equilibration, easily convince the reader that he thinks language unimportant. But, just like social influence in general, language is a necessary though not sufficient condition for cognitive development. Its importance was already mentioned in connection with the semiotic function and mental imagery, but the further the child advances in development, the more this importance increases. Formal, hypothetical thought as well as "meta-reflexion" (thinking about structures of thought) are evidently impossible without language.

The relation between language and logico-mathematical development is a complex relationship. As he has done no research himself, Piaget often quotes the research by Sinclair (**435**) that has his full approval. Sinclair's best-known experiment is, in fact, a training experiment. Of two groups of subjects one group were conservers of length and number, while the other were complete non-conservers. All the subjects were asked to describe and compare objects, such as a short thick pencil and a long thin one. Sinclair found that the language of the two groups differed at a highly significant level. The non-conservers used what the linguist Bull called "scalars" (large, small, many, few), while the conservers used "vectors" (more, less, etc.). I shall leave out other analogous differences in the language and limit myself to the general conclusion that a high correlation between the development of operations and that of language was found. The question now concerns how to explain this correlation. Sinclair decided to train the non-conservers in the language of the conservers and to check whether this would teach them to conserve. The language training was successful, but only 10% of the non-conservers improved in the same conservation task that had been used before the language training. This is a very small result, and in quoting Sinclair Piaget wonders whether even this progress is really due to the language training or to the development of schemes over time. His final conclusion is therefore that these experiments (together with a number of comparable ones) verify his theory that it is operativity that leads to the structuring of language (preferably within the framework of pre-existing models of language, of course) rather than the other way around (e.g. **53**, p.77/ p.43).

More recently Ferreiro followed Sinclair in the field of what can be called ''genetic linguistics''. In his Foreword to her book Piaget briefly discusses the relationship between logico-mathematical structures and language, somewhat modifying the view summarized above. Here he says that he no longer believes that cognitive pre-operations (constituent functions) and operations lead language development ''from the outside''. He sees rather a more general regulatory mechanism leading at the same time to progress in language and the construction of logico-mathematical structures (**63**, p.XIII).

7.2.2.2 Cultural transmission

Children grow up in an adult culture and the hypothesis that the adult has a formative influence in general undoubtedly contains a certain degree of truth. The adult is more advanced than the child and might therefore help him and speed up his development in the course of educational processes in the family and the community. As I mentioned, Piaget agrees that children of the present generation evidently know much more than those of several centuries ago. Furthermore differences have been found between children living in isolated villages and in the capital of the same country. However, this only shows that the speed of development is influenced by experiences and/or cultural transmission without showing that there are different structures of the epistemic subject.

7.2.2.3 Schooling

Piaget has published quite a number of papers and articles on educational topics (e.g. **77, 79, 80, 82**). He often tells us to stimulate intellectual development so that children will later be creative and critical adults. This evidently represents a system of his values and therefore his philosophy. As far as science is concerned psychology studies the facts and it is not the task of the psychologist to create a pedagogical system (**80**, p.32). The psychologist may offer his ideas to the educator who then is free to use them or not. The ideas offered by Piaget are varied: the training of teachers should be multi-disciplinary, the teacher should be able to evaluate the level of the child's structures, and his role then ''consists essentially in arousing the child's curiosity and in stimulating his research'' (**80**, p.33). This stimulation implies that the child has materials to manipulate actively, testing hypotheses all the time (**82**, p.X).

☐The active stimulating role of the teacher in the class is often forgotten by educators who oppose Vygotsky's idea of guiding the child to the next higher level to the idea of just waiting until the child gets there that is supposed to be Piaget's ideal.

As far as Piaget sees possibilities for more detailed applications of his research in the school, he usually emphasizes that children often cannot assimilate what they are taught, e.g. if ''new maths'' are taught in ''the old style''. He often finds in his research that children know all sorts of mathematical and logical terms but fail in Piagetian tasks because they cannot actively use the concepts they have memorized.

☐This warning may have led to the erroneous interpretation mentioned above.

All in all, education will influence the individual speed of development of structures, but for Piaget the genetic epistemologist this individual subject is far less important than he is for Piaget the man and Swiss citizen.

☐This conviction on my part explains why I have given so little space to education here (and none in Volume II) though I know that this will disappoint many educationalists in the United States and even some Genevans.

8 The Subject in the Subject-Object Interaction

☐Chapter 19, corresponding to this one, is only a very short chapter. There is a little criticism on ''abstraction'', and what there is is so closely related to biological development that it is summarized in Chapter 23. There are a few critical comments on correspondences (19.1) and consciousness (19.2).

In Chapter 7 I concentrated on the contribution of material and social reality to the interaction between subject and object. Turning now to the contribution of the subject, one might say, generally, that the subject contributes his activity, either in the form of behavioural actions or as interiorized action, that is to say, as mental activity. Through his activity the subject transforms reality and, as we saw in Chapter 7, the subject is always active in knowing: the figurative aspect cannot do without the operative aspect, empirical abstraction is impossible without reflective abstraction, in causality the subject attributes his structures to the object, and in learning from others he assimilates information into his schemes.

Turning to a more detailed consideration of the subject's activity takes us back to the difference between structures and procedures. The subject wants to understand his world and to solve problems. In all the years that Piaget concentrated on the first aspect, he only paid attention to the transformations this requires. But recently he has turned to another aspect of understanding, i.e. comparing. In making comparisons the subject is also active, but he does not change what has to be compared. Recent developments in mathematics stimulated Piaget's interest in comparisons, resulting in his publication of books on morphisms and categories. Piaget now sees the subject as active in three ways: understanding and transforming (8.1), understanding and comparing (8.2), and understanding and succeeding (8.3).

Considering these activities from a genetic point of view evidently requires a theory of development, which for Piaget means a theory of equilibration. The topics discussed in this chapter were, in fact, elaborated after the publication of Piaget's book on equilibration. In consequence of the change of order in the presentation, I shall return in Chapter 10 to those aspects of equilibration related to the topics of this chapter.

☐ The reader who prefers to read Chapter 9 first, can do so without a loss of coherence.

8.1 Understanding and Transforming

8.1.1 Introducing Abstraction and Generalization

Abstraction and generalization are two functions which are closely related to each other. *Empirical abstractions lead to inductive generalizations, while reflective abstractions lead to constructive generalizations.* I shall first describe these concepts in general—with some unavoidable repetition of what has been said in foregoing chapters—and then turn to more details, specifically as far as the developmental aspect is concerned. *Empirical abstraction extracts information from the objects themselves*, retaining some of their properties while excluding others. Such properties (e.g. colour, weight) exist in the object independently of the subject's activity. However, in order to know these properties the subject has to use instruments of assimilation (schemes, operations, structures) constructed by the subject. While the object gives the content, the subject contributes the form.

Inductive generalization is a "dangerous" term, according to Piaget, because of the unresolved disagreements concerning the method of induction. However, in this context, Piaget is not interested in logical issues, but in the epistemological frontier between what is contributed by the object and what is contributed by the subject (**110**, p.219). In this sense, inductive generalization uses empirical abstractions. *Inductive generalization starts with observables attached to objects·and abstracted by empirical abstraction, and uses them in order to verify the validity of observed relations in order to find their degree of generality.* Thus inductive generalization is purely extensional, leading from "some" to "all" (or some proportion of "all"). But, just as empirical abstraction cannot do without reflective abstraction, inductive generalization cannot do without the framework given by constructive generalization.

Reflective abstraction is not directly related to objects but to actions and operations of the subject. It always consists of two components: *projective reflection* and *reconstructive reflection.* The former consists of a projection on to a higher plane *B* of what was taken from the lower plane *A*, while the latter reconstructs at *B* what was already present at *A* (**102a**, p.6). Piaget also expresses the same notion by saying that the reconstruction at *B* uses what was present at *A*. He says as well that reconstructive reflection is the mental activity of reorganization (**102a**, p.91). The essential point is that the reconstruction leads to a new structure, that is to say, a qualitative change is made. The only problem is that Piaget does not say explicitly whether this refers to any new structure or scheme constructed within a stage, or only to the new structure of a next higher stage. On the one hand he gives examples of stage transitions, e.g. reconstructing at the stage of representation what was already available in actions. On the other hand, when asked whether microgenesis also proceeds by reflective abstraction, he answered that he had done no research on microgenesis and therefore could not give an answer (**103**, p.75).

□Piaget's "abstraction réfléchissante" is usually translated as "reflective abstraction", though sometimes as "reflexive" or "reflecting". Both these terms are confusing because Piaget uses them with different meanings.

Originally Piaget used the term "réflection" for both components of reflective abstraction, adding that the first one was like a physical reflection or projection, the second one being a mental reflection or reconstruction. Later he used these terms interchangeably with the new terms "réfléchissement" and "réflexion". As these variations are rather confusing, I have preferred to use two terms that come closest to Piaget's meaning: "projective reflection" and "reconstructive reflection".

Constructive generalization is a necessary framework for inductive generalization, but also goes much beyond it. While inductive generalization is limited to the assimilation of new observables into existing schemes, *constructive generalization creates new forms and new contents, that is to say, a new structural organization.* This is especially clear in logico-mathematical thought.

Example: Piaget illustrates the difference with a humorous example: although he spent years of his life on observations of molluscs, finding regularities by inductive generalization, he has never been able to create the tiniest mollusc. In the meantime his mathematical colleagues had the good fortune to create new forms and contents by constructive generalizations (**110**, p.220).

In contrast to inductive generalization there is not only an increase in extension here, but also one in intension.

The relationship between reflective abstraction and constructive generalization is as close as that between empirical abstraction and inductive generalization. This is due to the fact that the reconstructive aspect of reflective abstraction always implies an extension of level B with new (intensional) characteristics, in comparison to the foregoing level A.

Finally, there is *pseudo-empirical abstraction, which is a sub-variety of reflective abstraction and is also called an "application" of operations and structures to objects.* The child in the concrete operational stage needs extralogical objects as content for his logico-mathematical structures which give the form. Usually "pseudo-empirical abstraction" is used when Piaget wants to emphasize that the child cannot yet reason by the use of verbal hypotheses and "application" when he is emphasizing the difference between application and attribution of operations and structures in causal explanations. However, sometimes they are used as synonyms. For the psychologist there is a fundamental difference between empirical and pseudo-empirical abstraction, but there is none for the child.

There is no parallel to pseudo-empirical abstraction in generalizations.

8.1.2 Introducing Conscious Thought

Consciousness is an example of a notion Piaget had many years ago, which was then taken up much later in experiments. As early as 1932 Piaget had written that thought always lags behind action. Later, in *Insights and Illusions,* he wrote that consciousness proceeds from the periphery to the centre (**15**, p.183/p.135), and this is also the conclusion reached on the basis of the experiments that he published in 1974 (**85**, p.264f/p.335f). The more Piaget's interest turned to higher levels of thought, the more important conscious thinking became. Thus we see him take up this topic in the books on reflective abstraction and generalization.

8.1.2.1 Levels of consciousness

An *elementary level of consciousness already exists in animals.* This can only be studied by neurophysiologists or psychophysiologists in research on "vigilance". From this point of view the sensorimotor level—where an elementary consciousness, in the sense of awareness without conceptualization, may well be present—is not an absolute beginning. We must, indeed, *accept the possibility of a great number of intermediate levels between biological release mechanisms and conscious perception.* The considerable "know-how" of the sensorimotor level with its schemes and assimilatory functions is very important—even though it does not know itself—as it forms the basis of conceptualizations.

With the development of the semiotic function *a higher level of consciousness* is reached. This consciousness cannot be compared to a light
thrown upon an action, making the action visible without changing it.
True to his constructivist approach *Piaget considers conscious thought an
active reconstruction. It is,* in fact, *a transformation of an action scheme into a
notion, or in one word: a conceptualization.*

□The French term "prendre conscience de" (literally "taking consciousness of") is a current one. It has the advantage of corresponding to the
idea of activity. The title of Piaget's book *La prise de conscience* has been
translated literally as *The Grasp of Consciousness*, but in the text this awk-
ward term is avoided and replaced by "cognizance".

Though the first conceptualizations appear with the semiotic function, it is extremely difficult to study the first conceptual assimilations,
as the child who is just beginning to talk cannot explain his actions or
answer questions. A great amount of research remains to be done on
the period from 1½ to 4 years of age. From the age of approximately
4 years on, the child can answer questions during or after his actions
and it is for this purely practical reason that Piaget has only studied
cognizance in children aged 4 years and older.

At a still higher level of development, the child—and also the scientist—becomes conscious of his operations and structures. This *thinking
about the structures of one's actions and thoughts is called "thematization".*

Reflected abstraction and reflexive abstraction are sometimes used
as synonyms and sometimes distinguished by Piaget. In either case,
they are opposed to reflective abstraction which may be totally unconscious. *Reflected and reflexive abstraction refer to the "grasp of consciousness" of
the actions and structures used in reflective abstraction.* When they are distinguished, reflected abstraction is seen as consciousness at no matter
what level of cognitive development, and can be quite primitive.
Reflexive abstraction is used by Piaget for a higher cognitive level at
which the subject thinks about structures. This higher level of conscious
thought is also called *"metareflexion"*, defined as *"a reflection on the
products of reflected abstraction".* Reflexive abstraction or metareflexion
is often described as "a reflection on a reflection" in the sense of "a
conscious mental activity on the result of such an activity".

□Piaget explains that he called conscious abstraction "abstraction réfléchie" because the tense indicates that it comes after the completion of a
problem by reflective abstraction. I have therefore followed the translator
of the book in her use of "reflected" for "réfléchie". As for reflexive
abstraction, I prefer to use "reflexive thought" as some translators use
"reflexive abstraction" instead of what I call "reflective abstraction".

However, when following Piaget closely I sometimes use "reflexive abstraction"—the reader is warned that it is not the same as reflective abstraction!

8.1.2.2 Research on consciousness

Piaget divided his research on consciousness over two books, one concentrating on cognizance in tasks that are easy for the child (**85**), the other on cognizance in more difficult tasks of practical intelligence (**86**). As the latter is a forerunner of procedures and significant implication, I shall concentrate on the former for the time being.

As usual, there are many experiments, but two of them are often quoted by Piaget.

> **Example:** *Walking on all fours:* the child is instructed to walk on all fours and when he has done so is questioned about his actions. Which hand or foot did he put down first, which one followed, etc.? Then he has to demonstrate the action on a teddybear, and— if necessary—instruct the experimenter what to do.
>
> *The path of an object launched by a sling:* the child is shown how to turn around holding a ball attached to a string. Then he is told to send the string off in such a way that the ball will fall into a box opposite the place where the child is standing. Afterwards the box is displaced more or less to one side and the instruction is repeated.

The most striking result is that children under 7 or 8 years of age are completely incapable of describing correctly what they have just done perfectly.

> **Example:** The child describes a sequence of hand- and foot-movements which it is impossible to execute. More interestingly he insists that he launched the string in front of the box even though he executed the action correctly.

The question is therefore how this discrepancy between the adequate sensorimotor scheme and the inadequate answers to the questions that should make this scheme conscious, can be explained. The fact that the young child is incapable of such a description is called a *"repression"* by Piaget—especially in the task with the sling—comparable to repression in the affective domain as described by psychoanalysis (**57**). As this repression is not general, the question is why such a repression should take place in a number of tasks. Piaget explains this by the influence of a strong, consciously formulated notion which the child has that contradicts what he should observe in the new situation. This idea prevents a correct observation in the same way that an idea coming from the superego, for instance, keeps an impulse out of consciousness. In both cases the mechanism of repression is unconscious. Though in some theories the notion of an unconscious cognitive mechanism would not be acceptable, this is not the case in Piaget's theory in which the structure and functions of endogenous mechanisms constitute the cognitive unconscious. We should note, however, that the information given by reality is not unconscious (**103**, p.121). The child does see the problem, but he does not want to admit what does not fit into his notion. An interesting detail is that the child can observe correctly what an adult does in the same situation, because his preconceived notion only concerns his own actions and not those of others.

More generally, it was found that the first thing of which the child becomes conscious is the goal to be reached and the result of his actions (success or failure to reach the goal). This is called the "periphery" because neither the goal nor the result depend on the subject or the object alone, but on both at the same time. In other words: the periphery is the most immediate and external reaction of the subject towards the object: to use it according to a goal (called by the observer: to assimilate it into a scheme!), and to take notice of the obtained result. The goal and the result are always conscious in any intentional action, but the mechanisms leading from the goal to the result are not. The development of consciousness thus shows that cognizance develops from the periphery to the central mechanisms of the actions of the subject, on the one hand, and on the other hand, to knowledge of the intrinsic properties of the object (i.e. properties that are independent of the actions of the subject). *The development of cognizance to the centre of the subject is called "interiorization", leading to the construction of logico-mathematical structures, and that to the centre of the object is called "exteriorization", leading to physical causality.* Thus the study of the psychological problem of consciousness is linked, once more, to an epistemological issue.

8.1.3 The Development of Abstraction and Generalization

8.1.3.1 The sensorimotor stage

At this stage empirical abstraction dominates over reflective abstraction. Reflective abstraction coordinates actions, and later, action schemes, but it takes time to develop these. Thus, at the beginning of life reflective abstraction which must give a frame for empirical abstraction is still very limited. However, this is not such a serious handicap as one might think, because one and the same action scheme or coordination of actions (e.g. looking and grasping), enables the infant to get a lot of information from the environment. In other words, a limited result of reflective abstraction gives a frame for a nearly unlimited amount of empirical abstractions. Furthermore, the infant first observes single experiences by means of empirical abstraction. But then the recurrence of the same events and situations in daily life enables him to experience regularities by means of inductive generalizations. Thus the infant can make the most of his elementary logico-mathematical frame for acquiring knowledge of the world. But the fact that such a frame is present, however modest its beginnings, is essential because it forms the basis for further development.

By insisting on the importance of empirical abstraction at this early stage I have not dwelt on the two components of reflective abstraction, i.e. projective and reconstructive reflection. Further development does require a projective reflection of foregoing coordinations to a higher level, or in Piaget's terminology—preferred by myself—a use at the higher level of foregoing coordinations between actions of the subject or parts of them. Only then does reconstructive reflection lead to achievements of a higher level. Both components are important whenever new conduct is drawn from an earlier level.

☐ In his book (**102b**, pp.289-296) Piaget gives an example of an experiment on reflective abstraction in the sensorimotor stage. Though it is interesting because it is one of the few experiments with infants, limitations of space make it impossible to include a summary here.

8.1.3.2 The pre-operational stage

The organization of Piaget's experiments is influenced by his wish to talk with the child in question and to choose tasks which interest children between 4 and 12 years old. Hence he has done far more research on the second half of this period than on the first. The achievements of ± 4- to ± 7-year-old children correspond in the analysis of the data to stage I, with a slight but evident progress between the first part of level or stage I (called IA) and the second (called IB).

During the pre-operational stage, especially the second half of it, there is, of course, a lot of improvement in the child's knowledge through the development of representation and the semiotic function in general. But there is still the same predominance of external or exogenous knowledge achieved by empirical abstraction and inductive generalization, while consciousness is still directed towards the periphery.

The experiments show that the relation between empirical abstraction, with the physical knowledge it leads to, and reflective abstraction, with its structures, is a complicated one. There are many situations in which empirical abstraction facilitates reflective—or rather pseudo-empirical—abstraction and reflected abstraction.

> **Example:** This can be seen, for instance, in an experiment using a vertical stem on which seven wooden discs can be mounted in such a way that the whole forms a mushroom. The discs are given to the child in a random order. The child is then asked what he could make by putting them on to the stem. The youngest do not succeed in getting them into the correct order, but the older pre-operational children do succeed in this task.

Empirical abstraction gives the child a perception of the final goal to be achieved. This allows the child to read off the necessary sequence of actions in a pseudo-empirical abstraction, i.e. the concrete material helps the child and this help also extends to cognizance. In general, reflected abstraction lags behind the actions executed by reflective abstraction, but in situations where empirical abstraction offers help, reflected abstraction improves as well.

> **Example:** For instance, in the experiment with the mushroom the pre-operational children of level IB give a good conscious and verbal description of the order followed and understand and explain the necessity of the sequence.

In some experiments, like the one with the mushroom mentioned in the foregoing, empirical abstraction is a help. In others, however, earlier knowledge, given mainly by empirical abstraction, can have an unfavourable influence in a new situation. This was illustrated by the experiment with the sling, where the poor result was explained by "repression". The following example, from another book, shows how Piaget's interpretation of empirical results is influenced by the theoretical frame in which he is working at that moment.

> **Example:** The basic idea of this experiment is very simple though there are, as usual, many variations (**110**, p.47ff). In a plank measuring 80 cm × 8 cm there are twelve holes in a straight line at 6 cm distance from each other. In every hole a vertical stick can be inserted. Elastic bands of different lengths and different colours are also supplied. The main question is simply to determine how many elastic bands are needed to form couples of two

adjoining sticks, of three adjoining sticks, etc.—a different total number of sticks being given each time.

At level IA the child can perform the action with couples, but triples already cause some problems. The main difficulty, however, is that all the children tend to generalize to the rule that there are as many elastic bands as there are sticks, though they have no difficulty when actually counting them. When they are made to see their mistake, they give all sorts of reasons that are irrelevant.

The mistakes made in this experiment can be explained by the observation that every stick is touched by an elastic band. This gives the notion of a one-to-one correspondence. This notion is wrong, but it is one to which the child has become accustomed from the early sensorimotor stage on. Already at this stage it is one of the main forms of coordinations of actions and its importance increases at the level of representations. As a form for what the child does, this idea is due to reflective abstraction and constructive generalization, but these take place prior to the reasoning in the experimental situation. Notwithstanding the use of this correspondence, the child believes that he perceives observables and generalizes from them. In other words: he behaves as though he were generalizing inductively from observations, while in fact he falsifies his observations due to the use of the wrong frame.

☐One might explain the sling results by saying that inductive generalization had led to the rule: "I have to stand in front of the box". This rule then leads to a falsification of the observation.

Reflective abstraction with its two components is essential for the transition from the sensorimotor stage to the pre-operational stage.

We saw that there is already an elementary form of reflective abstraction at the sensorimotor stage, but its effectiveness is limited because objects have to be present. When actions or schemes are linked together, this is still a purely motor act. More generally, limitations are due to a lack of representations. The fundamental step from the sensorimotor stage to the next one is taken when projective reflection projects the recognition of objects in the presence of objects on to the level of their invocation or representation in their absence. At the same time the semiotic function is developed through the interiorization of imitation, also implying a projective reflection.

☐Piaget says that the semiotic function is in the first place due to the

interiorization of imitation, but he does not deny the influence of maturation.

This projection then requires a reorganizing or reconstructive reflection (**102a**, p.107). The great advantage of this level in comparison
with the sensorimotor level is that it becomes less tied to the present,
though the research on mental imagery has shown that the evocation
of what is not present is still quite limited (**24**).

The next question concerns how much of the child's achievements
becomes conscious. Piaget tried to stimulate the child's conscious
thinking by making him compare two tasks structured in the same way.
This requires reflected abstraction, that is to say, a retrospective representation or reconstitution of what has been in solving a problem.

> **Example:** Making and then undoing the mushroom is followed
> by building a cube with eight small cubes and then dismantling
> the big cube afterwards. The child is questioned during both tasks
> about the order of constructing and taking down, and then about
> the difference between the two tasks—the order being fixed in the
> mushroom and free in the cube.

At the pre-operational level the child who is able to describe correctly
each separate task, including the differences between them, still only
mentions some irrelevant detail (usually a difference) when comparing
them. This tendency is found in all the experiments, showing that
reflected abstraction lags behind the correct execution and even correct
description of separate acts. Thus the research on reflected abstraction
confirms the results of the research on cognizance, done some years
earlier.

8.1.3.3 The stage of concrete operations

The fundamental progress of the child at the beginning of this stage is
his construction of operations, i.e. of interiorized actions which are
reversible and combinable into structures that are experienced as
necessary. Though this stage begins around 7 to 8 years of age (in
Western cultures), this does not mean that all the operations and
structures of this kind are achieved at the same time. The concrete
operational stage is, in fact, a long period of elaborations.

After levels IA and IB of the pre-operational stage, levels IIA and
IIB are found during the stage of concrete operations. In general, IIA
is a period of preparation and IIB one of consolidation, the latter often
coming close to level III (formal stage).

Recently Piaget has often been struck by what looks like a regression around 9 to 10 years old, that is, at stage IIB. In many situations younger children at stage IIA seem to be sure of their answers without looking for many justifications. In contrast, the older ones show a different attitude. They feel a need for justifications or explanations of their answers. If the problem is easy for their age, like the first conservation tasks, this elaborate justification is correct, only giving the impression of being over-elaborate. When the problem is difficult, the younger children do not fully realize the difficulty and are therefore satisfied by their answer. The older ones give the impression of a regression because they hesitate more, look for irrelevant details, etc. In fact, there is no true regression, their behaviour being the result of the more advanced insight that there is a problem, combined with their incapacity to solve it to their satisfaction. Hence the irrelevancies (**114**). In the following I leave this aspect out of the picture.

The construction of operations is a fundamental change in the unconscious and conscious mechanisms leading to knowledge. At the concrete operational level the knowledge of the child and his mechanisms for improving it are much closer to those of the non-scientific adult than those of the pre-operational child. However, the concrete operational child is still far more tied to extralogical content than the young adolescent and adult who have become capable of hypothetico-deductive thinking. Concentrating on empirical and pseudo-empirical abstraction, this means progress by comparison with the pre-operational stage, on the one hand, and limitations by comparison with the formal stage, on the other.

The fundamental point is that there is now an absolute increase in the quality of empirical abstraction, combined with a decrease in its importance compared with reflective abstraction.

The increase in quality is due to the fact that operational structures as a framework for empirical abstraction lead to much better empirical abstractions than pre-operational structures. The main advance is the quantification that can be applied to reality in pseudo-empirical abstraction (e.g. conservation and classification). However, foregoing experiences and developing operational structures make the child depend less on empirical abstraction and therefore the frequency and importance of empirical abstraction decreases. But, as the child is not yet capable of hypothetico-deductive reasoning, there is still a limit to his structures.

When the child is asked to compare several tasks, he is now much better at it than at the former level. However, he still needs pseudo-empirical abstraction. Even when the specific example the child is questioned about has been constructed by the child himself, he is only capable of reading off the results as though it were a physical object.

> **Example:** In one of the tasks, the subject had to add, subtract, etc. numbers and then reconstruct the sequence, beginning at the end. Numbers do not belong to reality, but the results can be read off as though they were real.

Analysing inductive and constructive generalization at the concrete operational level, it is evident that progress in empirical abstraction, due to operations on which they are based, will lead to an improvement in inductive generalization. As one might expect, there is a fundamental advance in constructive generalization as well, but there are also still many problems in the transition from inductive to constructive generalization, the latter being independent of empirical abstraction.

> **Example:** In the experiment with the elastic bands (8.1.3.2) level IIA shows the improvement of inductive generalization and the passage to a beginning of constructive generalization. The reactions of the children can best be understood through the three levels found in the experiments on cognizance: at the first level there is a consciousness of the periphery. The child succeeds in reaching the goal without understanding how. At the second level there is a consciousness of the material action, due to empirical abstraction. At the third level there is an understanding of the endogenous mechanisms of the action, i.e. its necessary coordinations (source of logico-mathematical operations) and cognizance of this "praxeologic" type of logic due to reflective abstraction.
>
> When the task is simple, the children reach the second level with momentary glimpses of the third level at which constructive generalization becomes possible. But when the task is more complicated, the children execute it well without understanding their action. At level IIB there are numerous remnants of inductive generalizations which support a constructive generalization of which the child is still not sure. The improvement in constructive generalization is due to the fact that the children do reach the third level of cognizance, attaining the scheme of the construction, or in other words, the coordination that gives the reason for the rules.

Thus generalization shows again how fundamental the difference is between pre-operational and operational children. But when we turn to the formal stage, it will become clear how far the children still have to go to achieve the higher levels of generalization.

8.1.3.4 The stage of formal operations

The importance of empirical and reflective abstraction at this stage is the opposite of what it was at the beginning of life. While empirical abstraction dominated in the sensorimotor stage, reflective abstraction dominates in the formal stage. This is most clearly seen in the development of logico-mathematical structures that no longer require extralogical content. In the use of the combinatorial of sixteen binary operations and the INRC group, the adolescent shows that he can reason hypothetico-deductively on purely verbal material. To avoid misunderstandings: the combinatorial and the INRC group are used by the subject, but formalized by the scientist, just as the groupings are used but not formalized by the child.

Originally Piaget gave the impression that formal logico-mathematical structures do not need extralogical content, and that therefore empirical abstraction loses all of its importance. However, this only holds true for logic and mathematics. In general, the tendency described for earlier stages continues: improvements in reflective abstraction lead to improvement in the quality of empirical abstractions. So nowadays Piaget says no more than that extralogical content becomes relatively unimportant. What is essential is that formal thought consists of transformations on transformations, or operations on operations.

□In introductions to Piaget one often finds that concrete thought is replaced by ''abstract'' thought. But this is not a Piagetian term. For him the couple is concrete-verbal, or concrete-formal.

The change from operations to operations-on-operations clearly illustrates progress due to the two components of reflective abstraction. The child is already capable of the operations which are to be combined at the formal stage, but only separately. Reversibility by reciprocity as well as reversibility by negation are both within his capabilities. But the combination of the two in the INRC group requires a reconstruction (integration) of what was separately constructed (differentiations) at the foregoing stage. As has been shown in recent research conducted by the Centre, operational children can use all the sixteen binary operations, but only one of them at a time, and not in combinations as in the formal stage (114). This requires a reconstruction in which the acquisitions of the earlier stage are ''enclosed'' (''englobé'') in the later ones. However, this does not mean that the earlier structures are no longer available.

Though the adolescent is incapable of formalizing the combinatorial, he becomes much more conscious of his actions and structures. Conscious thought now takes the form of reflexive abstraction or meta-reflexion. However, the highest level is only reached in scientific thought. The same is true for higher levels of generalization. Though Piaget did experiments with children and adolescents, his examples are mostly taken from scientific thought and therefore this topic is included in the next paragraph.

8.1.3.5 Scientific thought

At this level the progress made at the level of formal operations continues. *While formal operations are a reconstruction leading to operations on operations, further reflective abstractions lead to progress in the same way. Thus there are finally operations to the nth degree.*

Operations to the nth degree without any extralogical content are only found in logic and mathematics. Other sciences have to take reality into account. This requires empirical abstraction. At this level, the same tendency described for earlier stages continues. Every progress in the frame given by reflective abstraction brings with it a progress in empirical abstraction. Properties of objects and actions which were not observed, or were interpreted in a wrong way, become observables at higher stages. This can be seen in all the experiments, but also in the development of sciences which concern reality: microphysics, astronomy, etc. Their progress is on the one hand due to a higher frame of logico-mathematical structures, allowing better explanations through the attribution of these structures to reality, but on the other hand to the improvement of empirical abstraction which gives the basic data and is necessary for the verification of deductive hypotheses. These empirical abstractions have been so well enclosed in a total of structures due to reflective abstraction that some scientists working on abstract models tend to forget the contribution of reality which exists independently of the scientist who improves his approximative knowledge of reality through reflective abstraction.

Thus, at the end of development, reflective abstraction can function at a nearly pure level of forms while empirical abstraction improves accordingly but is always subordinate to reflective abstraction.

When I turn to inductive and constructive generalizations, an analogous development can be seen. In logic and mathematics, constructive generalization becomes completely independent of extralogical content, not only constructing new forms but also new content. In other sciences, however, extralogical content cannot be excluded.

A closer look at this statement takes us to the fundamental concepts of "intension" ("compréhension") and "extension" ("extension"), as well as to extrinsic and intrinsic differentiations. The latter are so closely related to equilibration that I shall return to them in Chapter 10.

The essential point concerning extension and intension is that in all Piaget's experiments on generalization one finds a direct relationship between extension and intension, while everybody knows that in a hierarchical system of classifications there is an inverse relationship between them. The difference can be explained by means of the distinction between form and content.

Any structure has a form and a content. The form has an intension and an extension when we compare forms of structures of different levels. There are, e.g. fewer groups than monoïds. As for the content of the structures, we again find an intension (e.g. that of being a whole number) and an extension. As long as one only studies forms of different levels, the relationship between their intension and extension is inverse, and the same is true when studying their contents. But the situation is different when one compares, on the one hand, the intension of the form of the elements of a total structure ("structure d'ensemble") with, on the other hand, the extension of the content of the elements of the same structure. This relation is a direct one. An analysis of such structures shows that this is only true of total structures in which there is no extralogical content as both the form and the content are constructed by the subject, e.g. the system of numbers. In contrast, in a classification such as the biological taxonomy of animals the content is extralogical. In that case the "forms" at different levels of the classification have no specific structural characteristics; they cannot be deduced from each other. There is no logical way to get from the characteristics of a class to those of a species, these characteristics being given to the subject by reality. In such a total structure intension and extension have an inverse relationship, whichever way we look at it.

Any exceptions to the foregoing can be explained by distinguishing extrinsic and intrinsic variations, and strong and weak structures. The latter distinction, again, concerns form and content and can be summarized as follows: in a strong structure one can deduce the properties of the total system from those of the sub-systems and reciprocally, while properties of the sub-systems can be deduced from one sub-structure to another. In the strongest structures there is thus no extra-logical content. The logico-mathematical structures of a high level are therefore the strongest structures. In weak structures the content is extralogical, while the form is constructed by the subject. A classification of natural thinking, including the systematic biological classifications, is of such a type. To understand this we must follow Piaget in an excursion into set-theory, giving the different levels of complexity of structures.

In set theory, type 0 indicates objects that form no collection or set. Type 1 is a collection or set of which the elements are of type 0. A collection whose elements are of type 1, is itself type 2, etc.

In a biological classification, individuals are united but neither these individuals nor their characteristics have a logical ''form'', that is to say that they are of type 0, or are extralogical. The class uniting them has a ''form'' and is of type 1, etc. The higher classes do include the lower ones but these inclusions are only based on the generality of observed characteristics and as these remain extralogical it is impossible to deduce them.

As for intrinsic and extrinsic variations, the former can be determined by necessary deductions from the variable characteristics of objects.

> **Example:** For instance: the properties of Euclidean triangles imply the possible transformations of the lengths of the sides, these being necessarily equal or unequal. Thus considering the variations, the intension as well as the extension of unspecified Euclidean triangles would be larger than those of the sub-classes because an isosceles triangle, for example, can only vary within more restricted conditions.

Conversely, facts and experiences due to empirical abstraction lead to extrinsic variations.

> **Example:** Extrinsic variations can be illustrated by the fact that there are mountains of 1000, 2000, and 3000 m high. Analogously the fact that vertebrates do or do not have mammary glands is an extrinsic variation as long as there is no deductive link between this characteristic and the vertebral column.

Combining the two we find that a class is by definition more strongly structured when the sub-classes are linked to the whole or among themselves by intrinsic variations.

Example: A group and its sub-groups is a strong structure, while a class and its species is a weak one.

However, all intermediates are possible.

Example: A seriation in which the differences between *A, B, C,* etc. are unequal is weaker than one with equal differences and this is weaker than one with more complex relations between the elements.

Yet, extrinsic variations can always be considered temporary. The more knowledge we acquire, the more variations might be deduced and thus become intrinsic. The efforts of some biologists to find a causally related taxonomy show such a development.

This possibility leads to the hypothesis of a psychogenetic law according to which all generalizations tend to develop in the direction of intrinsic variations. This is another example of the development from exogenous to endogenous.

So far an example from mathematics has been compared with an example from biology. In the latter case there are weak structures with extralogical content, and extrinsic variations in which inductive (i.e. extensional) generalizations dominate. In the former there are strong structures without extralogical content, and intrinsic variations in which constructive (i.e. extensional and intensional) generalizations dominate. Having compared mathematics and biology, the problem arises as to the type of generalizations used in physics. As Piaget attaches much importance to this problem I shall briefly summarize his reasoning (**75**, p.217ff).

In the domain of experimental reasoning and generalizing the physicist must always take reality into account, however mathematical or theoretical his work might be. In studying the relationship between logico-mathematical structures and extralogical content in physics, we must, however, return to the distinction between application and attribution of structures to reality.

The description of a fact by means of adequate measurements and the formulation of a law by means of calculations and a symbolic elaboration, may lead to a more or less advanced structuralization. But all this supposes no more than an application of logico-mathematical structures constructed before their use. Then the scientist wants to know whether the facts and relations he found are more general and he has to apply the "form" he found to more or less extended samples. But even if this requires new calculations, the physicist does no more than establish whether his law can be verified for "all" the facts (with their fluctuations) and his generalizations are no more than extensional or inductive.

The situation becomes quite different when he passes from laws to causal explanations. In this case the operations attributed to the objects lead to a new formal content consisting of inferential coordinations that go beyond the observables. They thereby tend to join a new extra-logical content which is not yet realized but is a possibility opened up by the operational forms of the subject. The generalizations which make this progress possible are constructive generalizations. This is true notwithstanding the experimental controls and notwithstanding the fact that the contents which were constructed with the forms of the subject as their starting point, insert themselves amidst the extralogical contents and are considered an essential part of them. In other words: at the level of explanation generalization ceases to be purely inductive and consists of inventing new notions linking known facts to necessary deductive constructions.

Up to this point the problem as to how far all these scientific developments are conscious or not has been left out of the picture. Of course the scientist is conscious of his thoughts, but does he use only conscious instruments in his theorizing? Piaget's answer can be summarized as follows (**87**, p.229ff): reconstructive reflection may well remain unconscious, even at a high level of cognitive development, but there may follow "reflexive thought" which gives a thematization of what remained instrumental. In other words: thematization consists of a way of conscious thinking which is both reflexive and retrospective, being directed at the structures of the present level and at those of the former. This thematization has a content and a form. The content is the sum of all the operational compositions and newly discovered transformations with the correspondences between them in so far as these transformations are dependent on each other (in the sense of functional dependence). The essential point is that the form does not consist of instruments of transforming but of instruments of comparing. Thus the thematization finds the general properties of the new system, only adding their combination into a coherent whole. In other words: this form consists of correspondences and categories which are themselves not yet thematized but only serve as instruments. (See 8.2.1 for a definition of mathematical categories.)

☐ An "instrument" is what one uses, at whatever level, without thinking about it. A thematization consists in thinking about the instrument in order to make a theory about it.

At the level of scientific thought, this form itself may be analysed and this new thematization may lead to explicit categories. That is to say, there is a thematization of the instruments of thematization, or a reflected abstraction to the second degree.

☐This is called a "reflection on a reflection", a "reflection on the reflected", "reflected abstraction to the second degree", "reflexive thought", "formal thought", and "metareflexion". Piaget's love for playing with words can be very confusing for the reader!

At the scientific level one often sees how structures are used implicitly while their thematization follows much later. The comparisons, morphisms and categories which have demonstrated this in recent times, take us to the next paragraph.

8.2 Correspondences and Morphisms

8.2.1 Introducing Correspondences, Morphisms and Categories

Piaget was very much impressed by the structuralism of Bourbaki. When McLane and Eilenberg built a theory of morphisms and categories on Bourbaki's structuralism, Piaget was inspired to study whether children's activities of comparing objects and relations might lead to structures that would ultimately be comparable to morphisms and categories in mathematics. This would then be something analogous to the way transformations lead to logico-mathematical structures and finally to mathematical structures.

Piaget read a preliminary paper on correspondence (**101**) and wrote two books on morphisms and categories (**120, 121**). The latter has not been used here because it would require a very detailed summary and, even then, might be too mathematical for many psychologists.

As definitions differ between schools of mathematicians, Piaget's own definitions have been given.

☐The translator of the book on equilibration translated "classe" by "category" instead of class. This might cause confusions. Mathematical categories are not the same as classes.

Correspondence is taken in a very broad sense, including mappings and morphisms, but also a comparison of characteristics or parts of objects. This does not mean that any relation is a correspondence, because the relation must be repeatable, as in $b:b' = a:a'$. That is, it must be a sort of "correlate" in Spearman's sense of the word, but tied to actions and intentions without necessarily being conscious. Correspondences in this sense can

already be seen in the application of sensorimotor schemes to new objects
or to new situations.

Mappings ("applications" in French) *are a type of correspondence in which
elements of one whole (set) are brought into relationships with those of another, but
under more limiting conditions than in correspondences in the above-mentioned
sense.*

> **Explanation by Piaget:** Different types of mappings are "injec-
> tion", "surjection" and "bijection", the terms being the same as
> in French (formerly "one-to-one", "one-on to", etc. were used in
> English). If one compares the elements x of a set E (Ensemble) with
> those of a set E', all the x of E must correspond to the x in E'. In
> the case of an injection each element of E' receives 0 or 1 x from E.
> In the case of a surjection each element x of E' receives at least 1
> element from E. A bijection is an injection as well as a surjection,
> resulting in a one-to-one correspondence of 1 x in E with 1 x in E'
> (**104**, p.54/p.352).

*Morphisms are still more restricted because the structure of the systems that are being
compared is also conserved. There are different levels of morphisms, i.e. morphisms
can be compared to each other.*

A category is the total system of operations that can be performed on morphisms.

8.2.2 The Development of Correspondences and their Relation with Transformations

Though I roughly follow age-and-stage trends in the following, it is
important to note beforehand that there are no stages in the development of correspondences.

8.2.2.1 The earliest sources of correspondences and transformations

Right at the beginning of life assimilation comes before accommodation, as an innate or developed scheme must be present before it can
accommodate. This basic importance of assimilation is clearly seen in
the fact that the function of assimilation is the basis of correspondences
as well as of transformations. This early assimilation has several functional aspects, called by Piaget "coordinators". There are nine coordinators of which Fig. 8.1 gives an overview.

Three of the coordinators—substitution, ordering and displacement—imply a change, while the others concern differentiations and
integration. These purely functional coordinators are the common
source of correspondences and transformations. They lead, on the one

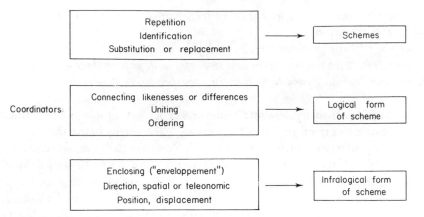

Fig. 8.1 Overview of coordinators

hand, to knowledge of objects by being applied to them (assimilation of objects), which is the basis of correspondences. On the other hand, their compositions (reciprocal assimilation of schemes) are the basis for transformations.

Example: An example given by Piaget is the infant who hits a suspended object in the same way as he succeeded in doing at an earlier moment. There is a repetition of the action, an identification of the new situation with the foregoing, and a substitution of the earlier suspended object by the present one. All this leads to the constitution of a scheme. We can also express this by saying that there is a ''correspondence'' between the earlier situations and the present one, or that the infant put the earlier situation and the present one in correspondence (''mise en correspondance'')'

When an infant pulls at a cloth to obtain an object put on top of it, he coordinates the schemes of pulling and grasping by reciprocal assimilation, thus forming a new scheme which is at the same time differentiated and integrated.

Once the earliest correspondences and transformations have been formed, they are independent of each other and this relationship changes very gradually.

There are no stages in the development of correspondences, i.e. there are no qualitative changes. Whatever the tasks are, one always finds bijections, injections and surjections. However, this does not' mean that there are no changes with development as there are corrections, generalizations, reciprocity and compositions.

Example: A simple example of corrections is found in the improvement of copying a model by drawing (**120**, Chapter 1). Paying more attention to what is a relevant characteristic for the comparison allows an improvement in generalizations. In an experiment the child is given eight sticks of different lengths and a box with a paper lid. The child is told to cut a slit which will allow certain sticks, indicated by the examiner, to go into the box (horizontally). The child begins by thinking that only stick 5 can be put into slit 5, then that this is possible for 4 as well, and finally he generalizes to the sticks smaller than 6 (**120**, Chapter 5; also Berthoud-Papandropolou (**171**)). Reciprocity has also been demonstrated in an experiment that is, however, too complicated for summary in a few sentences. Compositions mean that two or more correspondences are required at the same time, e.g. between the different parts of a seriation, preparing the operations required for seriation.

More important for general cognitive development than these improvements is the change in the relationship between correspondences and transformations. There are six levels in this development which cannot be called "stages" because they depend too much on the nature of the transformations. If the transformations are easy to understand, e.g. a rotation, children already understand them at 4 years old. But in a difficult transformation the same level of understanding will be shown at much later ages. The essential point of this development is that correspondences prepare transformations and then become subordinate to them. This gradual development is due to the fact that transformations take a long time to reach the operational level. During the whole pre-operational period the subject still has to check his inferences by experience and reading of the facts ("constatations"). In other words, before the subject is able to modify content, he has to know the content and furthermore to verify—step by step—the effect of each change because these effects cannot be deduced. Transformations require a conquest of the contents because one has to dominate them in order to change them. In other words, one has to know them in their unchanged state and in their variations before one can understand the change.

Thus it is evident that correspondences are not the source of the transformations but definitely play a role in the preparation of every transformation, providing the information necessary for seeing, analysing and understanding the transformation. What makes correspondences indispensable is the fact that they give us knowledge of extralogical content without changing it, only enriching it by assimilatory frames, constantly accommodated to the specific characteristics of the content. This situation changes once transformations have become operational and inferential.

The construction of operational structures coincides with a subordination of correspondences to transformations. This subordination does not mean a replacement of correspondences by transformations, as the former continue to exist within the operational structures and their functioning. Though transformations play the leading part, correspondences continue to prepare the content before the transforming actions give them new and endogenous forms, leading to morphisms of a higher level.

Considering the whole of development, we see that correspondences and transformations have a common source in the coordinators and end up in a synthesis. Why then, the long and laborious period in which their collaboration is completely lacking at the first level and only fragmentary and difficult at the second? The answer is to be found in the facts which should be well-known by now: consciousness proceeds from the periphery to the centre and this implies that material and external aspects of actions are known before their transformations with their reasons. Furthermore the passage from exogenous to endogenous is not a simple internalization but requires a more or less complete reconstruction by means of new instruments.

In sciences as well as in individual development there is an effort to subordinate correspondences which are at first simply observed, to operational systems based on transformations. Once correspondences are subordinate to operational structures, they thereby become morphisms because the comparisons concern structures instead of isolated observables. This shows, once more, but from a very different approach, how important operational structures are—the first morphisms being the starting point for higher levels of morphisms and finally for categories.

   □Piaget treats the development of morphisms and categories in far more detail, and introduces many new technical terms. Because I supposed that such details would be of little interest to psychologists without an extensive training in modern algebra, they have been "included in all that was excluded" in order to keep this book within a reasonable number of pages. I hope that I have given the interested reader a taste for what he may find when turning to the full text (**120, 121**).

8.3 Success and Understanding

Piaget's second volume on consciousness was called *Success and Understanding* (**86**). It was the precursor of an elaboration of two systems of knowing (**105, 119**) that are important for the opening up of new possibilities. Though these topics had already been indicated in *Success and Understanding,* they were elaborated after the theory of equilibration and will therefore be summarized in Chapter 10. For the moment only the main points of *Success and Understanding* will be mentioned, because they illustrate yet another aspect of the activity of the subject.

Though one might easily think that the problem-solving tasks concern no more than psychogenetic development, Piaget explicitly stresses their epistemological importance. The relationship between understanding and succeeding that Piaget studies is the psychogenetic aspect of the fundamental epistemological question concerning the relationship between technology and science (**86**, p.7/p.VIII).

☐The original says "la technique et la science", translated as "technical skill and knowledge" in the official text. To me this does not suggest an epistemological question, but that may be my fault.

The main difference between the experiments in this book (**86**) and those in many others, is that in them the child manipulates the material in order to reach a goal set by the experimenter, instead of trying to understand what the experimenter demonstrates.

Example: In the research on causality a marble was released and the child had to understand, i.e. to predict and later to explain what happens when it touches other marbles (see Chapter 7). In the same type of situation, the child now has to cause a specific movement of one of the marbles. A number of marbles are suspended on a horizontal plank in such a way that the child can make one of them move, without touching it, by using one of the other ones. After his efforts the child is questioned about the reasons for his actions, etc.

In the book on cognizance (**85**) Piaget had defended two hypotheses: action constitutes an autonomous form of knowledge which only becomes conscious later on, and the grasp of consciousness develops from the periphery to the centre (see 8.1). The new experiments confirmed these results but with the restriction that, from a higher level (about 7 or 8 years of age) on, conceptualizations influence actions. This is due to the fact that conceptualizations reinforce the capacity to anticipate future actions and to make a plan. But this does not imply that the subject becomes conscious of the structures he uses. This reflexion on his own structures is not found before the highest level, around the age of 14 or 15. At this stage (IIIB) the situation is completely reversed compared with that at the beginning. The child started with actions, followed by conceptualization (IA). Then, during a long period (mainly stage II), actions and conceptualizations were approximately at the same level, with a constant exchange between them. Finally, the situation has become reversed because now conceptualizations determine the actions. This means more than a succession of limited and temporary plans, as it is a total program, comparable to adult technology based on a theory.

So far we have seen that the problem-solving tasks in this book led to the same type of results as its companion volume showed for precocious actions. But their importance goes beyond this because the analysis of the results raises many new questions.

Succeeding in an action, and far more, failing to do so, stimulates the subject to ask why this happened. The answer to a "Why?" question gives us reasons. In other words, succeeding means no more than using things with success, while understanding means that the reasons have been found, and, as became clear in the foregoing, this allows for anticipations. In the end understanding may even do without actions. This sounds very unproblematic and perhaps even rather self-evident. But a closer look shows that the experiments raise new questions for the experimenter: "How does the child find reasons?" "What cognitive development makes it possible to end by understanding without acting?" *Success and Understanding* contains some tentative answers but its main importance lies in the fact that it led to the study of new topics: signifying implication, and the possible and the necessary.

9 A Model for Development: Equilibration

□The corresponding chapter is Chapter 20, but the title differs because critics not only discuss equilibration but also learning. Though in Volume I training experiments have only been briefly mentioned (in Chapter 6), they are important for Piaget's opponents. Therefore 20.1 contains arguments against equilibration and 20.2 concerns learning. However, as equilibration is also a biological process, the topic is taken up again in Chapter 23.

In the foregoing chapters the genetic aspect of Piaget's theory has often been mentioned but never analysed in detail. Yet, for a genetic epistemology, the development of knowledge is the basic issue and in the long run the study of this development cannot be limited to the description of successive structures. In fact, Piaget has paid attention to the processes of development from the very beginning of his theorizing, but—as has already been mentioned in Chapter 5—he found it difficult to find a satisfactory model. Piaget even criticized the 1975 book (**90**) at a symposium in honour of his eightieth birthday in 1976 (**103**).

The 1975 theory of improving equilibration ("équilibration majorante") *was meant to be a general model for the causal explanation of what the subject does in the constructions of his progressive cognitive development as well as for the way scientists proceed from one theory to the next.* In this sense equilibration is a theory of the psychological subject and of the scientists in contrast to the logical analysis of the epistemic subject and the "content" of scientific theories.

Considering development as a progressive construction of cognitive structures by way of equilibration raises a number of questions:

1) As any equilibrium implies that "something" is in equilibrium with "something else", the first question is, "What is in equilibrium with what?"

2) If every state of equilibrium is followed by disequilibrium, the next question is "What causes disequilibrium?"
3) In a healthy organism disequilibrium must be followed by a new equilibrium or a reequilibration. So, "What causes a return to a state of equilibrium?"
4) If Piaget is right in assuming that equilibration is "majorante", the next question is, "How is this improvement explained?"
5) "If equilibration is a model, can it be validated experimentally?"
6) The final question is, "Does Piaget give an explanation or no more than a description?"

9.1 What is in Equilibrium with What?

There are two closely related ways of answering this question, the second being an extension of the first one. The first answer is that assimilation and accommodation must be in equilibrium, and the second that affirmations and negations must be in equilibrium.

9.1.1 Assimilation and Accommodation

The three levels of assimilation-accommodation have already been described in Chapter 5. There are thus also three levels of equilibration.
a) The first level concerns the subject and external objects: assimilation of the object to the subject's scheme must be in equilibrium with the accommodation of the scheme to the object.
b) The second level is the relatively simple reciprocal assimilation and accommodation of schemes of the subject. There is an improvement in this equilibration, but there is no qualitative difference between a separate scheme like looking, and another separate scheme like grasping, in comparison with their coordinated scheme of looking-grasping (eye-hand coordination).
c) The third level is the highest one, consisting of differentiations followed by an integration. Accommodations lead to a differentiation of a scheme or system into sub-systems. Then these sub-systems are assimilated into a new total system which is qualitatively different from the foregoing sub-systems. This form is very important because the integration means that what had been "overtaken" ("dépassé") becomes a part of the "overtaking" ("dépassant") thus combining conservation of the earlier sub-structures with innovation in the new structure (**103**, p.39). This level of equilibration had been insufficiently

emphasized in the book on equilibration (**90**) and was therefore elaborated in later books. These later results will be summarized in Chapter 10.

9.1.2 Affirmations and Negations

In order to understand this description of equilibration, a short detour to the topic of contradictions is necessary.

9.1.2.1 Contradictions

While thinking about equilibration Piaget was struck by the notion that affirmations and negations must compensate each other. This insight led to a series of experiments on contradictions (**84**).

In this book Piaget is not interested in logical contradictions, but in natural ones. A logical contradiction consists of the simultaneous affirmation of the truth of p and non-p or, if $p \supset q$, it would be contradictory to affirm that both $p.q$ and $p.$non-q are true, taking into account the total of definitions, axioms and theorems formerly admitted as well as rules specifying the use of negation and implication. *A logical contradiction is thus an error in a formal calculation that might have been avoided by a better use of the procedure, and that can be corrected by using the right procedure as soon as the mistake is noticed* (**84b**, p.153).

In contrast, natural contradictions seem to be unavoidable, because the subject often does not have enough information to know beforehand whether an action a *is compatible with an action* b. The young child can only try them out and though the older ones can anticipate the results or conceptualize them, there will still be errors due to a lack of complete formalization.

The experiments showed up three different classes of contradictions: a) the child thinks that different actions can have the same result in a situation where this is not true, or that the same actions can have different results, b) the child makes an incomplete opposition of classes that should be disjunctive, c) the child makes wrong inferences, usually due to the conviction that $p \supset q$ allows the conclusion that $q \supset p$.

> **Example:** An example of b) can be seen in an experiment that is often quoted by Piaget because it concerns, again, transitivity (**84a**, pp. 15-31). The material consists of a plank with seven circular holes, each with a disc fitting into it. The smallest one, A, has a diameter of 5.88 cm and the largest, G, of 6 cm. They are arranged in two rows $A \diagdown B \diagup C \diagdown D$ etc. A chain is attached to each disc in such a way that A can only be compared to B, B to C, etc.

The only one that is unattached is G. The task is to compare the discs, but as the differences are subliminal, the child concludes that they are all the same size. After this preliminary, the main part of the interview follows, consisting of the comparison of G and A, resulting in the experience that $G>A$. How will the child explain what is evidently contradictory for the adult? The youngest children (4 or 5 to 7 years) see no contradiction. If forced to realize that $G = A$ (as they said), and $G>A$, their best solution is that G changed in size when being compared with F ($G = F$), and with A! At the second level, the child (from 7 years on) can use transitivity and is therefore conscious of the contradiction between $A = B = C = D = E = F = G$ and $G>A$. The children up to 9 or 10 years of age try to solve the problem by finding two classes, one composed of the small discs and one of the big ones, usually without a complete disjunction. However, in contrast to the subjects of the first level, they see that their solution is unsatisfactory, trying different ways of separating the two classes or giving up. The children from 9 or 10 years on do grasp that there are imperceptible differences but are unable to accept that adding them might lead to a perceptible difference. Finally the children from about 11 or 12 years on find the correct solution.

The important characteristic of all types of contradictions, which gives at the same time a definition of natural contradictions, is that there is an incomplete compensation between an affirmation (that is, attributing characteristic a to class A) *and a negation* (attributing non-a to class A', if $A + A' = B$).

The incompleteness of the compensation can be explained by the observation that affirmations are the most natural and spontaneous behaviour, while negations are far more difficult to construct (as a number of examples will illustrate in the next paragraph). In general, the use of the negation only advances with the gradual progress of structures and is not systematic before these become operational.

9.1.2.2 Affirmations and negations in equilibration

Looking at the levels of assimilation and accommodation from the point of view of affirmations and negations, one can easily see that all the levels require an equilibrium between affirmations and negations.
a) In the case of a successful assimilation of A', B', etc. into the schemes A, B, etc. the subject has to see that A' has characteristics suitable for the use of scheme A. This is a positive characteristic or affirmation.

But at the same time this implies that the subject must distinguish A', having the characteristic a' from all the objects characterized by non-a', and the scheme A from all the schemes that are non-A. For the young child the negations remain implicit, but at later stages they require a more or less systematic explanation.

In the case where an accommodation is necessary, the original scheme A is modified into A_2 but without the disappearance of A, which now becomes the sub-scheme A_1. Thus the original A is differentiated into A_1 and A_2. But, in order to reach a state of equilibrium, A_1 must only be applied to objects A' and A_2 to objects A'', and the partial negations $A_2 = A.\text{non-}A_1$ and $A_1 = A.\text{non-}A_2$ are indispensable.

> **Example:** A child who accommodates the grasping scheme for a large object (scheme A) to scheme A_2 when grasping a small object, is still capable of grasping the large object, i.e. he has scheme A_1 (the original A) and A_2 (the new scheme). But he must only apply A_1 to large objects and A_2 to small ones.

b) The mechanisms of reciprocal assimilation and accommodation are the same as those mentioned under a) but they require in addition the structure of an intersection with new negations. In order to coordinate the sub-systems S_1 and S_2 the subject has to discover their common operative part $S_1.S_2$ as opposed to $S_1.\text{non-}S_2$ and $S_2.\text{non-}S_1$.

c) Differentiating a whole T into sub-systems S requires finding the characteristics of each sub-system but also excluding, i.e. denying or negating the properties belonging to any other sub-system. Analogously, integrating sub-systems into T involves finding what they have in common but also what does not characterize them.

> □ Piaget uses A, A_1 etc. in a) because classes of objects, A', A'', etc. are integrated into the schemes. In b) there is no relation with objects, and therefore the letters S are used.

In summary, the answer to the first question is that assimilation and accommodation must be in equilibrium, which implies that affirmations and negations must be in equilibrium too.

9.2 What Causes Disequilibrium?

If it is true that affirmations and negations must be in equilibrium, the presence of an affirmation without a negation necessarily implies a disequilibrium. As was already indicated, the predominance of affirmations is "natural".

Example: Perception gives us affirmations while the absence of an object has to be inferred. Any displacement is primarily experienced as an approach to the goal to be reached and not as the distance from the starting point. All motivational actions are directed towards a positive goal, even where this involves taking away or avoiding an obstacle. Where failure to reach a goal is experienced, understanding of the negations to which it is due often requires a long period of construction.

The motivational aspect, mentioned in the examples, takes us to assimilations. The first postulate (see 5.3.2.2) states that every scheme tends to incorporate objects. But what is the driving force that makes them do so? Here Piaget sees a possible link between his structuralism and functionalism (Dewey, Claparède, etc.). In Piaget's terminology, an essential place must be reserved for needs and interests. *An "interest" is the motivational aspect of a scheme, as an object is only interesting when it can be integrated into a scheme.* In other words, from the point of view of the subject, an assimilatory scheme gives a signification to objects and a goal for actions (or mental activity) related to that object.

Example: An object hanging from the roof of a crib is given the meaning of "something to swing" and thus becomes interesting, and leads to the goal-directed activity of "swinging-it". The same reasoning is true for the scientist reading a scientific critique of his work.

A scheme may be activated by an object, but also by internal stimuli (e.g. hunger making the subject interested in food and actions for finding it). If the activated scheme does not succeed in finding the necessary food for assimilation, this is experienced as a need. From the cognitive point of view this means that there is a perturbation. *Perturbations, i.e. states of disequilibrium, take a positive form when there is an obstacle which prevents assimilation-accommodation, or a negative one when there is a "lacuna", that is, when the food for the scheme is lacking.* However, something is only a perturbation when it is experienced as such by the subject, that is to say, when the subject wants to reach a goal but cannot do so because of an obstacle or a lacuna.

Relating disequilibrium as the consequence of an obstacle or a lacuna to the predominance of affirmations in any motivational action explains why there are so many occasions for disequilibrium in the life of the young child. As long as the figurative aspect of knowledge and empirical abstraction dominate, it is very difficult to infer or construct negations. But as disequilibrium is necessary for reequilibration, even if the next equilibrium is only a temporary one, these frequent states of disequilibrium are favourable for development.

9.3 Reactions to Disequilibrium

Reactions to disequilibrium may be non-adaptive, in the sense of not leading to a new equilibrium, or adaptive, in the sense of leading to a new equilibrium.

9.3.1 Non-Adaptive Reactions to Disequilibrium

Perturbations caused by external obstacles often lead to unproductive reactions, especially in the young child, but even an adult may regress to unproductive behaviour.

Piaget mentions a number of unfavourable, primitive reactions to perturbations, though without the pretence of giving a complete inventory. One example of these is the reaction which is a mere repetition of the original action as though this might suddenly lead to success, notwithstanding the fact that the obstacle has not changed or been removed. Another reaction is to give up the action or even the goal. This may be done unconsciously, e.g. when a child is distracted by a new aspect of the obstacle and changes his course accordingly, or when a child represses the disturbing observation. The same behaviour may, of course, occur consciously, even at the highest level of development. In the case of a lacuna it is evidently also possible to give up the unfulfilled need. In some cases the lacuna leads to behaviour that is intended to fill in the lacuna, but causes in fact an undesirable effect.

> **Example:** The only example Piaget gives is a material one: a fire "finding food" will increase, but from our point of view this is an "error".

In the cognitive domain such unfavourable results of the effort to fill in a lacuna are exceptions, because the error leads sooner or later to contradictions that will then be corrected.

> ☐Piaget gives no examples, but just refers to his experiments on contradiction. However, the tasks are all rather easy for the oldest subjects so that they do see the contradictions. One wonders whether it is always true that errors in filling in a lacuna lead to contradictions which are corrected. Many students and scientists seem to persist for quite a long time in their errors so that Piaget's "sooner or later" might well be "much later" indeed.

9.3.2 Adaptive Reactions to Disequilibrium: Regulations and Compensations

The equilibrium mentioned in 9.1 gives a description but no explanation. The explanation of the process of equilibration is to be found in regulations and the compensations they lead to.

There is a close link between the two—so close, in fact, that Piaget often writes about ''regulatory compensations'' or ''compensatory regulations''. The fact that Piaget says that regulations lead to compensations would make one expect that regulations are an activity while the resulting compensation is a state. This is indeed often correct, but on the other hand *Piaget defines a compensation as an action in the opposite direction of a given effect, which is meant to undo this effect or to neutralize it. Regulations are then called instruments for reaching this goal.* So the reader will have to come to his own conclusion whether compensations are actions or not. In the following, regulations are described first, followed by compensations—though the separation is evidently rather artificial.

9.3.2.1 Regulations

In general a regulation means that action A *is not repeated as* A *but is modified into action* A', *the modification being due to the effect of* A.

There are two types of regulations: *corrections* (negative feedback) in the case of obstacles, and *reinforcement* (positive feedback) in the case of a lacuna.

An example will illustrate what Piaget means by ''negative feedback''.

> **Example:** Somebody learns to ride a bicycle. He is still rather unsure, leaning over too much to one side, then correcting himself when he feels that his motor behaviour is incorrect. He now leans over too much while taking a corner and again corrects this by straightening up, etc. (Incidentally this example, taken from Piaget, shows that sensorimotor behaviour is not limited to the first stage of development.)

Looking at this example from a theoretical point of view we see that the learner has developed a scheme (riding straight on). He still has to adjust his behaviour on the basis of the information he gets, either about his own behaviour or about an external obstacle, each of them forming a perturbation. Getting the information that the continuation of his behaviour will lead to dire consequences or has done so, he does indeed change his behaviour. In more general terms: the effect of his behaviour A modifies this behaviour into A'. The fact that this modification is due to information about a perturbation (often in the form of an external obstacle) and that this information then leads to a correction, is called ''negative feedback'' by Piaget.

> ☐This is rather confusing as Piaget does use the term ''feedback'' in his French text but includes the information and the correction in his definition. He writes explicitly that ''negative feedback'' consists of corrections (**90**, p.25/p.19). He also calls them ''instruments of correction'' (p.32/p.26). In other theories the information that something is going wrong is called ''negative feedback'' without including the correction which is the result of the feedback.

The second type of perturbations are lacunae. There is no example in Piaget, but the reader can take any example of reinforcement in a learning theory. Where the object is not available, but the behaviour is changed in order to reach it, there is positive feedback. One might think that positive feedback does not include a correction but, though it is less obvious than in negative feedback, there is also a correction in positive feedback. In fact, reinforcement is only superfluous in situations in which the fulfilment of the need is given immediately by an already established scheme. In all other cases a correction is required. But though there is indeed a correction this is not the most important aspect of positive feedback. More essential is the fact that the subject comes to attach a value to the goal. This gives him the feeling that the satisfaction of his need—whether practical or purely cognitive—is indispensable and, as was said in the foregoing paragraph, the fact that there is no ''food'' to give this satisfaction is experienced as a lacuna.

Separating negative and positive feedback in this way is rather artificial. As soon as behaviour is even slightly complex, negative and positive feedback are combined. For instance, a habit is usually considered the result of positive feedback, but it is evident that its formation requires a lot of trial and error with its negative feedback. The same holds true for what Piaget calls ''active regulations'', i.e. the conscious choice of another way of reaching the goal, or a conscious choice between alternatives. In general one can distinguish between quasi-automatic regulations and active regulations. The former characterize simple sensorimotor regulations. These need not be conscious. However, active regulations require consciousness and are therefore the source of a representation or conceptualization of a material action. This will lead to a subordination of the regulations to a higher level and constitutes the beginning of a ''second grade'' regulation or regulation of regulations. However I shall first turn to the role played by affirmations and negations in regulations because they do not require consciousness either.

Regulations always consist of a retroactive process and a proactive one. Even though an action A is changed into A', one may say that the action is resumed. Therefore, any regulation implies the resuming of an action and this is called the "retroactive aspect". But the fact of the change to A'—due to a correction, reinforcement or their combined effect—is "proactive". The retroactive and proactive processes, going in opposite directions, form a "loop" in the cybernetic sense, because resuming the action may be considered an affirmation and the change a negation. That negative feedback is a negation is clear because it always implies a suppression.

> **Example:** An external obstacle can be suppressed; one movement can be suppressed to the benefit of another; the strength of a movement can be suppressed, etc.

However, positive feedback is a negation as well. Positive feedback is directed towards the filling-in of a lacuna. However, a lacuna is in itself a negation: something is missing. Positive reinforcement is directed toward the suppression of this negation, in other words, it is a negation of a negation and—as Piaget explicitly states—this is more than playing with words.

Reading about the retroactive aspect of a regulation and the corrective effect of feedback, the thought comes to mind that the regulation may not only be due to the experienced effect of an action A but also to the anticipation of this effect.

> **Example:** The boy on his bicycle may well anticipate that he will fall and correct his behaviour before actually falling. Alternatively, having fallen once, he may anticipate the effect of his behaviour the next time and therefore correct it.

Piaget does indeed write that sooner or later retroactions lead to anticipations (**90**, p.35/p.30). However, he does not go into details here in the way he did in *Biology and Knowledge*. Here Piaget writes about anticipation in terms of feedback loops. Anticipation is a function—organization, assimilation and accommodation being other examples of functions. Anticipations are found at the level of classical and instrumental conditioning, but also at all higher levels of cognitive functioning.

> **Example:** A child of 11 or 12 months pulls at a support (action A), and thereby accidentally sets in motion an object lying on the support (result B). There is immediately a feedback loop linking the result B to the action A which is then repeated. The chance

action became a scheme of "pulling at a support to obtain an object".

At the simplest level, anticipation only changes a chance action into a scheme, but at all levels of cognitive behaviour, including that of the scientist, anticipation of failure or success influences behaviour in the form of feedback loops of a proactive nature.

So far I have described simple regulations in which the negative feedback is supposed to remove the obstacle while positive feedback leads to filling up a lacuna. However, these *regulations may not be successful or the problems may be more complex. In such cases the first regulations have to be regulated, a process called "regulations on regulations".* Thus a whole *hierarchy of regulations* is found, the highest level being that of autoregulations of the system, with a modification and enrichment of their original program by differentiation, multiplication and coordination of goals to be reached and the integration of sub-systems into a total system. This takes us well into the problems of improving equilibration to which I shall return in 9.4.

After this elaboration of regulations at the behavioural level, *there is still the far more fundamental problem of what the regulator guiding regulations is* (**90**, p.28/p.22).

The answer to this question is that *the regulator guiding regulations is the totality of the system.* Any regulation requires a regulator or programmed control, like a thermostat regulating temperatures. One might look for this program in the "nature" of reality, that is to say in the properties of objects which are at first unknown but to which the subject's knowledge approaches asymptotically. But this would be incorrect because we get to know objects through empirical abstraction which does not function without reflective abstraction by the subject. Therefore "objects", i.e. "reality", cannot be the regulator for the subject's knowledge of the physical world. It is even less acceptable to consider reality as a regulator for the logico-mathematical structures of the subject as these go beyond the physical nature of objects. As far as there is a harmony between mathematics and reality this exists through the operations of the subject, their characteristics being due to their organic roots. In fact, *the organism is a physical object amongst others, but a more active one than the others, hence we see at the same time that the organism and reality are in harmony and that the organism goes beyond reality* (**90**, p.28/p.22).

Now if the physical world outside the organism cannot be the regulator of cognitive regulations, there must be an internal regulator.

the regulatory process is not hereditary, the only possibility is to consider the mutual conservations inherent in the functional process of
assimilation the regulator. This looks very much like a vicious circle,
as the cycle of interactions would thus be the cause and the result of
regulations. In fact there is a circle, but not a vicious one. In every
biological and cognitive system one must consider the whole primor-
dial and not the result of an assembling of the parts, the latter being
the result of differentiations starting from the whole. This fact gives the
whole a cohesive strength and therefore properties of autoconservation,
which distinguish it from non-organic, physico-chemical totalities.

Piaget quotes a number of authors who have found in very different
fields of science that the whole is more stable than the composing parts.

The whole or totality of the system thus *plays the role of regulator of its partial
regulations and imposes a stringent norm on the regulations:* they must either
submit to the conservation of the whole i.e. to the closure of the cycle
of interactions or end in a complete dislocation comparable to the death
of the organism. As the continual play of assimilations and accommodations incessantly provokes reinforcements and corrections, both
take the form of regulations or feedback as soon as they continue in
retroactive and proactive processes, but under the permanent dynamic
control of the totality that demands its conservation (**90**, p.30/p.24).

9.3.2.2 Compensations

As I have already mentioned, regulations are very closely linked to
compensations. The notion of compensation is so fundamental for
Piaget that he has been accused of attaching far too much importance
to it. However, Piaget himself does not believe that it is possible to
overestimate its importance. It is true that he does take the concept in
a very broad sense—*anything neutralizing a perturbation is called a "compensation"*—but the study of its variations and their common characteristics is fundamental. I shall first summarize the general aspects of
compensation and then follow Piaget in its detailed analysis. The latter
is a necessary basis for recent notions described in Chapter 11 and for
the issue as to whether the process of equilibration is the same in the
sensorimotor period as in the rest of life, which has also been postponed
to this chapter.

*A compensation is defined as an action in the opposite direction of a given effect
tending either to undo it or to cancel it ("compensation by inversion") or to neutralize it ("compensation by reciprocity").*

In the case of a cancellation of the perturbation there is a complete negation. This process is called a "compensation by inversion" consisting either of a feedback loop or, at the operational stage, of an inverse operation. In other situations the subject has to accommodate his scheme, differentiating it into a new sub-scheme. In this case there is a neutralization, called a "compensation by reciprocity". Also, in such a case the correction does not consist of removing an external obstacle, undoing its effect, but is internal. As the original scheme still functions after the differentiation, the reconstruction by differentiation is only a partial negation of the original action, called "compensation by reciprocity". Such a differentiation may occur when there has been an external obstacle to the original scheme or when the reciprocal assimilation and accommodation of two schemes has led to a perturbation.

□At first sight it is confusing that having been used to reading about reversibility by inversion and by reciprocity one now sees the latter term being used in the sense of a differentiation of a scheme into a sub-scheme. However, the term is in fact applied to analogous situations. In the conservation experiment reciprocity consists of neutralizing an increase in height by a decrease in width. The increase is not undone, but neutralized by an opposite effect or negation. This is a partial negation, while pouring water back is a form of undoing, i.e. a complete negation. In compensations by reciprocity there is also a neutralization. In more technical terms one may say that there is in both cases the "same" action, but with a permutation of the (+) and (−).

Both forms of compensation may be the result of negative feedback or positive feedback. In fact, feedback always leads to a compensation, apart from the errors resulting from positive feedback. This does not mean, however, that all perturbations lead to compensations because we have already seen that there are unadaptive ways of reacting to a perturbation.

Furthermore, it should be mentioned that the reactions to any form of perturbation cannot be classified into "all or none". Between failure and success there are many intermediates. One of the most striking partial compensations was found in Piaget's research on contradictions. One of the characteristics of pre-operational thought is the fact that an affirmation need not be completely compensated by a negation, thus leading to what the adult calls a contradiction.

Compensations due to regulations are at the same time constructive and conserving. In itself a regulation is already a construction because retroactions or loops are added to the "linear" trajectory of the original action. Even if the result is only a stabilization without improvement, the action is enriched by the construction of new relations, e.g. implicit negations. But in general the intervention of disturbing elements and the accommodations by compensations lead to new knowledge, either of objects or of the subject's actions. Reequilibration then involves a construction at a new level, which takes us to improving equilibration.

9.4 Improving Equilibration

9.4.1 Improving Equilibration in General

Improving equilibration leads to a higher state of equilibrium. This raises the question of how one state of equilibrium can be characterized as higher or better than another. One of the expressions Piaget used more often in earlier work than he has done recently is that the equilibrium "becomes more stable". *Stability of an equilibrium is achieved by the integration of sub-structures into total structures.* Isolated schemes or structures are more vulnerable, more open to perturbations, than schemes or structures that are part of a whole. Therefore structures in a stable state of equilibrium will not change so easily. However, this does not mean that there can be no more change. Even in a science like mathematics where structures are never given up, there are constantly differentiations and integrations. The end of the foregoing chapter illustrated this by showing the development from structures to categories. Another of Piaget's expressions is that equilibrium is higher when the organism "becomes better adapted to its environment". But, can one really say that an adult is better adapted to his specific environment than an infant is to his own environment? For Piaget *a better adaptation means that the organism has more possibilities in interacting with a wider environment.* Equilibration is seen as a spiral, widening out from a very narrow base to a wide loop at the top. In this sense an adult can certainly be said to interact in far more ways with far more aspects of reality than the infant; and as a species humans have more varied ways of interacting with a more varied environment than species at a lower level of evolution. Thus it is reasonable to conclude that there is an improved adaptation in ontogenesis as well as in phylogenesis (**114**).

During cognitive development equilibration leads to improvement because a compensatory regulation does not imply a return to the former level of equilibrium, but to a higher one. Furthermore, the result of a regulation often ends in a new regulation of what has already been regulated. Coordinations of actions at the sensorimotor stage imply a regulation, but then these regulations have to be regulated again at the level of representations. Such regulations on regulations have already been described as "reflective abstraction" with its two components. Though Piaget is not very explicit about the relation between equilibration and reflective abstraction, he does say that there is a close link between them. He writes that reflective abstraction constantly interferes with the regulations on regulations so that it seems to be the same mechanism described in two different languages and from two points of view (**90**, p.41/p.35). Also some pages later he talks of the collaboration (if not identity) of regulations and reflective abstraction (**90**, p.43/p.37—the text between parentheses has been left out in the official translation).

> ☐I think that it would be best to consider equilibration as being the most general causal model and reflective abstraction as being identical with regulations on regulations.

9.4.2 Details of the Interaction Between Subject and Object in Equilibration

Perturbations by obstacles with the ensuing regulations/compensations clearly show a contribution by the subject who experiences the perturbation and the object that causes the perturbation. However, this is only one aspect of the interaction, expressed in rather general terms. Therefore Piaget proceeds with a detailed analysis.

9.4.2.1 Definitions of observables and coordination

Observables
An observable is what experience allows us to read off straight away from the facts themselves. But as Piaget is not an empiricist, *an observable is what the subject believes he perceives* and not simply what is "perceivable". In other words, an observable is never independent of the subject's assimilatory instruments in the form of pre-operational or operational schemes applied to the actual perception, leading either to greater precision or to a deformation. But these schemes have been constituted by prior coordinations, beginning with the newborn's reflexes or innate schemes.

The subject can observe his own actions, to be called "Observables S" (= "Obs.S"), or those that belong to the objects, to be called "Observables O" (= "Obs.O"), the two often going together.

Coordinations

Coordinations go beyond the "facts", being characterized by implicit or explicit inferences. The subject has the feeling that these inferences are imposed upon him, ranging from a feeling of subjective evidence to one of logical necessity. *The essential characteristic of all coordinations is that they construct new relations beyond observables.*

As Piaget considers notions of physical causality as pre-operations or operations, applied or attributed to the object, coordinations between objects are not essentially different from coordinations between actions. In addition to coordinations between objects and coordinations between actions, there are coordinations between objects which are momentarily introduced into the objects by the subject. Such applications or pseudo-empirical abstractions have already been defined in Chapter 8.

9.4.2.2 The interaction between subject and object

There are two types of interactions, each with a variety A and B. In type I, observables on actions become related to observables on objects, but without coordinations. In type II such coordinations are constructed. Variety A are causal interactions and variety B are logico-mathematical ones.

Type I-A

This type is already found at the level of very elementary causal interactions. Even then the subject needs pre-operational instruments to register the observables, but these instruments are not yet used in an inferential way.

> **Example:** A child pushing an object, or any such simple action is an example.

This elementary interaction is represented in the model of Fig. 9.1 (**90**, p.55/p.48).

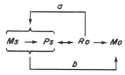

Fig. 9.1 Observables, type I-A:

Ms = movement of subject in the direction of object or movement given to the object
Ps = pushing power exerted on the object, indissociable from Ms
Ro = resistance of object
Mo = movement of object dependent on the action by the subject and the resistance of the object

The two functions indicated by a and b are themselves observables that are related as covariations, without any inference transcending these observables. At a later stage the subject may, however, become conscious of them or conceptualize them. In a the complex $(Ms \rightarrow Ps)$ depends on the resistance (Ro), as the amount of effort required of the subject is a function of this observed resistance.

In b the movement of the object (Mo) is experienced as a function of the complex $(Ms \rightarrow Ps)$, as this movement varies according to the action of the subject.

Type I-B

This type combines observables and logico-mathematical actions and is represented by the model of Fig. 9.2 (**90**, p.57/p.50).

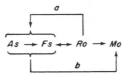

Fig. 9.2 Coordinations, type I-B:

As = the activity or operation of the subject (ordering, seriating, classifying)

Fs = the application of the operations, i.e. the form imposed by the subject on the object (e.g. sequence of relations, classification, etc.)

Ro = the resistance that may or may not be offered by objects (objects may or may not fit into a classification)

Mo = the modification of the objects that have become enriched by a new form

The first important difference between I-A and I-B is that in the Obs.Ms and Ps (I-A) the subject "loses" something (effort of the movement), while the object "wins" (Mo = movement). In I-B, on the contrary, the application of the form Fs means no expenditure by the subject but only a morphism enriching the knowledge of the subject. A second difference is that, though in both types the observables always depend on former coordinations, these are based upon a mixture of empirical and reflective abstraction in type I-A (where the properties of the object play a role), but on pseudo-empirical and reflective abstraction in type I-B (where activities are applied to objects).

In summary, these interactions of type I are the simplest form of equilibration (symbolized by $\rightarrow$) between assimilations by means of a scheme ($Ms + Ps$, or $As + Fs$) and accommodation to objects (Ro and Mo).

Type II

In type II there are observables as well as implicit or explicit coordinations, type II-A being the higher level of type I-A and type II-B being the higher level of type I-B. The separation between type I and type II is clarifying, on the one hand, but artificial, on the other; an interaction of type I is always preceded by coordinations though these are of a lower level than this interaction of type I.

Type II-A

In the construction of a model of type II Ms and Ps (or As and Fs), etc. are united into the global term "Obs.S" (= "observables relative to the actions of the subject") and Ro, Mo, etc. are united into the global term "Obs.O" (= "observables relative to the objects"). To these observables the coordinations S and O—as inferential coordinations of actions or operations of the subject (Coord.S), and inferential co-ordinations between objects (Coord.O)—are added.

If one only considers one state of type II-A without successive levels, the model is represented by Fig. 9.3 where ⟷ indicates a global equilibrium of short or long duration (**90**, p.59/p.52).

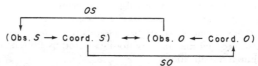

Fig. 9.3 Coordinations, type II-A

The processes OS and SO do not show the symmetry of a and b in type I because the one concerns observables and the other coordinations. Nevertheless they show the fundamental interaction between subject and object in every cognitive act: on the one hand the subject only cognizes his actions by their results on objects, on the other hand he only understands objects by way of inferences tied to the coordinations of these same actions. Obs.S are often incomplete or wrong until they are put in a precise relation to Obs.O. The process SO also takes us back to causality as it expresses the fundamental fact that in order to understand and even to discover causal relations between objects, the subject has to use his own operations.

This model of a state of equilibrium may be considered the starting point of a sequential process of equilibration. In the first place, as has been mentioned before, every observable is influenced by former coordinations and their results. In the second place, the coordinations of a given state will lead to the discovery of new observables, either because of a better reading-off or because of a search for verification.

Example: When a ball hits another one on the side, the child begins by thinking that the second ball will start off in the direction of the first one. When he begins to understand why the passive ball cannot continue in the direction of the active one, he begins to observe the directions, the point of impact, etc. much better than he did before.

The state of equilibrium represented in Fig. 9.3 is therefore only a temporary one and no more than a link in a chain of sequential equilibrations. Figure 9.4 gives the model for such sequential equilibrations.

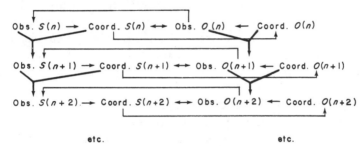

Fig. 9.4 Sequential equilibration

Beginning with the reading-off of new observables the four terms used end in a cycle in the following order:

Obs.O→Obs.S→Coord.S→Coord.O→Obs.O→etc.

In actual acts this cycle is seen in three different forms.

a) There is no discrepancy between the observables and coordinations and the cycle is rapidly closed. That is to say, there is no change, but a relatively stable equilibrium.

b) There are contradictions and local regulations leading to a short period of trial-and-error with a new, more-or-less stable, equilibrium.

c) The contradictions are more serious, leading to a more fundamental change, that is to say, from n to $n + 1$ along the dark lines in Fig. 9.4.

This model can be generalized to pure interactions between objects (type C) as Piaget explains in detail (**90**, p.68/p.63).

Type II-B

A subject can apply his pre-operations or operations to material objects or his operations to pure symbols. The application to material objects is the only possibility up to the formal stage, but may still be found at that stage (e.g. for combinations, permutations, etc.) and even in some steps of scientific thought.

The model for type II-B is the same as that for type II-A (Fig. 9.4), but with the following meanings:

Obs.S express the cognizance of the operational intentions of the subject. At the pre-operational stage they may be vague and modifiable by experience, while they correspond to an exact anticipatory scheme, i.e. are dominated by earlier coordinations, at later stages.

Obs.O are the material realization of the intentions of the subject (Obs.S), e.g. objects are seen as arranged in a series, as classified, etc. Coord.O and Coord.S are identical as the objects are not independent operators as in causality (type II-A) but are only coordinated in so far as the subject gives them properties by his very operations (order, classes, etc.). There is therefore only a simple though precise application of operational compositions to the objects, or in other words, a morphism allowing us to read off from the objects the operational structures of the subject.

Going on from this basic idea, the passage from a state n to $n + 1$ can only be due to contradictions at the pre-operational levels. As soon as the level of concrete operations is reached, the progress from n to $n + 1$ is due to new needs that may arise through the resistance of objects or as the result of a new problem. But such a construction does not change the foregoing operations and only enriches them through an integration into a larger system.

>   **Example:** Arithmetical multiplication based upon addition is an example.

This process may be described as "the construction of operations on operations". During such a construction the role of the objects (Obs.O) is gradually modified completely. This modification is possible because the observables do not change physically, but are only changed in their form. At the level n the observable is the content of the first form applied to it, but at the level $n + 1$ this form becomes the content of a higher level form. The object is then no more than the content of the content. If we continue this process, the concrete object is at some time replaced by symbolic objects and finally by formalizations.

Type II-B differs from II-A in that the model of II-A is a mixture of observables through experience (empirical abstraction) and logico-mathematical structures (reflective abstraction) applied or attributed to objects, while model II-B is limited to the equilibration of the logico-mathematical structures themselves. In this process experience initially plays a role as well, but in the form of abstraction starting from the coordination of actions and not of objects. Only in the most simple logico-mathematical structures (classes and relations) is there a content that is not determined by the form (e.g. of objects classified by qualities that have been given in advance), but development leads to forms that completely determine the content (e.g. numbers). In other words: progressive equilibration leads to a purification of the form.

9.4.3 Progressive Compensations

Returning to the subject of compensations I shall now add the changes in their characteristics during improved equilibration to their common mechanisms already described.

In order to understand these characteristics all misunderstandings about the meaning of cognitive systems in Piaget's theory have to be avoided. *The concept of cognitive systems is used in the broadest possible sense.* At first they may consist of very simple descriptions like Obs.O and Obs.S, conceptualized by the subject when a particular event or action takes place. In such conceptualizations the subject may use—implicitly or explicitly—certain cognitive instruments like classifications, seriations, etc., first at the pre-operational and then at the operational levels. These belong to the cognitive systems as well. We must then add operational compositions, due to Coord.O and Coord.S, elaborated either for a specific problem or as causal explanations. At a later stage these local compositions as well as the causal explanations will refer to larger structures (groupings and groups) that form the higher levels of these different types of systems. The result of this diversity is that the frontiers of a cognitive system generally remain mobile until the final level when operational structures end in a closed cycle.

Within this perspective three types of conduct must be distinguished as far as the relations between modifications and compensations are concerned.

Type α

□Piaget uses α, β and γ and I do so too in order to avoid confusions. Furthermore the use of these letters is easy for referring to these types of compensations.

In the simplest experience a new fact causes no modification at all.

Example: Adding a new object into a given classification.

The experience is a little more complicated when the new fact cannot be integrated without modification of the system. In this case the new experience gives rise to a perturbation. What happens then will depend on the strength of the perturbation. When this is weak, the subject will compensate the perturbation by a modification that undoes the perturbation.

> **Example:** A small child is used to hitting a ball with another one while standing in front of the ball to be hit. If the experimenter displaces this ball a bit to the side, the child will modify his own position in order to be again in front of the ball, thus compensating the displacement.

If the subject considers the perturbation a larger one, he shows another type of behaviour. The child will then undo the perturbation by ignoring it or by deforming it in such a way that it is no longer experienced.

> **Example:** In one of the experiments on causality a marble hits a row of marbles, making the last one go off but without moving the intermediate ones. Even though the child has his hand on top of the immobile marbles he will say that they did move a little.

It is evident that reactions of type α are no more than efforts to neutralize a perturbation resulting in a temporary equilibrium between the assimilation of an object and the accommodation to it.

Type β

The second type of conduct consists in an integration of the perturbation into the existing system. This requires, of course, a change of the system so that it may contain the disturbing element.

> **Example:** A fact that contradicts a causal explanation will no longer be ignored, but the explanation will be changed in order to incorporate the fact.

Piaget feels justified in calling this process a "compensation" because the changes in conceptualization due to the integration of the perturbation into the existing system transform them into variations within the system. These variations still form only partial compensations, but of a type which is superior to the one mentioned under α.

In terms of assimilation and accommodation it is clear that the change of equilibrium is performed with the minimum of cost: as much as possible of the assimilatory scheme is conserved while the maximum of gain is achieved by integrating the perturbation into the system, thereby eliminating it as a perturbation.

The equilibrium achieved is that between sub-systems coordinated into a larger system.

Type γ

The highest type of conduct, possible for all logico-mathematical situations and certain well-elaborated causal explanations, consists of anticipating all the possible variations. As far as these can be foreseen and deduced, they lose their characteristic of being perturbations and become part of the possible transformations of the system.

> **Example:** Thus, for subjects who have achieved the structures of perspective, the projection of a shadow or of a luminous cone, etc. no longer forms a perturbation as it is part of the transformations which can be inferred.

It is, however, still possible to speak of compensations though with a new signification. Each transformation in such a system may be completely undone by its inverse or be reversed by its reciprocal and this is comparable to a perturbation and its compensation. The fundamental difference lies in the fact that all these transformations already form part of the existing system. The closure of the system thus eliminates any contradictions from outside the system as well as from inside, while the intrinsic necessity goes beyond the level of simple resultants of opposed but contingent factors. The equilibrium achieved is that of differentiated and integrated structures, a topic that will be elaborated in Chapter 10.

9.5 Is Equilibration Empirically Verifiable?

If a theory of equilibration is a causal model of development, the question arises whether such a model can be verified empirically or not. Yet this is not the kind of question Piaget asks. For him there is a general problem, followed by experiments and the interpretation of the results, which requires a model (see Chapter 6).

After he has developed a new model, like the present model of equilibration, Piaget applies it to the results of earlier experiments in an effort to explain these results in a more satisfactory way. In the book on equilibration this is done for the "classics"—object permanence, classification, seriation/transitivity and conservation. The results are summarized in Chapter 11. Apart from these re-interpretations, Piaget gives two types of more direct "evidence".

In the first place there are his two books with experiments on reflective abstraction, which is another form of regulations on regulations. Just like his other experiments, they are cross-sectional. Thus they cannot possibly show the process of "projection" and "reconstruction" directly. What Piaget tries to do is to demonstrate that changes take place from one level to the next which can only be explained by the process called "reflective abstraction".

In the second place, one can try to provoke transitions from one level of development to the next in a training experiment. Piaget himself has done no training experiments of this kind, but he likes to quote with appreciation the experiments of Inhelder, Sinclair and Bovet (**300**). These authors have done a lot of experiments of this sort, of which only a few are published in the book. The basic notion is that "progress" is "a reequilibration following a conflict", to use Piaget's older terminology, or a "perturbation", to use his more recent one. Therefore the material is structured in such a way that the pre-operational child who actively manipulates it will end up with contradictory inferences and, hopefully, experience these as contradictions. This "conflict" will then lead to a reequilibration, and the pre-operational child will take a qualitative step forward by constructing the operational structure. In more concrete terms : the non-conserver becomes a conserver, the non-classifier a classifier, etc. The results show an impressive difference between children who have been completely non-conserving, etc. at the pre-test and those who had reached an intermediate level.

> □According to Piaget the term "intermediate level" means that the child alternates between operativity and pre-operativity in the same task. He may conserve when the difference after a transformation is small, but not when it is large; he may give a conserving answer but change it after a counter-suggestion.

To take the conservation task as an example: children who were at the pre-operational level in the pre-test, either showed no progress (87.5%) or progressed towards an intermediate level (12.5%), while 77% of the children who started at an intermediate level benefited from their experience—only 23% not achieving conservation (**55**, p.715).

Thus the conclusion is that the same material only leads to an experienced conflict when the child has already reached a favourable level of development. Otherwise there is no perturbation and no progress. Such results are very important, because they show the close union of constructions and compensations (**90**, p.45/p.39).

In summary, empirical results found in experiments on reflective abstraction, in re-interpretations of earlier experiments and in training experiments are in accord with the theoretical model.

9.6 Does the Theory of Equilibration Describe or Explain?

In answer to the critical argument that he gives no more than a description, Piaget has said that he neither claims to have given an advanced deductive theory, nor to have given no more than a number of cross-checks between the results of various researches. He believes that he has gone beyond the level of description and gives a number of *"functional reasons"*, i.e. reasons that indicate why an observed functioning is necessary, and a number of *"structural reasons"*, i.e. reasons that correspond to causal mechanisms (**90**, p.180/p.191).

Piaget does not go into details of the functional reasons because it is clear that assimilation and accommodation must be in equilibrium if knowledge is due to assimilation and accommodation.

As for structural reasons, he mentions seven of them (**90**, p.180ff/ p.192ff). I shall only enumerate them, summarizing each reason in a few words, because Piaget does not add anything new to what is contained in his books (**90, 102**).

1) The cyclical nature of every assimilatory scheme is the essential reason on which all the others depend.

2) The fundamental factor of a cognitive equilibrium is the conserving influence of the whole of a system on its parts.

3) Any totality is only temporary because a regulation is not only retroactive but also leads to anticipations with projective reflection as a result.

4) These projective reflections leading to a new level require a reconstructive reflection with a compensation of ($+$) and ($-$). Thus regulations on regulations are explained by reflective abstraction.

5) The paradoxical result is that every structure is based on the foregoing but also sustains the foregoing, clarifying and completing it.

6) Improving equilibration is not explained by the need for alimentation of the schemes alone, because this would only lead to a cumulative collection. It means that forms of former structures become the content of higher ones. As a limit of this progress the problem of improving equilibration is fused with that of the productivity of mathematics, that is at the level where regulations on regulations become operations on operations, or operations to the nth degree.

7) But this interiorizing construction is accompanied by an exterior-ization attributing the subject's structures to objects, hence the succes-sive levels of causality and the functional interactions between logico-mathematical thought and physical thought.

10 The Highest Level of Equilibration: Differentiations and Integration

□The publications used in this chapter are very recent, or are still in press so there is no corresponding critique.

As I said in the last chapter, Piaget distinguished three levels of equilibration. But he soon became dissatisfied because the highest level, that of differentiations and integration, had not been elaborated enough. This is a serious omission because differentiations open up new possibilities while integration gives them their characteristic of necessity. This process is not due to a better knowledge of reality, but to endogenous mechanisms of the subject. In a constructivist epistemology the question of how the subject opens up new possibilities, constructs what was not yet available and changes possibility into necessity, is a fundamental issue.

This question has two aspects. In the first place, logic is a deductive science and one can therefore study how something new is "deductively" possible, being deduced from what was actualized at an earlier moment.

> **Example:** Before having achieved operational seriation the child has to count the seriated sticks from A to Z and from Z to A in order to answer the question whether there is the same amount in the two directions. After the structure of seriation has been achieved, the child deduces that the numbers must be the same.

This sort of opening up of new possibilities is an aspect of generalization. Thus the summary of this topic in 10.1 forms a continuation of 8.1.3.

In the second place, one can look at the process of making "possible", asking what the possible "is" before it was actualized. Within constructivism the central problem is that of the construction or creation of what did not exist, unless it were in the virtual state of a "possible" which had to be actualized by the subject (**97**, p.281, left out in the translation). The answer must be that "possibles" are due to the activity of the subject, but then "necessity" has to be due to this activity as well. This theme will be elaborated in 10.2 where we shall see that it forms the continuation of 8.3.

The study of deductive generalizations and that of the possible and the necessary lead to the research on dialectics which will be summarized in 10.3.

10.1 Differentiation and Integration in Generalization

In Chapter 8 (8.1.3.5) I ended on the theme of extrinsic and intrinsic variations and I shall pick up the thread here.

☐Piaget's book on generalization is highly abstract with many different types of generalization. A very detailed summary would be necessary to give them all, and as it is not clear to me what their importance is, I shall leave out a lot and concentrate on differentiations and integration. But I want to emphasize that where the concise text is incomprehensible, this is my fault and not that of Piaget.

Extrinsic and intrinsic variations are also called "extrinsic and intrinsic differentiations". *Extrinsic variations or differentiations lead to a form of integration called "coordinating"* ("coordinatrice") and concern extralogical content. *Intrinsic variations or differentiations lead to a form of integration which is called "totalizing"* ("totalisante"). Every totalizing integration is constructive but there are two complementary forms. One of them is directed at enriching the original structures by adding new operations, while the other tends to unite structures of the same level into a total structure in which the differences between the original structures become intrinsic variations. Both types are necessary for the progress of knowledge, intervening alternatively in the course of cognitive development (**110**, p.233ff). As the equilibration of differentiations and integration in generalization can be understood without details of these types, they have been left out.

As was described in Chapter 9 a cognitive system becomes disequilibrated through obstacles (= conflicts) or lacunae, and reequilibrated through compensations. In constructive generalization the disequilibrium is experienced as a need and the constructions are compensations which are at the same time productive. The need may be to strengthen a structure which is too weak to solve a problem, the compensation consisting of filling a lacuna. Or the need may be to bring coherence into data by finding a common structure when the

sub-structures are too much differentiated and therefore in contradiction. The compensation then consists in eliminating the conflict
by an interplay of differentiations and integration. The need for a
common synthesis of a higher level than that of the sub-systems
imposes itself when a problem resulting from a sub-system can only be
solved by operations borrowed from another system. This is clearly
seen in the construction of numbers where disregarding the qualities of
the elements to be counted forces the subject to use ordering for the
distinction of equivalent units, while preserving inclusion. This leads
to substituting the tautology $A + A = A$ by the iteration $(1 + 1) > 1$, thus
forming the structure of numbers which is richer than the composing
structures of ordering and including.

The ever-returning need for reequilibration with compensations is
caused by the fact that every new differentiation is a source of conflicts
or lacunae. The characteristic of constructive generalization, in contrast to inductions, is that these differentiations come from "within",
being directed at the intension and not only at the extension. If one
does not limit intensions to artificial definitions, intrinsic variations of
characteristics are unlimited and such intrinsic variations then form
differentiations requiring reequilibration by integration.

The mechanism of these equilibrations is that of constructing negations
and I have already mentioned that this is far more difficult than finding
affirmations. This is all the more true of generalizations with their elaboration of new forms or content as the negations depend on the activities
of the subject. The first role of negations is a functional one. The first
condition for any constructive generalization is to deny, explicitly or
implicitly, that the given situation is a definite one or the only possible one.

> **Example:** Having arrived at a "grouping" uniting disjunctive
> classes, the subject must first "decide" that this is not enough in
> order to go on to higher levels of thought.

It then follows that other combinations are required and this implies a
partial negation of the first ones.

Negations have a more specific role where intrinsic variations are
concerned. These variations may be given to the subject requiring an
explanation, or he may introduce them himself and then look for their
reasons. In both cases stronger structures have to be used where abstraction and reflexive thematization give the reasons. In such a situation negations are imposed by the internal logic of the subject and this
is often done in an exploratory way, e.g. when thinking about the possibilities of non-Euclidean geometry, non-commutative algebra, etc.

However, once negations of the original situation have been constructed within the system, the other pole, that of affirmations, has to be strengthened in order to reach a new equilibrium. This is true because the structure can only be closed when negations and affirmations have both reached a higher level. And this closure is then experienced as necessity. In other words: the necessity of *a* implies the impossibility of non-*a* and closure then indicates the total of possibilities and impossibilities within a system.

A system that has been constructed in this way has its own laws of composition, the laws of sub-systems being deduced from them. Its equilibrium is a necessary one giving the "reasons" for the system. These reasons, or the algebra of the system, answer the question "why" this system is the necessary one. However, such an answer is always a temporary one. A reason which has been found leads sooner or later to the question of what the reason of that reason is. Therefore a closure does not exclude the opening-up of new generalizations. The thematizations related to every closure thus lean on constructions which cannot yet be thematized but are being developed, and thus there is a proactive productivity which does not contradict the rigorous requirements of its retroactive aspect.

Thus Piaget gave his contribution to what he calls in the preface of the book on generalizations "the two great mysteries of knowledge". The first mystery is: how can knowledge constantly lead to new structures which were not contained in the earlier ones but are seen as their necessary result once they are constructed? The second mystery is the fact that this construction leans as much on that which is "becoming" i.e. on that which has not been achieved as on that which has been acquired (**110**, p.5).

10.2 The Possible and the Necessary

As far as the possible is concerned, other epistemologies might accept that operations exist at all times as "a universe of possibles" which is independent of the epistemic subject and which is discovered by the subject (**110**, p.239). Or, that all the possibles are predetermined in advance because their elements are given and one has to do no more than recombine these elements to find the unlimited number of possible combinations (**97**, p.281/p.65).

    Example: Explaining evolution by the combinations and recombinations of DNA is an example; or, to take an often used analogy:

the letters of the alphabet are given and any book consists of combinations of them.

Analogously one might suppose that "necessity" is read off from the
facts given in reality.

Evidently, none of this is acceptable within a constructivist epistemology and so the studies of the possible and the necessary are once more
steps in the defence of constructivism.

Piaget's hypotheses and constructions can be grouped around four
questions:

1) "What are the mechanisms leading to the opening-up of new possibilities?"

  ☐ Piaget uses "le possible" and "les possibles". In English one can use
  "the possible" with or without quotation marks, but the plural sounds
  unnatural and has therefore been replaced by "possibilities".

The answer is that there are two systems of knowing, one of understanding and one of succeeding, and that the latter gives us possibilities.

2) "What are the mechanisms leading to necessity?"

  ☐ Piaget distinguishes "nécessité" and "nécessitation", the first being
  the state of necessity and the latter the process of becoming necessary.
  Piaget's new term "nécessitation" is translated as "necessitation".

The answer is that reasons found by signifying implication give us
necessity.

  ☐ In *Success and Understanding* Piaget says that he uses "implication signifiante" because he cannot find a better term, emphasizing that it has no
  relation with the linguistic signifier-signified. It is translated as "signifying implication" (**86**, p.240n/p.221n).

3) As possibilities are differentiations and necessity is an integration,
there must be a relationship between the two. So the next question is:
"What is the relationship between the possible and the necessary?"
And, furthermore, "How does this relationship develop?"

The answer, which will be elaborated later, is that there is a close
relationship from the very beginning, but that fundamental changes
occur.

4) Necessity has always been considered a characteristic of operations.
Therefore the final question is: "What is the relationship between the
possible and the necessary on the one hand, and operations and operational structures on the other?"

The answer is that the possible and the necessary give a wider framework in which the development of operational structures finds its place.

Before going into these questions the tasks used for the research on the possible and the necessary will be briefly described to give a background for the answers to the questions.

Research on the possible. From a constructivist point of view the possible has no meaning apart from the subject who considers something possible, finds new possibilities, etc. The tasks were therefore structured in such a way that the child might invent the maximum number of variations, usually an unlimited number.

> **Example:** There were five types of tasks: a) to find as many solutions as possible, the number of possible variations being unlimited. For example, to put three cubes on to a paper in as many constellations as possible; b) to solve a simple practical problem, e.g. to make the largest possible construction with a number of different blocks; c) to construct different variations of a form, e.g. a triangle; d) to finish an irregular form, of which a part is hidden, in as many ways as possible; e) to find all the possible ways to use an object, e.g. a pair of compasses.

Research on necessity. Different types of problems, concerning physical, spatial and mathematical necessity were given.

> **Example:** The first can be illustrated by the problem of anticipating and understanding what happens when drops of water are added to a glass partly filled with water. Here the child does not manipulate the material. In another task the child himself builds. The task is to construct a slope of two planks supported by three pillars in such a way that a marble will roll down. The pillars have to be constructed from small blocks and the planks are made of such a material that they must both have an inclination in order to make the marble roll. Thus pillar A must be higher than B and this one higher than C. Finally, it is worth mentioning the task in which the necessary and sufficient conditions constituting a verification have to be found. A very irregular figure consisting of thirteen pieces (twelve straight ones and one curve) is covered by twenty small rectangular pieces of cardboard. The child is given twelve figures resembling the one which is hidden under the cardboard with the instruction to find the one figure which is identical to the covered one. The child must try to lift as many pieces as necessary, but no more than sufficient.

10.2.1 The Mechanisms Leading to New Possibilities

In 8.3.1 the difference between understanding and succeeding has been mentioned. This raised many questions for Piaget which were taken up in his publications on the possible and the necessary (**97, 118**).

Understanding and succeeding are two systems of knowing, based on three different types of schemes and their combinations. In Fig. 10.1 I give an overview which uses Piaget's terminology.

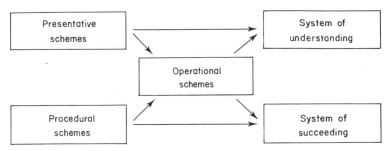

Fig. 10.1 Schemes and systems

Three types of schemes

Presentative schemes concern permanent and cotemporaneous characteristics of objects; they can easily be taken from their context and thus generalized; they are conserved even when enclosed in a larger presentative scheme. Though most of them are representational schemes or concepts (e.g. "the squares", "the cats"), there are already some sensorimotor schemes of this type (e.g. recognizing that an object is "far away" without having tried to grasp it). Because of the sensorimotor schemes of this type, the name "presentative" ("présentatif") is given them instead of "representative" ("représentatif").

Procedural schemes consist of sequences of actions serving as means to attain a goal, while the goal determines the actions. It is difficult to abstract them from their context as they are related to specific and heterogeneous situations. They are conserved to a very limited degree because the use of a later means replaces the earlier one which is no longer needed.

Operational schemes are a synthesis of procedural and presentative schemes. They are regulated and general means (operations) and this is their procedural aspect. But they are also coordinated into structures (the grouping of displacements, classification, seriation, etc.) and this is their presentative aspect.

Two systems of knowing

The different types of schemes are combined into two systems of knowing: that of understanding and that of succeeding. The former characterizes the epistemic subject, the latter the psychological subject.

The system of understanding consists of presentative schemes and the presentative or structural aspect of operational schemes. The logico-mathematical and infralogical structures constructed within this system are stable and allow the subject to understand his world through classification, seriation, etc.

The system of succeeding consists of all the procedural schemes and the operational schemes in so far as the latter are used to transform objects, i.e. their procedural aspect. The subject uses this system when he wants to succeed, to solve a problem, whether at an elementary level of sensorimotor actions or at the level of a highly abstract problem. In trying to solve a problem the subject uses classifications, seriations, etc. that he had constructed within the system of understanding. Thus the two systems closely interact.

The system of understanding with its operational structures was elaborated during the earlier part of Piaget's *oeuvre* on logico-mathematical structures and their use in notions of time, space, etc. As mentioned in Chapter 5 such structures are characterized by autoregulations.

The notion of the procedural system has been developed recently. It is this system which opens up new possibilities. This is evident if one realizes that a procedure requires a belief in the possibility of success and that the improvement of actions and methods used actualize new means within a wider range of possibilities. A closer analysis of this system shows the importance of comparisons and the way in which this system develops.

Procedural schemes are coordinated with each other, but not in the same way as schemes of the system of understanding are coordinated. While in the latter transformations are emphasized the former are mainly coordinated by correspondences and transfer of methods. The comparison of certain procedures with those that have been successful in other contexts leads to the development of new procedures. Such a progress, which need not be conscious, proceeds step by step, gradually contributing to the total system. As the progress lacks the auto-regulations of structural development, the opening-up of new possibilities takes a long time. The forming of new possibilities is, in fact, subordinate to two conditions. In the first place, the subject must be free to combine information concerning an unsolved problem with some procedure. In the second place, there must be a selection between combinations which is directed at a correction of errors. The correction is due to the results obtained, to the use of structures which have already been elaborated, or to procedural schemes which have proven their value. A characteristic of such a system is that it is never in equilibrium, but only consists of transitional states: as soon as a goal has been reached, the procedure ceases to exist as a procedure. On the one hand, the obtained result, which originally was a goal to be reached, becomes a presentative scheme. On the other hand, if the procedure leads to a mental reconstitution—a memory, understanding of the reasons of success—it becomes presentative or, at a later stage, representative. The progress in the coordination of procedures leads to the formation of operational procedures, e.g. the act of uniting classes into a total class.

The fact that this system always offers something new makes it into an instrument of reequilibration: to aim at a practical goal, to look for the solution of a problem, leads—in the case of success—to the filling of a lacuna or the removal of incoherence, thus leading to a new and richer equilibrium. "Generally speaking, then, the opening up of new possibilities amounts to the transcendence of a given state of affairs in the direction of a new reality, rich in possible actualizations and thus that much better equilibrated conceptually" (**97**, p.289/p.74).

A last remark on this system concerns the role of errors. While errors in a structural system are due to a lack of negation or to partial negation, and should be overcome as quickly as possible through autoregulations, errors in a procedural system may be very fruitful. Many new scientific discoveries have arisen from the correction of wrong hypotheses. This correction, being due to the comparison of the consequences of several hypotheses, shows once more the value of comparing. At the same time it shows the value of the procedural system for the structural system because the end result may well be an enrichment of the latter.

10.2.2 The Mechanisms Leading to Necessity

Necessity is the result of signifying implication. This concept is not easy to understand because it is part of the intensional logic the international Centre is still working on. As a result Piaget changes his notions from one tentative description to the next. At the moment, the publications on necessity (**105, 119**) and some personal explanations (**114**) give us his most recent notion, though this may well be elaborated on and/or changed when the work done in 1978/79 and 1979/80 is analysed.

Example: Inserting an example may make it easier to understand the following text, though its full significance will only become clear later on. At about 10 or 12 months of age, an infant has "learned" to pull at a support in order to get an object lying on it but out of his reach. If the infant only pulls when the object is on the support and not when it is next to it, he can be said to have connected the significations "object on support" and "pulling the support". This is an early example of a signifying implication, or rather of what the observer can interpret as such.

In 1963 Piaget distinguished causes and reasons (**14**). Causes are due to the attribution of our logico-mathematical structures to reality (see Chapter 7), while reasons are seen as the result of what Piaget then called "implication in a broad sense". This form of implication is called "signifying implication" in more recent work. At first Piaget thought that early signifying implications were due to empirical abstraction (**102**), but then he corrected this by emphasizing the role of reflective abstraction (**105, 119**).

Long ago Piaget had already become dissatisfied with certain aspects of classical extensional logic, especially concerning implication. In classical logic material implication can lead to conclusions that are formally true, but paradoxical in their content. An example of such a paradoxical implication is "If vinegar is sour, then some men have a beard." Many logicians tried to find a way out of this paradox, but others showed that these efforts were insufficient. However, recently a more satisfactory theory of natural implications seems to have been elaborated (**105**, p.242).

To return to Piaget's "signifying implication". The main point is that he is trying to find a satisfactory intensional logic of predicates instead of an extensional logic of propositions. In this frame, signifying implication consists of implications between actions and implications between statements ("énoncés"). The first can be seen as early as the sensorimotor stage, but here it is evidently the observer who has interpreted them as such.

□In **105** Piaget used ⊐ for signifying implication instead of ⊃, but he gave up that difference as he wanted to consider all implications as "signifying" (**114**).

The essential characteristic of a signifying implication is that there must be a relationship between x and y. At the sensorimotor stage, both x and y are a signification of a scheme in its intension and content, and there must be a relation between the two in such a way that the signification of y is part of that of x, or has something in common with that of x. To abbreviate: the signification of y must be "enclosed" ("englobé") in that of x. As this does not yet concern the extension of x and y, but only the intension and content, such "enclosings" can come long before class-inclusion with its property of extension. Another way of explaining the same notion is to say that x is a class of predicates and y is one of them, or—in yet another terminology—y is an "intrinsic variation" of the system which produces x or makes x possible. This takes us to necessity. According to Piaget the signifying implication $x \supset y$, becomes necessary in so far as the subject can determine its reason by a deductive construction. Starting from x, he finds that y is a necessary condition ("if, and only if") as it is an intrinsic variation within the total system of compositions. Seen this way it is clear that empirical abstraction plays a role in giving the original significations and establishing their link, but that reflective abstraction is required for the finding of reasons and thereby of necessity.

10.2.3 The Relationship Between the Possible and the Necessary and its Development

10.2.3.1 Different levels of the possible

All the experiments show three main levels of performance, running parallel to the levels of operational development.

The youngest, pre-operational children (level I) only see a very limited number of possibilities. These are called "possibilities by analogical succession" ("les possibles par succession analogique"). One solution given follows the next one, step by step, looking very much like the first one. Nothing really different is imagined. The first level of operational thought (II-A) coincides with what are called "concrete co-possibles" ("les co-possibles concrets"). Several possible solutions are now anticipated at the same time. At the next level (II-B) the child not only increases the number of anticipated solutions, but also realizes that they are examples of "many" possibilities. This level is called the level of "abstract co-possibles", though there is really nothing abstract about it. Finally, at level III the children spontaneously say, before any trials, that there is an infinite number of solutions, where this is indeed true.

10.2.3.2 Different levels of necessity

Before the child begins to realize what is necessary, there is a period of so-called "pseudo-necessities". The child believes that something has to be the way he experienced it, though there is no necessity from the point of view of the adult.

> **Example:** When constructing a triangle the youngest children believe that it has to be equilateral with its base parallel to the border of the table.

Once the child begins to see what is truly necessary, there are—again—three long periods, parallel to operational development.

At the pre-operational level there are local and isolated "islands" of necessity. At the operational level there are "limited co-necessities". This latter term indicates that there are necessary links but that they are still very limited due to their relationship with extralogical content, e.g. the necessity of inverse operations and conservations. Finally, at the formal level, the co-necessities become "unlimited", due to the fact that the subject can find the necessary consequences of any hypothesis and that he becomes capable of operations on operations, thus constructing "strong" necessities. Necessities can be "strong" and "weak" in analogy to structures which are strong and weak. Necessities are strong when the terms are linked by necessary connections. These terms are at the same time better determined in extension (more relations) and in intension (more significations). One can also say that a necessity is stronger if it has a greater power to lead to other necessities (**105**, p.237).

10.2.3.3 The development of the possible and the necessary

The levels found in the experiments do not tell us anything about the processes of development. These can be understood by realizing that at the beginning of development the possible, the necessary and reality are not differentiated from each other.

In the first years of life "reality" dominates in the experience of the child. Even if the constructivist genetic epistemologist is convinced that the known reality can never be a copy of an external reality, the child overestimates the "realness" of what is out there. For him reality is as it is experienced and it must be that way, as the pseudo-necessities show. In such a real world with these pseudo-necessities there is little room for new possibilities. Hence the limited number of extrinsic variations of the pre-operational child in tasks where he is expected to find new possibilities. One might argue that this description contradicts what was said about necessity due to signifying implication at the sensorimotor stage. Indeed, there is a beginning of true necessity at the sensorimotor level. At this time the possible characterizes the formation of schemes. But as we saw, schemes carry significations and these are linked by signifying implication. However, the necessities due to such signifying implications are still small, local systems. Furthermore, empirical abstraction plays an important role in their formation and this means that "reality" still dominates. So, even the beginnings of true necessities do not contradict the importance of reality and the indifferentiation of the possible (schemes), the necessary (links between them) and reality (empirical abstraction).

This indifferentiation lasts a long time because the real, the possible and the truly necessary impede each other's progress. Of these three the real exists outside the subject, though it is only knowable through the subject's assimilations. But the possible and the necessary depend completely on the subject's activity and this is still weak. The formation of new possibilities is prevented by pseudo-necessities, while true necessity requires schemes and therefore cannot proceed as long as possibilities are limited. Further development means that the lack of differentiation and the importance of reality must be overcome. Though this does take a long time, it is gradually achieved because the possible is due to procedures and procedures are directed at solving problems. Once the subject succeeds in finding some variations, some new possibilities, this means that pseudo-necessities begin to lose their power. It also means that the subject becomes confident that variations are possible. So, even if he cannot find them, he begins to believe that they must exist. Or, as Piaget says, they form "the domain of the virtually possible". Another aspect of procedures is that their results tend to be transferred to new situations which, again, opens up new possibilities.

When new possibilities are gradually opened up in this way, assimilatory schemes can be coordinated by mutual assimilation. These compositions are formed by processes of integration. Some of these compositions are necessary, but others are not. They are necessary if the composition C cannot be denied by non-C without a contradiction. Whether or not there is a contradiction is not determined by reality but can only be verified by the actions or operations of the subject. This necessitation proceeds by the use of reflective abstraction and generalization and—as has already been said—signifying implications.

The fact that there are close relations between the possible and the necessary is self-evident. Every necessity is a result of possible compositions and, reciprocally, co-necessities lead to new possibilities.

These interdependences are to be expected because both the possible and the necessary are products of the activity of the subject and are not observables given by experience. The empirical results confirm this parallelism.

10.2.4 The Relationship Between the Possible, the Necessary and Operations

Originally Piaget wrote that necessity is due to the closure of structures and is therefore not found before the operations of the concrete operational stage. Now he accepts that signifying implications already lead to the beginning of true necessity at the sensorimotor stage. The question is therefore what the relationship is between necessity and operations and, in consequence of the close union of the necessary and the possible, between the possible and operations. I have not followed Piaget's detailed analysis of the difference between ''strong'' and ''weak'' necessity, but the difference is important in this context. The strongest necessities always result from the compositions characterizing operational structures. But, in conjunction with the possible, the earlier and weaker necessities form a framework within which the operations can be constructed.

   ☐ Piaget's description of this construction is very concise (**105, 119**) and therefore difficult to follow. The reader who cannot understand the following summary is advised to go back to the original in the hope of finding a clearer exposé there.

Going back to signifying implications: we have seen that the necessary precedes the formation of operations though giving no more than local compositions of schemes and being characterized by the intensional nature of implications. Even at the earliest stage these signifying implications give a ''form'' to the content of the significations they combine. These forms are then the basis for successively elaborated higher forms. At about 7 years of age the child can construct operations that combine significations with their intensional nature and extensional considerations, but—above all—he can construct co-possibles and co-necessities. One essential aspect of this development is that inferences are found at the centre of cognitive levels at all stages of development, signifying implications implying inferences. Another aspect is that possibles express differentiations and necessities express integrations, and that the construction of operations therefore must be due to their union. However, the main point is that it is not so important to explain the construction of an isolated operation like the reunion of two classes. What is essential in operations is that they are built into general structures with their three levels of totality, sub-structures and elements. These general systems are due to reflective abstraction in which the possibles have the role of differentiations and necessities that of integrations, thus leading to the ever-higher levels I summarized in Chapter 8.

10.3 Dialectics

Piaget's book on dialectics (117) attempts to show his disagreement with classical dialectics, as well as to demonstrate the dialectical nature of the inferential aspect of equilibration as he sees it.

The main disagreement with classical dialectics concerns the nature of contradictions and their role in the traditional form of thesis-antithesis-synthesis. According to Piaget, *there is already a dialectical development when two systems that were separate but not opposed to each other become a new totality with characteristics that go beyond those of the original systems.* There are numerous examples in Piaget's earlier texts, where he calls this "a dialectic" or "a dialectical development".

□Piaget uses "une dialectique" and "dialectique" as substantives as well as adjectives. I use "dialectics" for the substantive and "dialectic(al)" for the adjective.

In his recent book on the topic Piaget gives an example in order to illustrate that there need not be an opposition, nor a sequence of thesis-antithesis-synthesis. This example is his "old" theory of the natural numbers. Numbers are constructed, according to Piaget, by the "fusion" of class-inclusion and ordering. This process of "fusion", or integration of structures into a higher level, is an example of reflective abstraction. The central notion of "going beyond" ("dépassement") what was given or developing is dialectical. Reflective abstraction and dialectics are evidently closely linked though Piaget does not mention reflective abstraction in his book on dialectics.

□When Piaget concentrates on a topic he tends to neglect other aspects of his theory, at least in the written text. The foregoing is based on a personal communication.

Looking for a more exact *definition of dialectics* we find it described as *"the inferential aspect of any process of equilibration"* (117, Introduction; italics added). This takes us back to the distinction between causes and reasons. The notion of causality must develop and this is due to a process of equilibration, called the "causal aspect of equilibration". But reasons found by inferences develop as well and this is what Piaget calls "the inferential aspect of equilibration".

☐I think that it should be "the equilibration of the inferential aspect of knowledge", because knowledge (not equilibration) has a causal and an inferential aspect.

Turning to inferences, one must distinguish states of equilibrium from processes of equilibration. Systems in equilibrium lead to discursive inferences (in Kant's sense of "discursive" as opposed to "intuitive"), while periods of equilibration lead to dialectical ones. Thus there is an alternation between dialectical and discursive inferences with variable periods of equilibration and equilibrium.

The dialectical periods of equilibration lead to the construction of new relations with internal necessity. But then the—by now well-known—question arises: "Do we have to accept that such a necessity is preformed, that is to say, innate, while the subject only had 'to lift a veil' in order to find it?" It seems hardly necessary to say explicitly that this cannot be Piaget's solution and that he is trying to convince his readers, once more, that genetic research confirms a constructivist solution of the problem. In fact, any dialectic contains circular (or rather "spiral", as we shall see) processes between proactive and retroactive development. At the end of these dialectical processes authentic necessity is constructed though it may seem to be innate. To avoid misunderstandings: Piaget does emphasize in this connection that he does not completely reject the influence of what is innate. Any behaviour, whether elementary or of the highest level, must contain a certain innate component, if for no other reason than because of the hereditary factors of the nervous system. But the importance of this innate component is limited, because by itself it cannot explain the interdependences between subject and object, even at the simplest level. When behaviour becomes more and more complex, the component of the innate becomes correspondingly less influential.

Before summarizing the general conclusions on dialectics I shall describe one of the experiments and its interpretation in more detail than in the other chapters. In the first place Piaget considered it important enough to publish it as a separate article, and in the second place it gives a good starting point for the rest of the summary.

10.3.1 The Dialectic of Predicates, Concepts, Judgements and Inferences: a Genetic Study (**113**)

Some authors claim that concepts are produced by judgements, while others consider concepts primary. Piaget, however, wants to enlarge this notion into a dialectical circle of concepts (C), predicates (P), judgements (J) and inferences (I). These form two sequences. If one looks at compositions, concepts are reunions of predicates, judgements form relations between concepts, and inferences are composed of judgements. Thus there is an ascending process: $P \rightarrow C \rightarrow J \rightarrow I$. But if one looks at justifications one finds the opposite order, or a descending movement: $I \rightarrow J \rightarrow C \rightarrow P$. Any judgement rests on inferences, concepts require judgements, and predicates result from the comparison of concepts. The two sequences are indissociably linked but without forming a vicious circle, because their significations are different. In fact, it is not so much a dialectical circle as a spiral because the content changes continually.

Piaget and his collaborators did two experiments to study this ascending and descending movement.

> **Example:** In the first one, the children were given twenty pictures of different animals in a random order. The experimenter hid his identical pictures and then picked out one of them. The child was allowed four to six questions in order to find out which one was chosen by the experimenter. I will not go into the results of this experiment because all the general conclusions can be related to the second experiment as well. In this second experiment eighteen figures were given in a classified order: nine big ones (three squares, three circles, three rectangles) and nine small ones of the same forms. Each of the three figures of the same form and size had a different colour (brown, blue, white). The experimenter gave information and the child had to show which one he thought was meant. Afterwards the child was allowed to ask questions.

At the first level (I, 4-7 years), the child is not yet able to distinguish questions with sufficient and with insufficient information for making a choice. He therefore makes a wrong choice though he does remember the information. When asking questions, he simply asks, "Is it this one?"

At the first half of the second level (IIA, 7-9 years), the child's questions are related to common properties of a number of figures (e.g. blue, square). But the child does not realize that having one characteristic excludes others. Knowing that the figure to be found is "square", he then asks whether it is round, and then whether it is a rectangle, even though he knows from the beginning that the number of questions is restricted.

At the next half of the second level (IIB, 8-9 years), there are no longer redundances, but the children do not yet realize that the amount of information should directly influence the certainty of their choice (indicated by a chip put under the figure chosen, to the left when completely uncertain, to the right when certain or any position in between).

At the final level (III, 10-12 years), judgements guided by inferences which are sometimes still incomplete, but are directed by considering all possibilities, are given.

If one analyses the results, the ascending line (O (object)$\rightarrow C \rightarrow J \rightarrow I$) forms an example of inclusions ("emboîtements"), while the descending line consists of establishing that a certain totality opens up several possibilities (e.g. a square can be divided into "big", and "small", and again into "white" and "blue" and "brown"), allowing the child to indicate why one of them is the correct choice. Both the ascending and the descending lines are different at the three levels.

At level I the child does not yet understand that the predicates ("blue", "square") apply to more than one object and so chooses one of them with perfect certainty. His questions being limited to "Is it this one?", the object he indicates can be called a "conceptual object". The predicates are the elements in the sense of observables that are "given", are located in the object. The conceptual object is the product of a number of predicates but is due to an immediate synthesis which is limited to this specific object. At level II there are inclusions due to judgements uniting several conceptual objects using their common properties (predicates). But there are as yet no inferential inclusions as the redundances show. At level III judgements are coordinated by inferences, giving intersections.

Thus the law of composition from predicates to inferences is: "agglomerated predicates"$\rightarrow$conceptual objects; union of such objects$\rightarrow$ concepts based on judgements; coordination of the latter$\rightarrow$inferences, source of higher inclusions (intersections) (p.247).

While there is thus a composition of totalities based on the organization of their elements or parts, there is at the same time an opposite line going from the totalities to the parts. These totalities are justified or enriched by new relations between the parts which were not given in the ascending process and which complete their significations by their subordination to the including totalities (p.247). Knowing that a figure must be round and brown, a child concludes that it must be the big one or the small one. The inference leads here to a judgement as conclusion and to two possibilities he has to choose from. Furthermore, it is the judgements that guarantee the conceptual inclusions of level II, while the conceptual object of level I presupposes the action of concepts on predicates, as the latter do not give unique properties that can be isolated, but properties known from other objects (e.g. the colour blue is not limited to the object searched for, but is known because the sky is blue).

Thus we see that the dialectical spiral with its ascending and descending movement enriches the theory of inclusions by its "overtaking" ("dépassement") of the real (to which ascendant compositions are limited), both in the direction of the possible and the necessary.

While this dialectical movement is very important, further analyses show a more fundamental "dialectization", consisting of implications between actions or operations. Its importance can be shown by comparing the above-mentioned conceptual spiral with actions at the sensorimotor level. At this level assimilation of observables gives objects their signification (e.g. "graspable", "solid"), just as predicates do later on. Assimilatory schemes, related to significations which a number of objects have in common, correspond to later concepts. New attributions and differentiation into sub-schemes correspond to later judgements, while the coordinations of schemes correspond to later inferences. Thus there is an ascending order, with compositions leading from elementary significations to inferential coordinations of schemes, and a descending one with justifications and an increase of possibilities. This dialectical spiral is very important, because it leads to implications between actions, long before the development of language and conceptual understanding.

10.3.2 Dialectics in General

To return to what was said at the beginning: not all cognitive activities are dialectical. Periods of equilibrium with discursive or deductive inferences alternate with periods of dialectical equilibrations. Only equilibration is a constructive process leading to the formation of structures. Furthermore, in any dialectical development, a special form of implication is found, called "implication between actions or operations". This is one of the two forms of signifying implication, the other

being implication between statements ("énoncés"). Signifying implications between statements give no more than what is already
given in the terms that are connected. The production of something
new, that is dialectical "overtaking" supposes a process of transformations and must therefore be due to pre-operational or operational
constructions. To be more exact: an action or operation already gives a
transformation and therefore implications connecting them are
transformations "twice over".

The experiments show that there are several forms of interdependences between developing actions or operations. In the experiment
described in detail there is a mutual and more or less simultaneous
enrichment of the sub-systems which constitute the total system. In all
the experiments together there are eight forms.

☐As the forms are closely related to the experiments chosen, they seem
to be a rather random selection of all the possible forms. Piaget admitted
that adding more experiments might enrich the theory, but he is also
convinced that the main points would not be changed by such an addition
(**114**).

The driving force behind all the forms of interdependence must be
the ever-closer relationship between the "possible" and the "necessary". Returning to the parallel development of the possible and the
necessary as described in 10.2, it is now possible to consider this the
most general expression of dialectics. Calling, for the sake of abbre-
viation, any already acquired knowledge "real", or R, the following
process takes place. R leads to the development of several new possibilities, P. Between some of these, necessary relations, N, are formed.
These then include R, but in a richer form, R_2, which contains R but
also goes beyond it ("le dépasse"). R_2 then leads to new possibilities,
P_2, with certain new necessities, N_2, and so on, and so forth, without
end. The most elementary form of such a spiral is seen in the interaction between subject and object. But elementary does not mean
simple, because every progress which makes the subject approach
reality, leads to a "retreat" of reality (see 5.1.2).

A closer analysis of the dialectical subject-object interaction shows
that there are, in fact, three dialectical movements. In the first place,
assimilations acquire "forms" that must be elaborated and become
interdependent in a process of interiorization, leading to logico-mathematical structures. In the second place, properties attributed to
objects must become interdependent during a process of externaliza-
tion. Finally, these forms and contents must become interdependent in

a dialectical synthesis of auto-organization of the forms and the reconstitution of contents discovered in the object. It is the latter that determines at the same time the progress of knowledge and the retreat of reality which poses new problems as soon as knowledge increases.

Piaget realizes that a comparison of this description with classical dialectics might lead one to the accusation that he pays too little attention to negations or contradictions. However, he does not believe that such an accusation would be justified.

As was elaborated in Chapter 9 the process of equilibration requires that negations compensate affirmations. And within a constructivist epistemology one must consider negations themselves as a construction and not as a "given". That is to say, negations are constructed in an elementary dialectic, being among the possibilities, P. Then, once constructed, the negation becomes an instrument of a higher dialectic. Piaget's research tried to follow this development of elementary to higher levels of dialectics.

11 A New Look at Old Friends

□Data on stages and the consecutive periods of cognitive development are discussed in Chapter 21. However the parallelism is only partial as most writers criticize Piaget's older work. As far as he still accepts these notions, the critique is included. Separate references are given after chapter sections.

·In developing his theory Piaget sometimes explores completely new experiments and topics, but also returns more than once to old favourites. In this chapter I turn to object permanence, conservation, numbers and other topics of research on which Piaget had worked well before 1965. Two topics are added though they were introduced in 1968—identity and (mathematical) functions—because they are of the same type as the other topics discussed.

Because the material is organized within the classical four stages, it seems appropriate to return first of all to the much debated subject of stages.

11.1 Stages

For many psychologists the first association with "Piaget" is probably "stages". Looking for stages, opposing stages, etc. became an aim in itself. Interestingly enough Piaget never intended it that way. Since he heard the psychiatrist Janet lecture on stages, he has used stages as a heuristic instrument. As he said in a paper in 1955,

"Why does everyone speak of stages? ...One tries to construct stages because this is an *indispensable instrument for the analysis of formative processes*."

(Quoted from the reprint in *The Essential Piaget*
(**277**, p.817; italics in original))

As a biologist Piaget was used to zoological and botanical classifications which are useful instruments preceding analysis, but no more. As he added to the foregoing, "I must vigorously insist on the fact that stages do not constitute an aim in their own right" (**277**, loc.cit.). This heuristic use is most clearly seen in Piaget's analyses of experimental data. The main stages of development were then based on the analyses and it is these main stages that began to lead a life of their own. Actually, a careful reading of Piaget's publications shows that he uses three different stage-concepts even though he never says so explicitly. There are the six stages of the sensorimotor stage, the stages and their sub-stages in the experimental analyses, and the main stages.

11.1.1 The Six Stages of Infant Development

In analysing the observations made on his three children, Piaget distinguished six stages within the sensorimotor stage. As far as I know he never compared these stages to the main stages. In more concrete terms: are differences between e.g. structures of stage IV and stage V comparable to differences between pre-operational and concrete operational structures? Or should one compare them to the sub-stages IA and IB within the pre-operational stage? Though there is no answer to this question, Piaget did study the problem whether the process of equilibration is the same during the sensorimotor stage as during later stages. As equilibration is so fundamental for his whole theory, this point will be summarized in detail in 11.2.1.

11.1.2 Stages in the Experiments

It is rather confusing that Piaget's system of numbering levels or stages of achievement differs from one book to the next. Sometimes levels or stages are numbered from I to IV, stage IV corresponding to concrete operations. In many recent books level I corresponds to failure, level II to relative success and level III to complete success. As the experiments are often chosen in such a way that progress from the pre-operational to the formal stage is possible, the three levels correspond to the three main stages.

More important from the theoretical point of view, is the fact that there is no abrupt progress from stage I to stage II, nor from II to III. There are not only levels or sub-stages IA and IB, etc. but often "intermediate" levels or reactions, e.g. between IA and IB, as well as IB and

IIA. The difference between IIB and III is often very small, or even non-existent.

11.1.3 The Main Stages of Development

In some publications Piaget distinguishes three stages, in others five, but generally there are four with sub-stages. In the latter case, the stages are called: the sensorimotor level, the first and second level of pre-operational thought, the first and second level of concrete operations, and the formal level (**48**, p.13ff/p.20ff). More important than the way in which the total development of the child and the adolescent is cut up, is the fact that Piaget is less and less interested in stages. Thinking in terms of stages one runs the risk of looking too much for periods of rest or equilibrium, while in fact development is never static. Piaget now considers development a spiral and though one may call a stage ''a detour of the spiral'' (**114**), this indicates that the periods of equilibrium are relatively unimportant.

One of the often-mentioned characteristics of a stage is the qualitative change at its beginning. Piaget certainly does write about qualitative changes, but in the context of reflective abstraction. The reconstruction of what has been constructed, the integration of what has been differentiated, implies a qualitative change. However, he is not sure whether this mechanism only takes place from one main stage to the next, or also in smaller steps. Furthermore, the process of reflective abstraction does not require that the changes in all structures, e.g. classification and conservation, take place at the same time.

The one thing impressing Piaget in the context of stages, is that he sees a change in all sorts of experiments around 7 or 8 years. After 7 or 8 years children show a period of elaboration and then one of consolidation.

So what emerges is the following picture: there are a number of small steps, sub-stages in the experiments, with differentiations that open up new possibilities. At a certain moment, there is a reconstruction or integration, and a qualitative change of structure. This structure is then demonstrated in some tasks, but not in others, though they are the ''same'' tasks in adult eyes. Gradually the tasks or situations in which the child can use the structure extend, while at the same time new differentiations are a preparation for the next integration. This description applies to the four main stages and their continuation in scientific thought. However, it raises a number of questions.

The first question is how any stage can possibly be a "structure d'ensemble", one of the characteristics often mentioned by Piaget and Inhelder (e.g. 23). The answer is that it cannot be one. This characteristic is used to stress the contrast with other stage-concepts like that of psychoanalysis. In the paper already mentioned, Piaget said that Genevans were looking for the common characteristics of all the manifestations of one stage. This seems reasonable. Groupings characterize the concrete operational stage and groups the formal stage. But it is still rather difficult to characterize the earlier stages by positive characteristics, though it could be done.

 ☐In a personal communication Inhelder confirmed that the "structure d'ensemble" was an unfortunate expression, which should not be taken literally. This is rather reassuring because when one tries to construct a total structure one gets into far more difficulties than the low correlations found in experiments. What could a total structure of the sensorimotor stage look like?

The second question is how the well-known time lags ("décalage horizontal") can be explained. Several factors are involved here. The first is the influence of the figurative aspect of knowledge and empirical abstraction. This influence may be either favourable or unfavourable. In the paragraph on classification an example of the former type of influence will be given, and in that on conservation one of the latter. The second factor is what Piaget calls the "resistance" of objects, seen in many causal explanations. Some applications of our structures easily fit "reality", while others do not do so because of all sorts of complicating influences. This can be easily seen in the time-lags between the conservation of substance, weight and volume with the two balls of clay. Weight requires a lot of experience with objects. It pushes down, but it can also uphold something either from the bottom up, or to the side. Volume is still more complicated and requires formal thought. Though quite a number of time-lags can be explained to Piaget's satisfaction, there is one type for which he cannot find a reason. Using marguerites and primroses with the question whether there are more marguerites or more flowers, many children of 7 or 8 years old give the correct answer. However, not all these children answer correctly to the same question about seagulls and birds, even though Genevan children see these birds at least as often as the flowers and both words are well-known. No difference could be foreseen and it cannot even be explained post hoc (59, p.11).

There might well be other questions, but as I said at the beginning, Piaget feels that he has more interesting problems to solve.

□Critical arguments are given by author to show how many points of view there are. See 21.1.

11.2 The Sensorimotor Stage

Piaget has done little new research on this early stage of development, but some theoretical considerations are important.

□I presume that the reader knows the six stages of the sensorimotor stage, but as a reminder Piaget's overview is given (**90**, p.87n/p.85n).

Stage I: reflexes and spontaneous movements
Stage II: first habits
Stage III: secondary circular reactions, i.e. the ability to reproduce inter-
            esting events which were originally discovered by chance
Stage IV: coordinations of means and ends
Stage V: discoveries of new means
Stage VI: inventions by sudden understanding

Piaget uses "phases" in his book on equilibration, the third phase coin- ciding approximately with the beginning of stage IV.

11.2.1 Is the Process of Equilibration the Same as in the Later Stages?

In 9.4.2 the details of the interaction between the subject and object were summarized. In the different models Obs.O (observables of objects) and Obs.S (observables of the subject) were linked together. But, as already mentioned, Piaget followed J.M.Baldwin in assuming that the newborn makes as yet no distinction between himself and external "reality", and in calling this a period of "adualism". There- fore the question arises whether the mechanisms of equilibration in this period are the same as those described in 9.4.2. This is a fundamental question. Adualism shows that philosophers who assume that at all levels there exists a separate subject and object, are wrong. This is only true after the first months of life. Does this imply that the interaction between subject and object, and the mechanisms of this interaction are also limited to the later period?

The answer to this question can only be found through a detailed analysis of the regulatory and compensatory mechanisms of the sensori- motor stage. The analysis, which is summarized in the following, shows that there is no fundamental difference (**90**, p.83ff/p.81ff).

11.2.1.1 Observables OS

The assimilatory schemes present at birth are innate, few in number and very general as far as the assimilable domain is concerned, e.g. sucking, looking, listening, touching.

At first all the possible perturbations consist in lacunae when a need cannot be satisfied. In a second phase a perturbation may, in addition, be related to spatio-temporal distances between the subject and the assimilable object.

> **Example:** An object disappears from the field of vision, or a total change of the perceptual field gives rise to a new tableau in which the ongoing assimilation is no longer possible.
>
> ☐Piaget uses "tableau" for what the child perceives in order to avoid confusion with the "object" which does not yet exist for the child.

It is only in the third phase, towards stage IV, that the perturbations concern an object or an event that is clearly defined and can be manipulated by the child. This late appearance is easily understood, as—until stage IV—Obs.O and Obs.S still form a whole, called "Obs.OS" (schemes are classified among the observables because they require no inferences).

> **Example:** A well-known example is when hands are treated in the same way as any other object by the infant. Furthermore, infants bringing an object to their mouth to suck it, only as yet know their mouth or head by tactilo-kinetic or taste perceptions and have no representation of the way from hand to mouth.

As long as there are only Obs.OS there can evidently be no distinction between Coord.O and Coord.S. The first reason is that causal coordinations between objects make their first appearance at a later moment than causal coordinations between subject and object. A second reason is that the first coordinations linking objects and the actions of the subject at first only use the whole Obs.OS. A third one is that the most primitive coordinations based upon Obs.OS consist of no more than reciprocal assimilations of schemes and even this form is not reached before stage II when the first habits are observed.

Thus, before model II-A (Fig. 9,3) there is a prior model represented in Fig. 11.1 (**90**, p.89/p.87).

The progress from these initial reactions leads, after many intermediate steps, to type II-A, a change called the "Copernican revolution" by Piaget. The lack of differentiation in Obs.OS, changing to the differentiation into Obs.O and Obs.S, and then to the formation of

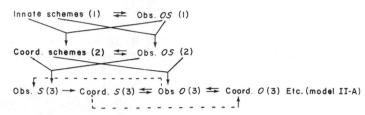

Fig. 11.1 Sensorimotor equilibration

differentiated coordinations, indeed means a complete reversal of perspective. In general, this forms a first example of the differentiation of schemes into sub-schemes, and of their integration into wholes, compensating this differentiation.

This process is so important that it is worthwhile studying it in more detail. From the level of innate schemes on, one sees certain regulations of type α for weak perturbations (see 9.4.3).

> **Example:** After a few days of breast-feeding the infant retrieves the nipple—when escaped from his mouth—with greater ease. The movement to retrieve it is going in the inverse direction to that made by the mouth of the child when losing its hold of it, thus forming a compensation.

The same is true for the first habits, which continue innate schemes, e.g. thumbsucking.

A detailed analysis shows a whole sequence of compensations of this type α, but with an extension of the regulatory process.

> **Example:** Thumbsucking by systematic adduction, rediscovering with a glance an object that has left the field, are good examples.

The same process is seen in the case of classical conditioning. The so-called "association" is in fact an assimilation giving meaning to the signal by incorporating it in the scheme on which the need and its satisfaction depend. The regulation during conditioning consists of separating this satisfaction, i.e. the alimentation of the scheme, into two steps, due to a momentary replacement of the food by its signalling index. In this case the perturbation in the form of a lacuna or a modification of the spatio-temporal distance is compensated by a replacement or modification in the opposite direction. According to this interpretation the signal would mean even more than an index of food; it would be directly assimilated as an aspect or part of the original whole "food + signal" by a sort of pure and simple substitution of the absolute stimulus by the conditioned one.

11.2.1.2 The coordination of schemes

At the next level of development schemes are being coordinated.

> **Example:** First seeing and hearing: looking in the direction of a sound to find the corresponding visual tableau. Then sucking and grasping: to bring to the mouth what is grasped without being seen.

The explanation of these reciprocal assimilations is a simple one: as there are many occasions in which an object can be seen and heard, etc. these intersections of schemes leave a lacuna when only one of them is being activated, e.g. when an object is heard without being seen. In general terms: starting from the situation of intersections where objects show the characteristics x and y, the opposite situation is characterized by a spatio-temporal distance between x and y (going beyond the field of vision though still being heard, etc.). This is a perturbation that will then be compensated by a movement in the opposite direction, that is to say relating x and y, a coordination which is still one of type α. In this way a new scheme xy is added to the schemes with characteristics x and y. This results in the possibility of secondary circular reactions leading in their turn to many others.

> **Example:** A child trying to grasp a suspended object only touches it, thereby making the object swing. This is an interesting new spectacle and the child immediately tries to reproduce it.

Trying to reproduce an incidental event seems paradoxical behaviour seen from the point of view of perturbations and compensations. A child who fails to grasp an object, thereby causing a swinging movement of the object, must experience at least a fleeting perturbation caused by the failure to grasp the object. Why then does he not return to the grasping effort instead of turning his attention to the new experience? The main point is that perturbations are never—even at the most advanced levels—absolute, but only relative. During the sensorimotor period two further considerations are important. One is that schemes are very general: after eye-hand coordination the goal is not so much to grasp an object as to exercise the abilities of the hands: displace objects, bring objects nearer to the subject, etc. If the hand causes a swinging motion this would then be a generalization and not a perturbation. The second one is, that there are still only Obs.OS. Swinging an object is therefore still an undifferentiated power belonging at the same time to the subject and the object. It is thus perfectly normal that the regulation started by this event tends to reproduce or conserve it (positive feedback) and not to undo it. Seen in this way the secondary circular response is still not behaviour of type β but only an intermediate step on the way to tertiary circular reactions that are true examples of type β.

11.2.1.3 Differentiations and coordinations

The infant, whose development we are following, has by now reached the very important stage IV, the level of differentiations and coordinations of means and ends.

> **Examples:** Some examples from Piaget's early observations of his children are: pushing away a pillow that is impeding the movement of the hand which is reaching for an object; pushing the hand of an adult in the direction of an object the child himself cannot reach.

Two important mechanisms are: the compensation of a perturbation with a beginning of negations constructed by the subject, and the compensation of a spatio-temporal distance. The same two mechanisms lead, shortly afterwards, to the construction of object permanence. At the earlier levels the disappearance of an object was a perturbation but without a compensation. As long as the world consists of global tableaux a disappearing object just becomes part of the following tableau without being experienced as a separate object in that tableau. But by the time schemes are coordinated into xy, and means and ends are being coordinated, the screen masking an object is no longer part of a new tableau, but becomes an object that can be removed. This possibility, together with understanding that objects are displaced instead of remaining at the place where they were found the first time, are manifestations of a generalization of compensatory regulations leading to the important advances of stage V and VI. But what is the driving force of this generalization?

In discussing behaviour of type α we saw a difference between the results of weak perturbations that are compensated by a movement in the opposite direction and a more serious perturbation that is simply ignored. As long as the infant lives in a world of global tableaux the disappearance of an object is a major perturbation that is ignored. But the multiplication of schemes (in the sense of coordinations like xy) allows for means-end connections and this changes the scale of perturbations. What was formerly a major perturbation now becomes a modification of a detail, and may therefore be compensated by a movement in the opposite direction. This is a very important step in development, as the changes of global tableaux consist of no more than differences, while removing a screen experienced as an obstacle constitutes a negation of a negation constructed by the subject, even though only at the practical level.

Thus level IV is an essential step in development: the coordinations of means-ends which mark the beginning of truly intelligent actions, and the first forms of object permanence are the beginning of the second level of sensorimotor development with a progressive equilibration of differentiations and integrations during the final stages V and VI.

As far as differentiations are concerned, it is evident that the bipolarity between subject and object introduced by the beginning of object permanence has important consequences. Accommodations will become far more differentiated when they are directed at individual, stable objects instead of global and moving perceptual tableaux. Furthermore object permanence not only concerns objects in the usual sense, but also includes persons. Persons as permanent objects give rise to object relations, as Gouin-Décarie has shown in a research project that is often quoted with full approval by Piaget (266). These relationships are in their turn related to the development of the self and are accompanied by imitations.

Stage IV therefore is an important total of differentiations linked to accommodations with all the compensations and implicit negations they contain, and this is at the same time true for the subject as well as the object.

During stage V another new conduct can be seen in the tertiary circular reactions or "experiences in order to see what happens" with variations in the factors involved. This experimentation leads to modifications that would have been perturbations at an earlier stage. We therefore see that already at the sensorimotor stage conduct of type α is transformed into reactions of type β, but of course only on the level of practical actions without conceptual representations. The child at this level intentionally varies factors in the sense of $(+)$ and $(-)$, which results in compensatory accommodations and practical differentiations between positive and negative aspects of an action.

> **Example:** To drop or throw a ball from lesser or greater heights, with more or less strength, to the left or to the right.

Finally, a third aspect of differentiations follows the former: the discovery of new means to an end.

> **Example:** To pull an object on a rug, or by a string, or to use a real instrument like a stick to reach an object.

All these differentiations would imply the risk of a total disorder or of a juxtaposition of independent reactions if there were not at the same time a step-by-step progress in assimilatory coordinations leading to integrations.

Object permanence is linked to coordinations of positions and displacements of objects, the child constructing during stage V and VI the practical "group" of displacements. Though this group proceeds step-by-step without a representation of the whole, it does give the sensorimotor universe a structure which is a remarkable unity and decentred from the subject's own body. Next, causality becomes spatialized and objectified by a system of interactions between the objects themselves.

It is self-evident that these integrations show two sorts of improving equilibration. On the one hand, there is in every particular situation a total of regulations necessary for the constitution of these coordinations. In the case of the group of displacements they are very evident in the trials leading to the acquisition of "returning behaviour" (reversibility of the group), and "detour behaviour" (associativity of the group). On the other hand, a more general process of equilibration intervenes between the differentiations and integrations as such, in the sense that every accommodation—source of differentiated novelties—corresponds to an assimilation relating it to more or less general coordinations. Without these coordinations the differentiations would remain chaotic and of short duration.

11.2.1.4 Conclusion

The reexamination of the sensorimotor development within the theory of regulations seems to justify the hypothesis that the genesis of new structures which are superimposed one upon the other, level by level, is not in contradiction with compensatory mechanisms as the elaboration of each of these structures starts with a phase of regulations which are at one and the same time compensatory and formative. Returning to our original question we may therefore conclude that there is no fundamental difference between developmental processes at the sensorimotor level and later levels, even though a slight adjustment of the model has been necessary as Obs. O and Obs. S are not differentiated at the beginning of development.

☐Only one author discusses this point and comes to the opposite conclusion (21.2.1).

11.2.2 The Permanent Object

Object permanence is one of the topics to which Piaget returns very often. But for him it is not important to know how old a child must be in order to find a hidden object. Epistemologically seen, the question is rather how the original adualism develops to the point where a clear distinction between subject and object exists, as far as the scientist can decide. Such a separation presupposes that the object does not depend any longer on the child's actions, including the actions of perceiving. Or, in Piaget's terms,

*"An object can be said to attain a permanent character when it is recog-
nized as continuing to exist beyond the limits of the perceptual field,
when it is no longer felt, seen or heard, etc. "*

(**11**, p.9, italics added)

As the adult must infer from the child's behaviour that he understands this, the child's active search behaviour is the best criterion. But this is not a purely practical decision as the permanence of the object is closely linked to spatial organization as was already mentioned in the last paragraph.

From this epistemological point of view it is understandable why Piaget attached so much importance to object permanence. His recent work has concerned three questions: "Can the attainment of object permanence be explained in terms of equilibration?" "What is the role of actions and representation in its development?" and "Is object permanence acquired at an earlier age for persons than for material objects?"

11.2.2.1 Object permanence and equilibration

The answer to this question is already included in 11.2.1 and can be summarized as follows: object permanence is always studied in a situation in which an object disappears. There is therefore a perturbation. The infant's reaction will depend on the strength of the perturbation. In the case of a weak perturbation there is a correction by a displacement in the opposite direction, while a larger one is simply ignored or avoided. As long as the infant has only a few schemes at his disposal, the disappearance of an object behind a screen is experienced as a total change of the global tableau. This is a strong perturbation and the infant, not knowing how to compensate it, simply ignores it. When the number of schemes increases and means-end connections develop, a gradual refinement takes place. What was a strong perturbation now becomes a weak one, because it means no more than a partial change of a tableau. Therefore the perturbation can be compensated by the opposite action, that is by removing the screen. This action shows once more how a negation is constructed by the subject as a compensation of an affirmation (the screen), confirming the importance of negations in equilibration (**90**, p.94/p.92).

11.2.2.2 Object permanence, actions and representation

In the early books about his children Piaget often writes that object permanence demonstrates that the child has a representation of the object. He now no longer says so and this is linked to the relation between object permanence and the group of displacements. In a very useful earlier summary Piaget said that "The object's permanent character results from the organization of the spatial field which is brought about by the coordination of the child's movements" (**11**, p.10). The child becomes able to return to his starting point and to change the direction of his movements. As was already mentioned such movements are characterized by "reversibility" and "associativity" Poincaré called such a coordination a "group of displacements" and Piaget took over this term. Since then, mathematicians at the Centre have drawn his attention to the fact that these displacements do not have the characteristics of a group and Piaget now speaks of a "group-like" structure.

☐The effect of going from A to B, B to C and C to D is equivalent to going directly from A to D. However, the most important characteristic of a group is that one can combine two elements into another element of the group. But in this structure one cannot combine A to B and C to D, so it is not a group, whatever Poincaré said and Piaget copied.

Anyhow, whether it is a group or only group-like does not change the notion that "The permanent object is then an invariant constructed by means of such a group" (**11**, p.10).

In other publications Piaget is less explicit about the relationship between the development of object permanence and the displacements. This is easily explained by the fact that both constructions take a long time to develop (from stage IV to stage VI), interacting in a dialectical way and progressing together.

☐The translation of Piaget's book on equilibration (**90**) is misleading. It says (**90**, p.96, English) "once objects have become permanent...", but this impression of a temporal order is only due to an inexact translation (**90**, p.97, French).

While this development takes place there are as yet no representations. According to Piaget it is certainly not true that object permanence presupposes a representation (**114**). In the "experimental" situation the child has just seen the object before its disappearance. At first the object is perceived and after its disappearance there is an evocation of what has just been there. This is still a prolongation of the child's action and not yet a true representation that would be independent of the action and take place in the "real" absence of the object. The successful search without representation is possible because there are all sorts of intermediates between a perception and a true representation and because the child could continue an action he had started. In recent terms such a successful action would be described as a "procedure that leads to the construction of a structure".

11.2.2.3 Object permanence and person permanence

Piaget has always supposed that persons become "permanent" objects sooner than material objects and his observations confirmed this. He was therefore very pleased when Gouin-Décarie verified this in a larger sample than Piaget's three subjects (**266**).

◻The "permanent object" led to much research from different points of view. See 21.2.2.

11.3 The Pre-Operational Stage

The stage from ± 18 months to ± 7 years is a very important one in the child's life. The semiotic function now plays a role in all aspects of cognitive development; the child begins to construct concepts, an intuitive logic develops, etc. It may seem rather absurd that it derives its name from what is lacking: the operations, but this name is due to the overwhelming importance attached by Piaget to operations with their internalization and reversibility. Another factor is that this stage consists of two very different sub-stages, so that it is difficult to find a suitable name covering them both. The later period, from the age of about 4 years on, is called the stage of "intuitive logic" with the development of identity and constituent functions. This indicates an effort on Piaget's part to find "positive" characteristics, a tendency also seen in Piaget's recent notions on egocentricity (see 7.2.1). But it remains difficult to find positive characteristics of the first period with its pre-concepts and pre-functions. As Piaget admits that a lot of research must still be done on this period of life, using different methods, the following concentrates on the period between 4 and 7 years of age.

11.3.1 Identity

11.3.1.1 The nature of identity

Piaget's research on identity studies the child's understanding of the invariance of an object or a movement. This "identity" is a qualitative one in contrast to the quantified "identity operator" (± 0) of groupings. The permanent object is an example of identity as the object remains "the same object" when it "disappears" and "reappears" for the child. Originally Piaget considered the permanent object an example of conservation but later on he wanted to limit this concept to changing objects, and the permanent object does not change. However, he is not consistent and one may well find him saying in a recent publication that the permanent object is an early manifestation of conservation. This shows that the concepts of identity and conservation are difficult to distinguish. This is all the more true because they may both be found in the same situation. When a straight wire is bent, it is still "the same wire" (identity) of "the same length" (conservation). When water is poured into a container of a different shape, it is still "the same water" (identity) and "the same amount" (conservation). The important difference is that identity can be purely qualitative while conservation must be quantitative. That there is a difference is clearly illustrated by the children who understand identity but without conservation.

There are many different aspects of identity. The changes of an identical object can be reversible or irreversible. Both the changes of the wire and of the water are reversible. But changes of growing things are irreversible, as are many others. Furthermore, changes can concern objects or movements.

> **Example:** A subject (A) can transmit a movement to an object (B) which then transmits it to (C). Is it still the same movement?

11.3.1.2 Experiments on identity and their results

Piaget and his collaborators studied many aspects of identity (**38**). The most interesting experiments are probably those concerning the identity of growing "organisms".

> **Example:** A grain of potassium ferrocyanide dropped into water to which copper sulphate has been added, gives within a few minutes a beautiful arborescence (called "grass" or "seaweed" by the children). Is it the same seaweed at all the steps of development?

The same questions are asked concerning the child's body and that of the experimenter. All the questions are combined with different types of drawings.

The comparison of these experiments with those concerning reversible changes clearly shows that understanding identity during "growth" is much more difficult. It is, above all, difficult to realize the continuity and the relationship between extreme stages of a transformation.

Example: The child does not believe that an experimenter has been a baby, and he cannot see himself as an adult.

As a result different stages of growth remain discontinuous classes: small, middle, big, instead of continuous transitions. Therefore differences become more important than the identity of the organism. A "continuous" identity is first accepted for the child, then for the experimenter and only at the last level (stage III) for the "seaweed". This level is reached by 75% of the 7-year-old children (size of the sample was seven). The earlier understanding of the identity of humans is due to the fact that they show a continuous activity that allows their recognition as individuals and makes them permanent centres of interest and values. Growing "plants" lack this individuality. Piaget sees an analogy between this difference and the earlier permanence of persons.

11.3.1.3 Explaining the development of the notion of identity

While 75% of the 7-year-olds attain level III with irreversible changes, 75% of the 5-year-olds reach this level with reversible changes. This leads to the question of whether the understanding is based on the same processes. The comparison shows how the notion of identity develops in general.

The source of the notion of identity is found in the assimilation of objects to schemes of the subject's actions. Now the self is essentially the totality of these schemes and the subject's body is for him its instrument. The assertion of the identity of the self as well as of the body refers to the continuity of their activity. This does not mean that identity implies an introspective experience or the influence of memory. Identity derives from assimilation itself, that is, from the constitutive process on which action is based and to which consciousness of the action is due. As action is necessarily an action on the object and as this object always reacts, identity is at the beginning by this very fact bipolar. It is, on the one hand, an identity of the object as a point of application of the assimilatory schemes and as a source of actions that correspond to the subject's own actions. On the other hand, it is the identity of the subject's own body or the self, as a system of assimilatory schemes and as a source of continuous activity linking it to objects and causing the body to be an object among other objects. Though the terminology is a different one, it should be clear that the description of this first general level of identity is the same as that of the constitution of the permanent object. At the second level of identity actions have become interiorized though they are still pre-operational. Identity by assimilation to schemes then becomes differentiated into "individualized" and "qualitative" identities. At this stage accommodations to the object lead to a differentiation of the assimilations of the first level that have proved themselves to be too global. The child becomes more conscious of changes and transformations, and therefore limits the domain of identities. Identity becomes rarer with the exception of the subject's own body and later on, by generalization, that of the experimenter. At the third level of identity quantitative considerations finally impose themselves, though still in a pre-operational form. The better differentiations lead to a distinction between constant qualities belonging to the object and variable qualities that are more or less accidental. This allows for a consolidation of identity but still without conservation.

Though there are differences in the ages at which identity is understood in the different experiments, the general results are analogous to the ones mentioned above. In general, the notion of identity progresses slowly during the child's development from its earliest form as seen in object permanence to qualitative identity and then to the identity operation. However, this identity operation—which might be considered a fourth level—is only possible for reversible structures. In the case of a growing organism no more than a global conservation is possible, as even scientists do not know in detail what the biological operations are that assure conservation during the changes in size that growth produces.

11.3.2 Mathematical Functions

At the same age that children begin to understand qualitative identity, they also begin to understand the qualitative or ordinal aspect of functions (37, 48). Piaget speaks of constituent functions in contrast to the quantified, constituted functions found at the level of concrete operations.

In a function, the variations of one variable depend on the variations of another variable: $y = f(x)$. A simple example is a string running over a pulley: lengthening one end of the string necessarily leads to a corresponding shortening of the other, while the total length of the string is conserved. This insight is called a "constituted" function. The young pre-operational child does not even realize that the differences in length must correspond to each other, nor does he conserve the total. At the next step he may understand the correspondence, but still without conservation. The latter, still limited insight is an example of a "constituent" function.

The subject constructs functions through empirical and reflective abstraction. In a function between material variables empirical abstraction plays an important role, because the connection between the variables is given in reality and is not introduced through reflective abstraction. Only in purely logico-mathematical functions does the covariance depend exclusively on the operational manipulations of the subject, that is, on reflective abstraction. These can evidently only be constructed from the operational level on as constituted functions.

Constituent functions are interesting from the epistemological point of view because they illustrate, once more, the importance of actions. *Constituent functions are dependences in one direction: lengthening part of a string implies a (corresponding) shortening of the other part.* It is this direction which reveals the connection between constituent functions and action schemes. Actions are always directed towards a goal and any scheme of action contains an element of orderly dependence.

> **Example:** There are many different dependences, e.g. between the conditions of the action's execution and its results; between the objects serving as means and the final objects, e.g. in instrumental conduct; between one action and the following one in more or less specific or generalized coordinations.

The connection between constituent functions and action schemes makes us understand why the constituent functions can be constructed before operations which require interiorizations and reversibility. It also allows us to understand why there are so many more functions than structures. Not every action is reversible nor can every action be included in a composition.

> □In the book on functions (37) Piaget analyses the relationship between action schemes and functions in terms of the different types of assimilation (reproductive, recognitive, generalizing). He then links these to three of the coordinators corresponding to the principal operators

distinguished by the combinatorial logic of Curry, Feys and others. However, it would take us too far to go into that aspect here.

Originally Piaget considered constituent functions of great importance as they supposedly were the common basis of later logico-mathematical structures and causality. However, when Piaget wanted to continue their study in turning to morphisms, he soon found that elementary correspondences cannot be the basis because correspondences are due to "comparing", while operations are "transforming". This led to the differentiation between the two in the books on morphisms and categories (**120, 121**).

11.3.3 Empirical Reversibility (= Revertibility) and Operational Reversibility (= Reversibility)

Originally Piaget only used the term "reversibility". Later on he had to admit that children already return to their starting point long before the stage of concrete operations. This return-in-action was then called "renversabilité" to distinguish it from "réversibilité", or in my terminology "empirical reversibility" as opposed to "operational reversibility".

□In his glossary Keats gives the terms "revertibility" and "reversibility" (**308**, p.XIII). Though it is very convenient to have one word and it is quite clever to find two different words, I think that the difference of a single letter is very confusing for the reader and therefore prefer to use my terminology.

The essential difference between the two is that empirical reversibility is no more than a return to the starting point, centred on the result of the action and without implying the identity of the paths followed. In contrast operational reversibility is a return that may take place in thought, in which the paths are identical, their opposite directions being the only difference.

At the sensorimotor stage the child becomes able to return to his starting point.

After the sensorimotor period the pre-operational child still shows empirical reversibility in much of his behaviour.

Example: The child who finds his way from home to kindergarten is able to find his way home, but only by doing so, not by demonstrating it with a model.

Experimentally, empirical reversibility is easily demonstrated in conservation tasks—the child sees that water has only to be poured back—but this does not imply conservation which requires operational reversibility.

In his study on reflective abstraction Piaget tried to create situations in which the action is reversed but without the complicating aspect of conservation. In order to check his understanding of reversibility the child is asked to compare two actions he has performed, and sometimes to construct an analogous sequence from other materials.

Example: The child is told to dress a doll and then to undress it. After that he is told to build a tower and to take it down again. He is now asked the question: "What is the same in the two tasks" and may then be given some other materials of which some lend themselves to analogous actions of doing and undoing, while others are unsuitable. The instruction with the new material is to make something "that is just like what you have just done."

The children are only capable of operational reversibility at the age of 7 or 8 years when they are able to understand the principle of returning or undoing.

In general, empirical reversibility is centred on the result of the action and this is to be expected if we think of the way consciousness proceeds from the periphery to the centre. Only when the child is fully conscious of his actions does he understand operational reversibility. He is then capable of choosing his own material in such a way as to construct an identical path from A to D as that from D to A.

☐Criticisms of this are given in 21.4.

11.3.4 What is "Pre-Operational" About the Pre-Operational Child?

The easiest answer to this question is that the child cannot yet classify, conserve, etc. But this answer, which seems to be indisputably correct, leads to trouble because Piaget writes about "classifying infants", etc. So the next question is whether Piaget contradicts himself or whether he just uses the same term with different meanings. In order to answer this question one must look at the different domains in which the operational child succeeds, and compare the achievements of pre-operational children with the successes of the older ones.

11.3.4.1 Can the young child conserve?

Challenged by his critics who claimed that very young children already conserve (Bruner, Mehler-Bever), Piaget finally answered that the natural tendency of young children is to conserve as long as they are not confronted with facts which they do not expect, and whose inexplicability leads them to change their opinion. In general, children expect conservation, but since they cannot know beforehand what will be conserved and what will not be conserved, they have to construct new means of quantification in every new sector of experience. The inadequacy of the means of quantification explains non-conservation, and it is worthwhile to note that non-conservation therefore indicates an effort to analyse and to dissociate variables. Very young children and severely mentally-retarded children pay no attention to these variables, whereas older, normal subjects pass through a stage of non-conservation as they reorganize relations which they cannot yet grasp in full (**41**, p.978). The main point is that young children do conserve, but have difficulties with quantification. I shall return to this difficulty in a moment, but first another aspect of these early conservations should be mentioned. Though Piaget has written for years that children are more capable in their actions than in their verbalizations, he has only elaborated this in the recent books on consciousness (**85, 86**). Linking this with conservation leads to the hypothesis that the young child will "conserve" in his actions, but without being able to conceptualize this. Only when the child is about 6-8 years old is he capable of giving justifications, that is to say, conscious reasons for what he might have done correctly at an earlier age. Before that he might either still believe in the "omnipotence" of his actions—e.g. the act of elongating adds clay—or he might act according to laws of conservation in a truly non-verbal situation. This would have to be decided with appropriate experiments, but Piaget has not done so. Nevertheless, he is quite willing to accept that young children might conserve non-verbally (**114**).

  □ Training experiments are discussed in 20.2.

11.3.4.2 Can young children classify?

As Piaget does not distinguish "discrimination" and "classification", the young child evidently classifies as well as many animals do. But one can go a step further and easily find examples of class-inclusion: what mother offers is edible but some edibles are nice while others are nasty. However, the child is again not conscious of the criteria for extension and intension of classes, that is to say, cannot quantify.

11.3.4.3 Early transitivity

To avoid monotony one example of early transitivity should suffice: the child wants to push an object but it is too far away. So he takes a stick, pushes the stick and thus pushes the object, but, of course without cognizance and verbalization.

□Bryant's theory of transitivity with arguments against his experiments are given in 21.3.5.

11.3.4.4 Common characteristics of the pre-operational child

In looking for common characteristics, identity and functions can be included with "pre-operations". Trying to express common characteristics in "positive terms" proves to be unexpectedly difficult. It is clear that the child can already act very intelligently, especially in situations where empirical abstraction is a help. Things go wrong when the perceptual data are misleading, e.g. in the classical conservation experiment. This shows what is lacking. Whether in identity, functions, conservation or classification, it is always the quantitative aspect that is lacking. This does not mean that the operational child measures, but that there is a complete compensation, specifically of negations and affirmations. The difficulty of this quantification is that it cannot be achieved by a reading-off of observables. Any "quantity" presupposes a complex construction of which the child is incapable before the age of 6-8 years. This remains true even though the younger child constantly uses terms that have a quantitative meaning for the adult: big, dark, heavy, etc. For the child, these terms still indicate qualities and not quantities, as can be seen in many experiments in which objects are grouped as small, middle and large instead of using their relations of smaller, etc. In terms of reflective abstraction one can conclude that the later part of the pre-operational stage is a period of differentiations which allow, at a certain moment, a reconstruction resulting in the beginning of the operational stage.

11.4 The Stage of Concrete Operations

Piaget is as much fascinated by concrete operations as his opponents are, though probably for a very different reason. For him the structures of this stage are the first ones that are basic for formal operations and thereby for scientific operations of the nth degree.

□This way of looking at structures is so evident that many readers believe that groupings are the first logico-mathematical structures, though Piaget explicitly writes about logico-mathematical structures of the sensorimotor stage.

The stage is characterized by groupings. Piaget had to defend this notion against many attacks of logicians and psychologists, though he never pretended to have given more than a formalization which is half-way between mathematics and psychology. Logicians then came to his defence with efforts to formalize groupings. The first attempts failed because formalizations for strong structures were used while groupings are weak structures. Finally the logician-mathematicians Wermus and Wittman succeeded in a form, satisfying mathematicians and Piaget (**457, 463**). Piaget then elaborated conservation, classification and seriation in terms of this formalization (**104**).

  □Because of its highly technical terminology no short summary can be given.
Before this latest effort to explain groupings Piaget returned to groupings in many publications within the period covered by this book. Sometimes he explained the results of former experiments by new aspects of his theory, sometimes he did new experiments. A complete overview would take up too much space. Therefore only the main theoretical aspects have been summarized.

11.4.1 Conservation

Before explaining the transition from non-conservation to conservation, the question as to what conservation is has to be answered.

11.4.1.1 What is conservation?

Piaget's experiments on conservation are epistemologically important because they illustrate the relation between conservation and transformation (see 5.3.4). This relation can clearly be seen in the definition Piaget gave in 1968—after having done research on the topic since 1941. He then wrote, *"We call 'conservation' (and this is generally accepted) the invariance of a characteristic despite transformations of the object or collection of objects possessing this characteristic"* (**41**, p.978; italics added). Piaget's many texts on conservation clearly show that one must add a number of characteristics in order to have a complete picture of the meaning of conservation as used in his experiments. In the first place the invariance is always a quantitative one, though this does not mean that the child does any measuring. In the second place one should add "all other conditions being the same".

  □In Piaget's experiments on the conservation of volume the question concerns how much the water level would rise if the form of the clay ball that might be submerged into it was changed. In this context Piaget writes explicitly that clay is neither penetrated by water nor compressed by it. Where the conservation of weight is concerned he never mentions the condition that the weight of an object before the transformation of its form must be compared to the weight of that object after the transformation under the same conditions of height, temperature, etc. This was probably so self-evident that he did not mention it, though it is, of course, a necessary condition.

As the stage of concrete operations is characterized by groupings, the question of the relationship between conservation and the groupings arises. The nine groupings are: transitivity (a sort of preliminary grouping for the others), four groupings of classes and four of relations. Thus conservation does not seem to come into the picture. This is also indicated by the title of Piaget's recent article "Some recent research and its link with a new theory of groupings and conservation" (**104**). Asked about the relationship, Piaget answered that conservation is a necessary condition for the groupings (**114**). After what was said about the dialectics of cognitive development (see 10.3) there is hardly any need to emphasize that this does not mean that conservation is completely developed before classification and seriation begin to develop, and even less that all conservation tasks have to be solved before success in any task of classification or seriation can be expected. Theoretically it means that in a class-inclusion, $A + A' = B$, the whole, B, must be conserved in order to understand that $B - A' = A$. In a seriation, the relationship between the seriated elements must be conserved.

☐ For critical arguments see 21.4.1.1.

11.4.1.2 Explaining the results of conservation experiments

In 1955 Piaget and Inhelder wrote a very interesting, though hardly ever read, passage (**12**, p.58/p.63). In conservation experiments with clay, cylindrical glasses etc. there are, of course, three dimensions. However, only two of them are distinctly perceived by the child and included in his reasoning. The three dimensions would, in fact, require a logical multiplication, but what the child does is more additive than multiplicative. The child has, above all, the impression that it is possible to displace certain parts of the object, which are taken from one dimension, to the other dimension, thus equalizing the result of the products (height × width = height × width). This remark about displacement, which was subsequently completely forgotten by Piaget, contains the essence of his later explanation of conservation, which is "simpler and relatively new" (**93**, p.59; also given in **84b**).

Conservation is now explained by "commutability". This is a more general form of "commutativity", meaning the insight that the whole is conserved when parts of the whole or elements of a collection that are taken away at one point are added at another.

Commutativity can be written as $n + n' = n' + n$. In commutability, written as $m + m' = m' + m$, m' is the remaining part and m the displaced one. This sort of displacement is a generalization of commutativity because the latter is linear and consists of a permutation, while this is not required in commutability.

There are two problems concerning commutability. The first one is how the development of conservation in terms of the mechanisms of equilibration dovetails with the notion of conservation as commutability. The second is whether there are differences between the development of logico-mathematical conservation and infralogical conservation. The former is the conservation of discrete elements and the latter is the conservation of a continuous whole.

□ Strictly speaking there is a difference between the conservation of logico-mathematical structures, e.g. number, and the conservation of infralogical structures, e.g. substance in the ball of clay or quantity in the pouring of water. However, in the book on equilibration, Piaget answers the first of the two questions mentioned, using the clay ball as illustration but writing about logico-mathematical structures (**90**, p.115ff/p.117ff). The difference between the two types of structures is discussed in detail in an article of which Piaget is co-author (**93**) to which I shall turn in answering the second question.

a) *Commutability and equilibration*

Conservation develops in four successive levels described in terms of observables and coordinations with the clay ball as illustration.

Level I: No conservation. Most subjects centre on the length of the clay sausage. Obs.S = action of elongating in one direction. Obs.O = increase in length. Coord.S and Coord.O = increase of quantity evaluated in an ordinal, qualitative comparison of the original and the final states.

Transitional level II: Obs.S continues to be centred on the action but the subject begins to see two sorts of Obs.O: increased length and diminished width. Coord.S and Coord.O form an unstable equilibrium, the child first concluding that there is more, then that there is less.

Level III: Around 6 years of age the children anticipate correctly that the clay sausage will become "long and thin". This is probably due to Obs.O as there are no separate aspects in the action, though there are in the observables. Obs.O then in its turn influences Obs.S. Coord.S and Coord.O are now seen as real coordinations and thereby the action is no longer seen as taking place in one direction. There is empirical reversibility but without conservation, because the quantitative aspect is still lacking. The important improvement is that the child no longer compares the end state with the beginning but pays attention to the transformation. In the case of small variations the child may even see the possibility of conservation but still without justifications.

Level IV: Obs.S and Obs.O (getting longer and thinner) are seen right away as effects of the action. This implies that the Coord.S and Coord.O of the preceding level have modified these observables, introducing a necessary union between them. Getting longer and thinner are seen as compensating each other quantitatively though the subject does not look for measures or empirical verification. Even though the child only conserves substance, and not weight or volume, he has taken an important step forward because the Coord.S and Coord.O go far beyond observables.

These levels show that the construction is dominated by one general process. At first the subject only reacts with predicative comparisons of a static nature (the sausage is fat, the sausage is long). He ends up with inferences about transformations with an evaluation of their relationship (it will be longer but not thicker). It is clear that a process of regulations has taken place. However, this leads to the question of what these regulations are. In order to understand their mechanisms a closer look at their outcome is necessary. This leads to distinguishing three aspects of what the child has achieved: commutability, vicariousness and compensation.

Commutability
□In the article (**93**) the presentation is slightly different from the book (**90**), all three characteristics being called "aspects of commutability". There is, however, no fundamental difference.
The child expresses commutability by the well-known justification "nothing was added or taken away", or "you only elongated it", or "it is the same quantity of clay".

Vicariousness
In a classification, a class B can be divided into $A_1 + A_1'$, but also into $A_2 + A_2'$. "Vicariousness" is defined as the insight that in whatever

way the breakdown into parts is done, and whatever their spatial disposition, the total is the same. Vicariousness implies partial negations, as a part is always considered "the whole minus the other part". Otherwise the sum would vary according to the disposition of the parts, and there would be no negation. The difference Piaget makes between vicariousness and commutability is a subtle one: in vicariousness the constancy of the whole or total sum is emphasized, while in commutability the identity of the displaced parts is stressed. When the child uses the second well-known justification "you can re-make a sausage into a ball", this reversibility can be an expression of vicariousness or of commutability.

Compensation

The third justification of the child is the compensation between the changes in the length and diameter of the sausage. However, this is again given without measurement.

In order to understand the mechanisms by which these outcomes of regulations are reached, one should first of all realize that the actions themselves need not be regulated, as every young child is capable of changing a ball into a sausage shape. It is the Obs. and Coord. that require regulations as a result of perturbations. In terms of perturbations, level I is characterized by the fact that there is no perturbation at all. The child simply ignores the observable of the sausage becoming thinner, thus showing behaviour of type α. The first perturbation arises when the child perceives the contrast between the Obs.O of elongation and the Obs.S in which he feels that he successively displaces bits while stretching out the sausage. But as the notion of displacements does not yet exclude that of elongation with increase in quantity, the child still accepts such an increase. A more serious perturbation arises when a new Obs.O shows that the sausage becomes thinner at the same time as it becomes longer. This leads to an unstable equilibrium in level III in which the fact that the sausage becomes thinner is no longer a perturbation, but a variation of the system. This is behaviour of type β. This variation then becomes deducible, and the child realizes that parts added at one end $(+)$ correspond to those taken off at the other $(-)$, and that additions in length $(+)$ correspond to diminutions in diameter $(-)$. This is behaviour of type γ.

The more general problem then is to understand why these compensations, once achieved, are experienced as a necessity even though no displacements of parts can be isolated nor variations in form be measured. In the first place, inferential necessity is always the result of the closure of a system. In the second place, the conservation of the whole is the common invariant of groupings of which the essential operations are identity ($\pm\, 0$) and reversibility ($T.\, T^{-1} = 0$), that is to say complete compensation of affirmations and negations.

Seen this way, commutability, vicariousness and the compensations of ($+$) and ($-$), which are three expressions of or derivations from groupings, would not constitute primary facts but would constitute the result of regulatory mechanisms ending in these structures. This is confirmed by the fact that the regulations proceed from type α to type γ.

b) *Logical and infralogical conservation*

In his early books Piaget had already distinguished logico-mathematical or logico-arithmetical and infralogical structures. *Logico-mathematical structures are composed of operations performed on individual objects while spatio-temporal relations are not taken into account. Infralogical structures concern the part-whole relationships within an individual object as a whole* (objects being of whatever size, including the universe), *taking their spatio-temporal relations into account* (**7**, p.332).

☐Some authors confuse infralogical and pre-logical structures. "Infralogical" does not denote an earlier level of what will become logical afterwards.

From the point of view of commutability, logico-mathematical conservation of quantity in which discrete elements are displaced should be easier than infralogical conservation in which a "displacement" is far less evident. Furthermore it should be possible to train conservation by cutting-up the displacements into two separate steps: first taking away an element, then adding it in another position. This training should have better results in logico-mathematical (or logico-arithmetical) conservation if the first hypothesis is to be confirmed. Both hypotheses were tested in a series of experiments with young non-conservers (**93**). The aim of the training was not to accelerate development, but to test the theory.

Non-conservers of number were selected in a pre-test. They were then given three tasks.

Example: In the first task the experimenter and the child each have a row of chips arranged in one-to-one correspondence. Then one of the chips of the child is taken away and added at a different place. After each displacement of this kind the child is asked whether there are still as many chips in front of the experimenter as there are in his own, new constellation. The second and third tasks are of the same kind.

No more than 75% of the answers to the questions on these tasks were correct. But, and this is the important point, a post-test on the same number-conservation task showed a very great improvement. Of the eleven non-conservers eight were conserving after the training while three were at an intermediate level. After three weeks the improvement was maintained, but this was no more than a favourable indication because it was unknown what the spontaneous progress of the children might have been.

    ☐It is astonishing that this realization rarely leads Genevans to the use of control-groups.

If commutability is essential in the conservation of discrete elements, the next question concerns what happens with a continuous object like a clay sausage.

From several previous experiments it is known that conservation of a continuous quantity lags somewhat behind that of a discontinuous quantity. This can be explained by the fact that the conservation of continuous quantity implies two "displacements" instead of one. In the case of a collection of discrete elements which are displaced, the elements themselves do not change their form. However, when parts of a sausage are displaced in its elongation, each displaced bit also changes its form. In order to conserve the identity of the displaced parts, the subject must construct two sorts of displacements: those of the parts one takes off and replaces (or that are simply pushed in an elongation), and those within each displaced (or pushed) bit. These difficulties were confirmed in a conservation experiment in which bits of clay of different colours were used in tasks of the same kind as those mentioned above. The result of the training was less spectacular but still evident.

The experiments discussed in this article thus confirm the hypothesis that logico-mathematical conservation of the quantity of discrete elements should be easier than the infralogical conservation of a continuous quantity or substance. They also confirm the explanation by commutability.

The question remains as to what the relationship between logical and infralogical "pre-operations" and operations is. At the pre-operational level there is clearly a lack of differentiation between the logical and infralogical. A quantity of objects still depends to a high degree on the spatial arrangement of the objects, as one of the experiments of this series showed. On the other hand, spatial arrangements depend on conceptualization in "intension" as thought cannot function without it. During the period of differentiation there are certainly differences between the two, but there are also common mechanisms that lead to a final isomorphism once infralogical and logical actions have become operational. Whether there are discrete elements or a continuous whole, there are always exact compensations between subtractions and additions. There is also an equivalence between the total quantity and the sum of the parts. This need not be true for the preoperational child, as the child who has been active in elongating a sausage may well believe that he has added to its quantity.

All in all, the study of commutability shows that it would be wrong to oppose infralogical and logico-mathematical processes in a radical way, as they are interdependent at all levels, though in different ways.

    □There are no critical comments on commutability, but alternative interpretations of conservation are mentioned in 21.4.1.2.

11.4.2 Class-Inclusion

The basic experiment for class-inclusion has remained the same during all the years since the first experiments, though the questions are more limited and less confusing. What is new about class-inclusion is its explanation in the context of equilibration theory and reflective abstraction theory.

11.4.2.1 Explaining the development of class-inclusion in terms of equilibration

At first the child only looks for similarities neglecting all differences, even though the instruction of putting together what is alike implies "to leave out what is different" and even though this is often specified. The child looks for a positive connection between two elements. He is incapable of anticipating the extension as determined by common characteristics of all the elements—an anticipation which would require the elimination of all the elements that do not have these characteristics. The collection is only seen as a totality when all the bits are part of a spatial whole in the infralogical or "mereological" sense. Differences between the elements are ignored according to the rules of behaviour of type α.

    □In this context "mereological" is used without any further explanation. In a footnote in another book (**110**, p.32n) we find that the Polish logician Lesniewski distinguishes the logic of classes from that of the part and the whole, when the parts are the pieces of a continuous object (e.g. the nose as part of the face) or the elements of a concrete collection (the furniture of a room). The latter are called "mereological structures" and his axiomatization shows the similarities and differences between these structures and those of classes or sets. In studying infralogical structures with their part-whole relations Piaget has concentrated on isomorphisms with logico-mathematical structures, because these are more important from a psychogenetic point of view than other aspects of part-whole structures. (See 21.4.2 for a more detailed description.)

At the beginning of the next level the child begins to pay attention to the differences, because the elements of one sub-collection have a characteristic that is missing in the other sub-collections. But the differences are still seen in terms of affirmative judgements, the negations not being understood. The child of this level does see that there are A' that are B, and that differ from the A. But saying that the A' are not A is purely verbal, and the child is incapable of concluding that there must then be more B than A. In other words, the lack of negations and subtractions leads the child to the comparison of A and A' instead of A and B, as the whole B does not exist any longer when subdivided into A and A'. This difficulty is really due to the lack of negations and not to a problem of counting, as the numerical comparison of A and B is easy by correspondence. The real problem is that the child has to understand the affirmation "all A are B", and the negation, "not all B are A". At this level the child then shows behaviour of type β. Finally, the differences and similarities are completely equilibrated in the sense that the first are understood as partial negations (A' becoming B.non-A). The child now shows behaviour of type γ.

11.4.2.2 Explaining the development of class-inclusion by reflective abstraction

In his research on reflective abstraction (102) Piaget analysed a sequence of experiments, including several tasks on class-inclusion and logical implication. The interesting aspect is that they were all given to the same subjects and therefore it would have been interesting to report them in detail. On the other hand they had already lost some of their importance because Piaget had changed his notions on signifying implication. Therefore only one important aspect has been given here. This is all the more justified because development is, again, seen in terms of the construction of negations.

The interesting point is that Piaget introduced a class-inclusion experiment using green figures of different forms, e.g. squares and circles. The question whether there are more green figures or more squares was answered correctly by most 5-year-olds though they failed completely when the traditional question about marguerites and flowers was given. Finding such results, Piaget was not satisfied by the conclusion that this was another example of a time-lag, nor by the conclusion that details of the task influenced the availability of a structure. His efforts to find an explanation led to a detailed analysis in terms of signifying implication. In signifying implication the subject recognizes in objects qualitative properties which have a signification for the subject. These properties are linked to each other by more-or-less constant relations which allow the subject to infer the presence of one property when another one is perceived. The important aspect is that the relations can be perceived by empirical abstraction. Therefore perception is a help instead of the hindrance it is in conservation. There are, however, limits to the use of signifying implication in a task of class-inclusion. In the first place, the significations of signifying implications are qualitative, because any quantity has to be constructed. The fact that words like "big", "small", etc. are no more than absolute predicates for the young child implies a limitation to intension and a lack of extension. In the second place, primitive systems of significations are seriously limited because of the lack of negations, especially negations constructed by the subject and not imposed externally. Thus a complete negation would be seen when a colour like green is opposed to non-green, but it is not a negation when it is opposed to another colour. So, as long as signifying implications are greatly influenced by empirical abstraction, some tasks will be easier than the usual class-inclusion tasks in which the child has to construct class B and which require a quantification for a correct answer. However, the help given by signifying implication is limited.

☐For critical experiments on class-inclusion see 21.4.2.

11.4.3 Seriation and Transitivity

Piaget had another look at seriation in the context of conceptualization (**85**) and reflective abstraction (**102**), and at seriation and transitivity in the context of equilibration (**90**).

11.4.3.1 Seriation and conceptualization

The question is whether the child's conceptualizations or his actions are the more advanced, or whether indeed the two develop at the same time (**85**). This question is most interesting for children who succeed in seriation tasks using the most adequate method. These children, who are at the concrete operational stage, cannot be more advanced in their conceptualization because their actions are perfect. So, either the two develop together or actions are more advanced than conceptualizations.

> **Example:** In the experiments the children are given some material with the instruction to make a sequence or series. After the child has succeeded, he is asked how he has worked and/or how he would explain to another child what to do.

In their actions, children of this level choose each time the biggest of the remaining sticks because a correct seriation requires that $B < A$, but that $B > C, D, E, F$ and G. In their verbalizations the children neglect the second aspect, only mentioning that $B < A$, $C < B$, etc. Many of them even use the more primitive level of verbalization by using the absolute terms ''small'', ''middle'', ''big'', instead of the relative ''smaller'', etc. Thus, in describing their actions these children only pay attention to the result, neglecting the method actually used in actions. The latter supposes a general coordination directing the actions from the inside, while cognizance proceeds from the periphery to the centre and this evidently is a later step in development.

11.4.3.2 Seriation and transitivity in terms of equilibration

The development of seriation is another example of the sequence of type α, β, γ behaviour (**90**). In terms of compensations one might say that there are two types of progressive compensations: those between similarities and differences, and those between positive and negative characteristics.

Transitivity is reached at the same time as the child reaches the highest level of seriation. At the foregoing level of seriation the child succeeded by trial and error, but this is impossible in transitivity tasks. As $A < B$ and $B < C$ are never seen together, the relation between A and C must be deduced. The child's reaction that he cannot know the answer because he did not see them together illustrates the importance of perception for the pre-operational child. Piaget does not accept the possibility that the child might have forgotten that $A < B$ when he no longer sees them (**86**, p.251/p.230). The child of this age is quite capable of remembering two isolated bits of information. The problem is that he is still centred on positive characteristics. Being told that $A < B$ he does not deduce that this excludes $A > B$ and $A = B$, nor that B in $B < C$ is not just *any* positive element, but is one that is already qualified as much by what is excluded as by its positive relation with C. Thus the conclusion is that a lack of reversibility is not a sufficient explanation of non-transitivity as Piaget believed at an earlier date. Transitivity has to be explained by taking negative implications into account as well as positive ones (**86**, p.251/p.230). This conclusion is repeated in slightly different terms in the book on equilibration (**90**). Transitivity results directly from the compensations of the $(+)$ and $(-)$. If one has $(+) + (-) = 0$, one has as well $(+) + (+) = (++)$ and $(-) + (-) = (--)$, or $(A < B) + (B < C) = A \ll C$ where $\ll$ indicates the reunion of two relations of $<$.

11.4.3.3 Seriation and reflective abstraction

In his research on reflective abstraction (**102**) Piaget returned once more to seriation, because the relations of order or sequence are very important in logico-mathematical and logico-arithmetical structures. Furthermore, he has always maintained that the notion of order, in the sense of a sequence, is a fundamental example of a construction by reflective abstraction. Even at the most elementary level the scheme of ordering is not simply acquired by an inspection of an already ordered sequence, because the actions required for finding this order (following with the eyes, the finger, etc.) have to be ordered themselves. If empirical abstraction and reflective abstraction both play a part, it is important to do new experiments in order to find their respective contributions, adding at the same time the study of pseudo-empirical abstraction.

The essential difference between the new experiments and the former ones is that the child not only has to order the given material and to compare the sequences, but that he has to construct a continuation choosing from a number of elements, or construct an analogous sequence with different objects. Furthermore, the differences between the successive sticks are not always equal, but may be twice as large successively. These tasks are far more difficult than the traditional ones and the highest level is only reached at the beginning of the stage of formal operations.

The main results are:

a) Logico-mathematical, specifically seriational, relations have to be constructed by the subject. As long as he is not capable of constructing them, he cannot understand them. This has, evidently, consequences for teaching.

b) The presentation of the series has an important influence on its degree of difficulty. The principle of *o oo ooo oooo* is far easier to continue than that of *RBRBBRBBBRBBBB* (Red, Blue, etc.). In the first one empirical abstraction (or the figurative aspect of knowledge—Piaget does not always distinguish them) helps. This is the same tendency as the experiments on classification showed.

c) The progress in seriation shows three levels due to repeated processes of reflective abstraction. Each level enriches the foregoing and leans upon it to reconstruct what has been taken from it.

11.4.4 Logico-Arithmetical Structures

Ever since Piaget began to study the concept of number, he has written that numbers require classification and seriation. However, as has already been mentioned in 10.3 this does not mean that the latter were constructed first. But it does mean that there is an important difference between counting and understanding numbers. A child shows his understanding by the conservation of number, by knowing without counting how many chips there are in a heap having just counted them when they formed a circle, and by understanding that $2 + 3 = 5$ and $3 + 2 = 5$ (asked in a suitably concrete form).

While one can easily teach a child to count, to do additions and even to recite the multiplication tables, the child only constructs numbers at the stage of concrete operations.

The problem that has interested Piaget recently is the fact that multiplication of classes is understood at the same time as the addition of classes and relations, while multiplication of numbers proves far more difficult than addition (**102a**).

> **Example:** In one experiment the child is given two heaps of counters, one yellow (A) and one blue (B). He is then told to make an equal amount of *A*s and *B*s taking two *A*s at a time and three *B*s at a time (six being the lowest common multiple). Having succeeded the child is questioned about what he has done, and about the possibility of succeeding with larger or smaller collections. The 7- to 8-year-olds anticipate the possibility of making equal amounts but they only succeed by successive trial and error. It is not until the age of 9-10 years that the problem is solved without hesitation.

The difference in difficulty between the multiplication of classes and that of numbers can be explained as follows. In a multiple classification there is no need to count and the child can construct "in intension" by association of the qualitative characteristics of each class. Given counters that are round or square, and white, blue or red, six sub-classes can be found in the same way as one multiplies 2×3 in order to get six numerical units. However, the child does not have to count but may look at the common characteristics of the counters in each sub-class, i.e. their intension. In the case of numbers with their equivalent units the relation "n times x" requires more. The units have to be counted in extension as they have no common characteristics in intension. Then the number of times one has taken x units has to be counted. As these "parcels" of two counters have no common characteristics, one has to count the number of actions or operations one has performed while taking n times the number of x units. Thus there is a difference in the level of cognizance. In adding the units x into "parcels" of two and three one counts the objects in the way one manipulates the concrete objects in multiple classification. But in a multiplication of numbers one has then to count the operations.

11.4.5 Logico-Geometrical Structures

11.4.5.1 The nature of logico-geometrical structures

Space is a very interesting epistemological issue. Objects have spatial properties like position, form, displacement, etc. independently of any subject. When the subject comes to know them by what Piaget calls "spatial abstraction", this abstraction always depends on these "real" properties of the objects. When logico-mathematical abstractions add deductive frames such as classification, relations, etc. to objects, these structures must always "fit" the objects. But in the case of spatial abstractions, the relationship with the characteristics of the objects is much closer because the objects had their spatial properties before being classified, etc. Space thus forms an extension of the objects and at the same time of the "geometry of the subject", that is to say, the system of his actions and operations. It is therefore, from the sensorimotor level on, a zone of intersection between reality and the operations of the subject. This means that the relationship between reflective abstraction and empirical abstraction differs from that in logico-mathematical structures: reflective abstraction gives the characteristic of necessity to spatial properties and empirical abstraction gives the already existing and continuing characteristics of the objects.

11.4.5.2 Experiments on geometrical problems

Recently Piaget did a number of experiments on spatial relations within the context of reflective abstraction (**102**). Though one of them, once more, takes up conservation and it is therefore tempting to summarize it, limitations of space do not allow this.

The experiments show that there is no fundamental difference between the development of logico-mathematical and logico-geometrical structures, notwithstanding the greater influence of empirical abstraction.

Though empirical abstraction is important, the experiments show that empirical abstraction by itself is not enough because it only gives facts without uniting them into a system of transformations and, above all, without giving reasons. But empirical abstraction remains necessary, because the deductive models of the subject must be applied to the objects. Reflective abstraction is the source of ever more novelties, leading to reconstructive reflections after every projective reflection in a never-ending sequence: from actions to representations, from representations to "telling about", then to comparisons and finally to reflexive thought. At every level "reflection" reorganizes a new system with a progress in coherence and integration, until the "reason" is found. Later on these reasons will lead to new reasons built upon them by metareflection. In a word: the double process of "projective reflections on projective reflections" and of "reconstructive reflections on reconstructive reflections" forms a continuous dynamic of which these experiments show some of the most simple steps (**102b**, p.227).

11.5 The Stage of Formal Operations

11.5.1 The Nature of Formal Operations

Once the structures of concrete operations have been developed, reflective abstraction can lead to a new integration. Thus the operations on operations are constructed.

In a very useful chapter on the epistemology of logic (**33**), Piaget summarizes the three "novelties" of the formal stage (p.390):

a) There is a generalization of classifications leading to the classification of the second degree, called the "combinatorial";

b) This combinatorial allows the addition of propositional operations ($p \supset q$, etc.) to the operations of classes and relations. This implies a more general form of logic in which the form is independent of the content;

c) This formal structure thus becomes completely reversible with $N(N$ of $p{\supset}q$ is $p.\bar{q})$, and $R(R$ of $p{\supset}q$ is $q{\supset}p)$. There is then a complete group of four transformations: $I = NRC$.

This summary gives nothing new, but in view of the many misinterpretations it may be useful to add some details. Piaget's favourite example is action and reaction. Their strengths can go in opposite directions and there is a relationship between the transformations of the action and the reaction. Another example is that of a snail on a plank, both being able to go into two opposite directions, their movements being seen in relation to an external point. Though it is an "old" experiment Piaget still refers to it in 1977 (**102a**, p.133). It illustrates the problem of integrating two systems of coordinations. N might be the transformation which gives the inverse of the direction in which the snail was going. R would then be the compensation for this action of the snail by the opposite movement of the plank. As the examples show, Piaget does not distinguish physical INRC groups and propositional ones. This is explained by the fact that he is not interested in the actual movements but in the adolescent's hypothetical thinking about them, and this is done in propositions. In other words: he is interested in the propositional description of the material actions. These thoughts may start from $p{\supset}q$, but could also do so just as well from some of the other binary operations.

> ☐ The easiest way to find the negation, N, of a proposition is to start from the "tautology" $(pq)v(p\bar{q})v(\bar{p}q)v(\bar{p}\bar{q})$. N is the complement of the original proposition. Thus pvq means $(pq)v(\bar{p}q)v(p\bar{q})$ are true. Its complement N is $\bar{p}\bar{q}$.

Just as in other formalizations, the adolescent uses the INRC group while the logician formalizes it.

As in other summaries, Piaget emphasizes that form and content become independent of each other at the formal stage. However, nowadays (**114**) he mitigates this by saying that they become "relatively" independent. As we have seen in earlier chapters of this book, only logico-mathematical structures become independent of extra-logical content, while other scientific structures contain extra-logical content. Piaget does not indicate whether this elaboration of his theory influences his hypothesis concerning the question of whether all adolescents reach the formal stage or not. This question became urgent when research showed that not all adolescents and adults succeed in Piaget's tasks for formal thinking (12). A careful reading of the book makes it clear that Piaget never pretended that they did. Anyhow, this result is a fact, confirmed by much research. Asking himself whether the poor results in those tasks really meant that the adolescents did not reach the formal stage, Piaget suggested three hypotheses. The first maintains that all individuals do reach the formal stage, but that some of them do so at a much later age. The second hypothesis says that adolescents may be talented in different fields and may therefore reach the formal stage in one field, but not in others. The third hypothesis, which is his own favourite, says that everyone reaches the stage of formal structures but in different areas according to his aptitudes and professional interests. As Piaget emphasizes, this hypothesis would have to be tested. Though this has not been done, Piaget continued to write about the stage of formal structures (54).

This position of Piaget is often quoted as his "weakened" notion of the relationship between form and content. What is never mentioned is the important suggestion, added in the same article (54), that further research would be required to decide whether other types of tasks would show the same underlying logico-mathematical structures or different structures.

☐The critique of formal operations is partly found in 16.3.5.2 and partly in 21.5.2.

11.5.2 Recent Research on Formal Operations

In many recent experiments, the oldest children have been 11 or 12 years old and have reached the beginning of formal operations. There are, however, few experiments specifically directed at the formal stage.

In the book on generalizations (110) Piaget describes an experiment showing how adolescents develop the two kinds of generalization, inductive and constructive generalization. Earlier experiments (12) had given many examples of inductive generalization and hence, as Piaget writes, this form of generalization did not deserve special attention (110, p.6). As for constructive generalization this experiment clearly showed that it is due to the system of actions and operations of the subject (pp.213-219).

In the book on reflective abstraction (102) Piaget pays special attention to the difference between the Klein group and the INRC group.

The Klein group is a commutative group of four transformations T_1 to T_4 in which the composition of any two of the operations T_2 to T_4

gives the third one and the combination of all three again gives the identical T_1. In this general form the Klein group is found in all domains. This is easily seen in the characteristics A and B of a multiplicative matrix of classes. This passage from one combination to the other thus forms a Klein group.

The INRC group is a specific case of this general Klein group with far more restricted characteristics, only being found in the "set of all subsets" (classifications of classifications, or "simplexes"), and especially in propositional logic. Comparing the two, the negation N of pvq, which is $\bar{p}.\bar{q}$, reminds one of "neither A nor B". Yet there is a fundamental difference. One can define N, R and C independently of each other. N is the negation of the operation, while in R the operation remains the same but the terms are negated ($R(pvq) = \bar{p}v\bar{q}$). This is not influenced by the fact that it may be written as $p|q$ (p excludes q). In C, defined independently, there is a permutation of (v) or (.) into the normal form of the operation that was the starting point. The essential aspect of these independent definitions is that their combination ends up in $NRC = I$. This shows how much more complex the INRC group is than the Klein group. The passage from $A.B$ to neither A nor B is only a reciprocity, R, and that from $A.B$ to non-$A.B$ is only a partial reciprocity which is completed by $A.$non-B. These partial passages are understood at 7 or 8 years of age when the child is able to construct a 2×2 matrix. The difference can be expressed in the well-known definition of the INRC group as "operations on operations", while the operations of the Klein group do not differ from those used in the construction of the matrix.

The gradual transition from the Klein group to the INRC group is due to reflective abstractions. Piaget tried to trace the beginning of these transitions in two experiments. However, a very important caution was included (**102a**, p.134). The composition of two or more couples, e.g. AB and $A.$non-B does correspond to propositional operations (pvq), but not to the operators N, R or C which operate on these propositions. In addition, there is another important difference between a propositional combinatorial and one of classes. In a propositional combinatorial each of the sixteen binary propositional operations has a specific, clearly delimited meaning (implication, disjunction, etc.). But a composed couple of classes shows no more than a weak degree of increase in complexity. The differences between the classes remain analogous to those opposing one couple to another. Psychologically one might compare such compositions of two, three or more couples to their isomorphic transformations N, R, C and I, but this would imply reflexive abstraction and not a construction by reflective abstraction.

Piaget did two experiments to study the transition from a simple Klein group to the INRC group; one with rotations and one with classes. In the second, comparisons requiring reflected abstraction were added. Though the experiments are probably simple to execute, it is difficult to summarize the material used and the interpretation of the results. Therefore only the conclusions are summarized though they do not add much news to the foregoing.

For Piaget it ''seems nearly evident'' that the reflective abstraction and generalization leading to the use of the INRC group (not its conscious thematization!) are prepared by successive abstractions to which the elementary Klein group leads. Thanks to the latter the subject learns to manipulate four basic associations and to relate them in couples of two or three. But in order to get from there to the INRC group the child must first differentiate the separate compositions which will become part of the combinatorial and then differentiate the inverse N, etc. This requires reflected abstraction and is therefore only a late development.

A final remark takes us back to propositions at the stage of concrete operations. Recent research and Piaget's related notions, emphasize once more the fundamental difference between the level of propositions and that of operators on propositions. Recent research at the Centre has studied propositional thinking in young children. According to a personal communication from Piaget, the researchers did succeed in finding all sixteen binary propositions when using suitable material. But the children were still incapable of integrating them. This confirms the results of the last experiment mentioned. It is to be hoped that the results will become available soon as they will throw further light on the development of the child's natural logic and might rectify a lot of misunderstandings and misinterpretations.

D || The Biological Foundation of Knowledge

12 Organic and Cognitive Regulations

☐The critique of Chapter 12 and Chapter 13 is combined in Chapter 23. After some general arguments (23.1), topics are arranged from the most specific (assimilation-accommodation) to the most general (evolution). When Piaget was still a schoolboy he published his first article on molluscs and in 1966 his last (**22**)! Fortunately, he only gave part of his time and interest to pond snails and an alpine plant, mainly building up his career as a genetic epistemologist. But the dates of the biological publications show how fascinated Piaget has been by a biological problem. This can easily be understood when one realizes that, according to Piaget, "psychogenesis can be understood only if its organic roots are exposed" (**48**, p.60/p.52).

The relationship between psychogenesis and the organism has several aspects: in the first place, actions which are the basis of cognitive development depend on the nervous system; in the second place, there are structural and functional "isomorphisms"; and in the third place, organic and cognitive development both progress as an "epigenetic system". All three aspects are discussed in *Biology and Knowledge* (**32**), one of Piaget's favourite books.

☐For most readers it is a difficult book, because Piaget writes for both psychologists and biologists, switching from psychology to biology and vice versa. Another difficulty is due to the fact that Piaget demonstrates how correct his own theory—that we give meaning to objects by assimilating them to our schemes—is. The "objects" are standard terms like "genome", "gene pool", etc. which are given their own "signification" through Piaget's notions. It is already enough of a problem for psychologists to understand modern genetics, and therefore Piaget's assimilations instead of accommodations do not make the reader's life any easier.

Finally, Piaget's study of the variations found in many successive generations of molluscs and sedum plants directed his interest to theories of evolution. These have been elaborated in two more recent books (**83**, **96**). However, again Piaget's interest is not limited to the biological aspect but also includes the analogy with cognitive development. This aspect of evolution will be summarized in Chapter 13. (I shall follow *Biology and Knowledge* in this chapter.)

☐ In 1966 Piaget published his Conclusion as a separate article (**26**), and in 1970 summarized some of the main ideas in Chapter 2 of *The Principles of Genetic Epistemology* (**48**).

12.1 Piaget's Guiding Hypothesis

Piaget's guiding hypothesis is

"*Cognitive processes seem, then, to be at one and the same time the outcome of organic autoregulation, reflecting its essential mechanisms, and the most highly differentiated organs of this regulation at the core of interactions with the environment,* so much so that, in the case of man, these processes are being extended to the universe itself." (**32**, p.49/p.26, italics in text)

A close look at this hypothesis shows how much Piaget puts into one sentence. Cognitive processes are the outcome of organic autoregulations, which takes us to the question of the role of the nervous system and to that of the epigenetic system. Cognitive processes reflect the essential mechanisms of organic organization which takes us to the question of "isomorphisms" between the two types of regulations. Cognitive processes are an organ, which raises the question as to what that means. I shall use these questions as a guide-line to the rest of this chapter, though in a different order.

12.2 Structures and Functions

12.2.1 Structural and Functional Isomorphisms

In comparing biological structures and functions with cognitive ones, Piaget often uses the terms "isomorphism" and "correspondence", adding a differentiation between "complete" and "partial" isomorphisms, and "general" and "specific" correspondences.

In structural isomorphisms two structures are compared. The simplest and most non-technical way of describing what this means is to say that *there is an isomorphism between two structures when the same structure is applied to two different sets of elements* (**32**, p.199/p.140).

Complete isomorphisms between structures are rare, but there are degrees of similarity. Logicians do not accept such degrees, being convinced that there is either a complete isomorphism or none at all. But Piaget thinks that the concept of *partial isomorphism* is useful. One must, evidently, accept certain conditions, otherwise one could always find that two objects have "something" in common. The first condition is that one must be able to indicate the processes by which one structure is transformed into another to which it is compared. The second is that these transformations must correspond to a real and observable process of a historical or developmental nature. Both conditions can be fulfilled in the comparison of organic and cognitive structures.

Partial isomorphisms are most useful in comparing structures of different levels of complexity, where the most complex structure is a reconstruction of the more primitive one.

> **Example:** Relations of order are found at organic levels, from the genes in the DNA on. In cognitive development there are activities of "ordering" from the sensorimotor level on to complex systems of seriation. These orderings are constructions and reconstructions, and the analysis of what all the organic and cognitive "orderings" have in common is most useful (**32**, p.92/p.58).

The problem of functional isomorphisms is more complicated because one and the same biological function can use very different structures. For instance, assimilation at the physiological level uses quite different structures to those used by assimilation at the behavioural level. Therefore one cannot compare functions in the same way as structures. However, it might be useful to compare them in a more general way which Piaget calls *"correspondence"*. In Piaget's words,

> "In this very general sense we may therefore make a functional comparison of the part played by the two regulatory mechanisms in widely different structures, insofar as they both have the final effect of reinforcing or inhibiting some activity in proportion to the result immediately preceding."
>
> (**32**, p.203/p.143)

> **Example:** An example of such a correspondence can be seen when biologists speak of "memory" as the conservation of information by an organism of a very low level. There is no similarity with human memory at the structural level, but in the sense of "conservation of an experience that modifies the following behaviour" there is a functional correspondence.

If there are "partial" structural isomorphisms, one might expect something analogous where functions are concerned. This is indeed true, but in another sense, that is to say, as *"general" and "specialized" functions.*

If the functions characterizing cognitive mechanisms were exactly the same as the main functions of organisms, knowledge would have no functions of its own, which would evidently be absurd. This takes us back to Piaget's main hypothesis. He supposes in this hypothesis that

> "certain general functions common to both organic and cognitive mechanisms do exist, but that, in the case of cognitive mechanisms, a progressive specialization of functions also exists."   (**32**, p.206, p.145)

These specialized functions will take us to the "organ" mentioned in the hypothesis.

12.2.2 A Comparison of the Functions and Structures of the Organism and Cognition

12.2.2.1 Organization

After all that was said about organization in Chapter 5, only some remarks concerning the comparison have to be added.

As a general function, organization is so all-pervasive that one might say that it is identical to life itself. And knowledge of any level contains an organization too. Functional cognitive and biological organization are both characterized by continuity and conservation, differentiation and integration, and by reconstruction.

There is, however, an important specialization as well, and this shows clearly the specificity and originality of knowledge. The main specific characteristic of knowledge is the progressive separation of content and form, and—in consequence—the deductive rigour of cognitive conservations.

In animal life and at the beginning of the sensorimotor stage, form and content are indissolubly linked. But at the pre-operational level the first dissociations can be seen and these proceed rapidly until the dissociation is more or less complete at the formal level. This "natural" logic then makes it possible for scientific thought to construct a reflexive or axiomatic logic and "pure" mathematics. In biological organisms no comparable dissociation of form and content is found and therefore this dissociation is a specialized function within the larger frame of organization (**32**, p.217/p.154).

Turning to the structures of organization, we see that cognitive structures are just as much characterized by cycles as biological organization is. This does not seem to be true of deductive reasoning or of mathematics, but this is due to the fact that reasoning has been ''constructed'' in a non-cyclical way. However, psychologically, every system of knowledge is ''circular'' and the extension of knowledge consists of a widening of the field of knowledge. Even the classification of sciences has this structure, as Piaget argues in several publications. Sciences can be grouped in a circle instead of being linearly linked as is often claimed. As the ''cycles'' are essential in adaptation I shall return to this topic in the next paragraph.

Another similarity is that classification and ordering are biological as well as cognitive structures. Piaget argues in detail that classification plays a role at all levels of life: instincts distinguish food from non-food, materials suitable or unsuitable for nest-building, etc. Cognitive classification differs from instincts in that it becomes intentional and reflexive—that is, conscious—whether the classification is pre-scientific or scientific. However, this is only a difference of degree, classification as such being found at all levels of organization (32, p.231/p.163). An analogous reasoning is given for ordering.

12.2.2.2 Adaptation

a) *The biological cycle and the epigenetic system*
Adaptation can refer to a state of adaptedness of the organism to its environment, or to a process of becoming adapted. The latter occurs as soon as the environment changes. In both cases there is a *cycle of adaptation.*

A state of adaptation might be represented as follows, using a very abstract presentation:

$$(A \times A') \rightarrow (B \times B') \rightarrow (C \times C') \rightarrow (D \times D') \rightarrow ...(Z \times Z') \rightarrow (A \times A')...$$

(32, p.220/p.156, and p.242/p.172).

A, B, C etc. are ''elements'' of a system and A', B', C' etc. are external elements that are necessary to keep it going. If '' $\times$ '' indicates ''interaction'' and '' $\rightarrow$ '' the result of this interaction, there is thus a system returning to its starting point. But when the environment changes a process of adaptation is required as well. Then B' might become B''. This leads to a local change of C into C_2, but without a loss in the cyclic form. Thus we get:

$$(A \times A') \rightarrow (B \times B'') \rightarrow (C_2 \times C') \rightarrow (D \times D')... \rightarrow (Z \times Z') \rightarrow (A \times A')...$$

In this case C_2 is an example of accommodation and as the cycle is not destroyed, the cycle is a case of a process of adaptation.

Thinking of the emphasis on "improving" equilibration (see Chapter 9), one might wonder why the cyclic form of the system implies a return to the original ($A \times A'$). This becomes clear in the later book on phenocopies (83, see Chapter 13), where Piaget gives the same cycle. He emphasizes how this adaptation gives the maximum of cyclic coherence to the system. But, at the same time, there is a dynamic and even innovative reaction which guarantees an adjustment of the system to unexpected circumstances (83, p.17). This cyclic form of equilibrium between assimilation and accommodation characterizes the first level of interaction between subject and object and should be distinguished from the hierarchical equilibration of the third level, that of differentiations and integration.

The fundamental functions of adaptation are embodied in all sorts of structures at all levels, from the genome to the highest cognitive mechanisms. Before going into the behavioural structures, the importance of assimilation and accommodation will be shown by a short passage on *the epigenetic system.*

In his research on pond snails and the sedum plant Piaget was fascinated by their variations in different environmental circumstances. This evidently led to questions concerning the relation between genotype and phenotype. I shall summarize Piaget's critique of Lamarckism and neo-Darwinism in Chapter 13 as a short introduction to his hypotheses on phenocopies. For the present, however, I will only go into his own interpretation of the epigenetic system. In studying other biological theories Piaget is above all interested in those theories that consider the organism active and developing in interaction with the environment. At the embryological and evolutionary level this implies that the organism's genetic endowment, the genotype, actively interacts with the environment in developing into the phenotype of the mature organism.

Though there are several biologists whose work Piaget appreciates for this point of view, he has been most impressed by the work of Waddington. Waddington is one of the neo-Darwinists, but Piaget prefers to see his theory as a *tertium quid* between extremes of Lamarckism and neo-Darwinism.

In his theory of evolution Waddington distinguishes four main subsystems, the epigenetic system being one of them. *Waddington defines the epigenetic system as "the sequence of causal processes which bring about the devel-*

opment of the fertilized zygote into the adult capable of reproduction'' (**452**, p.58). This process is due to the genes and their reactions to the stresses of the environment. The characteristics of the epigenetic system which interest Piaget most are *"chreods"* and *"homeorhesis"*. *A "chreod" is a predetermined trajectory of change along which an organ or a part of the embryo develops with a built-in time-tally, or sequence in time.* At certain points chreods may open up differing possibilities. The total of chreods, each of them more or less profoundly canalized, is called the "epigenetic landscape" by Waddington. The landscape symbolizes the chreods as more or less deep canals and valleys, some of them dividing into smaller separate valleys. The phenotype of an organ, a part of an embryo, or a characteristic is like a ball rolling through these valleys, making a choice at points of separating pathways. Piaget uses the more general name "epigenetic system" for the epigenetic landscape, as he is not impressed by the new name nor by the symbolic representation. For him the main point of interest is what happens under the influence of stresses from the environment. Under the influence of the environment a phenotypic characteristic may be forced to deviate from the chreod it is following. Unless this deviation is too fundamental, the phenotype will return to its chreod by the interplay of coercive compensations (**32**, p.39/p.19). This return to an equilibrium is due to a complex interplay of genetic regulations. Because of its dynamic character and the time factor Waddington calls it "homeorhesis" instead of "homeostasis" as a more static equilibrium in physics is called. For Piaget homeorhesis characterizes equilibration, and homeostasis equilibrium. The return of a phenotype to "its" chreod shows a tendency to conserve the predetermined way of development. However, there is also a certain flexibility as there may be viable modifications that take an "abnormal" form when the stresses are too strong. The latter is the most important aspect in a theory of evolution, but there is no need to go into that now.

One of the reasons why Piaget attaches so much importance to the epigenetic system is its close analogy with the stages of cognitive development. Intellectual growth has its rhythm and "chreods", just like physical growth, which explains why it is so difficult to change the speed of development (**32**, p.42/p.21). But, this does not mean for Piaget that knowledge is given ready-made in the genotype, or in the nervous system. It only means that heredity and maturation open up possibilities at certain moments of development. There is an analogous epigenetic process in cognition and organic development, but notwithstanding this similarity, one has to recognize that the influence of the physical as well as the social environment is much more important in the development of knowledge. However, for Piaget the essential question is not what the quantitative proportion of genetic and environmental factors is. From the point of view of qualitative analogies

> "it seems obvious that internal coordinations of the necessary and constant type, which make possible the integration of exterior cognitive aliment, give rise to the same biological problem of collaboration between the genome and the environment as do all the other forms of organization which occur in the course of development."   (**32**, p.45/p.23)

□Criticism of the epigenetic system is found in 23.2.3.

b) *Instincts and logico-mathematical structures*

Adaptation presupposes that animals and humans have a certain "know-how" and this leads us to instincts and knowledge. An epistemological approach to instincts must look for the necessary and sufficient conditions of the instinctive "know-how" of animals, which will then allow a comparison with human intelligence.

In view of this comparison, three hierarchically ordered levels of instinctual conduct must be distinguished. The first level is characterized by the general coordinations found in all instances of instinctual conduct. One example of such coordinations is seen in what Piaget calls "the logic of organs". Such a logic is seen in the sequences of actions which are a type of ordering, and in the inclusion of subschemes into total schemes which give them a significance.

> **Example:** The red belly of the stickleback is perceived by an instinctual scheme, which is a sub-scheme in relation to the total scheme of sexual combat.

Another example of coordinations is the transindividual nature of instincts. The example of the stickleback illustrates its meaning. Though the instinctual structures are imposed from within, they are coordinated with a different structure of the partner or partners.

> **Example:** A non-sexual example is the transindividual behaviour of parents and offspring, and the different types of behaviour of the members of a beehive.

The logic of organs, described in this way, is more than a simple metaphor. It

> "does in fact contain the basic structures of inclusion and relationship—in a form both additive and multiplicative—that

occur in the logic of acquired sensorimotor schemes and,
better still, in operational logic." (**32**, p.329/p.235)
The second level is the hereditary programming of the content of
behaviour. The third level shows individual adjustments to variations
in the environment. Some instincts are completely rigid, but there is
also—especially in the higher animals—a certain flexibility, as the
study of the epigenetic system shows. Though Piaget goes into many
details concerning instincts, there is no need to follow him, as our only
interest is in the possible comparison of them with human knowledge.

A look at the three levels mentioned shows that the second is nearly
completely lost in humans. As Piaget writes "instincts exploded" into
interiorization, which corresponds to the first level of coordinations,
and exteriorization, which corresponds to learning and experimenting
in the interaction with external circumstances.

In Piaget's theory the development of logico-mathematical structures through equilibration as described in Section C of this book, is
very different from learning. The difference can be illustrated by the
comparison of number-concepts and counting, as given in *Biology and
Knowledge* (**32**, p.427ff/p.309ff).

Piaget had argued in earlier works that numbers are a synthesis of
inclusion ((1) being included in (1 + 1), then (1 + 1) in (1 + 1 + 1), etc.)
and of order (taking 1,1,1, etc. in a specific order as these elements
cannot be distinguished otherwise). A one-to-one correspondence in
the comparison of two sets of elements is an expression of this synthesis.

The young child evidently needs objects to classify and to seriate, but
the actions of uniting, including, etc. are not taken from these objects
because such relationships are found as preliminary conditions in all
forms of coordinations, whether it be at the level of behaviour, of the
nervous system, of physiological functioning or, in general, the organization of living organisms. In such a case experience or drill may be
necessary to learn to apply these general relations to specific problems,
and/or objects must be handled in "pseudo-empirical" abstraction,
but the origin is to be found at a far deeper, biological, level.

As for the learning of animals, Piaget mentions that O. Koehler has
succeeded in teaching jackdaws and budgerigars to find the fourth
object in a row. But notwithstanding the admirable results, the learning of the birds shows clear limitations. Their success does not go
beyond five units and is influenced by spatio-temporal patterns. But,
above all, the bird has not learned an iterative system. When it is able
to find the fourth object of a row, it has not learned to find the second

and the third. Once a child has a real understanding of numbers—
instead of having been taught to count—he sees that $1 + 1 = 2$, $2 + 1 = 3$,
etc.

Notwithstanding the fundamental difference between a true number
concept and "counting" by the bird or by a pre-operational child,
there are common features between the two.

Considering what we have written so far about Piaget's theory, it is
not astonishing that he does not interpret the learning of the bird and
the pre-operational child as the result of a passive acquisition due to
endless repetitions. In itself repetition is useless, as is shown by the
failure to train lower animals. What happens is that the bird or the pre-
operational child can learn a correspondence in spatio-temporal patterns that are not numerical in themselves. This is possible because the
"numerical" aspect that is learned is an actualization of general coordinations available at this level. At the higher level these same general
coordinations will lead to immediate "insight". Thus we see a continuity between the beginnings of logico-mathematical experience and
later logico-mathematical structures.

If logico-mathematical structures are not learned, they might be
inherited. This notion is only acceptable if one takes "inherited" in a
very broad sense. "Hereditary" would then have to mean that these
structures are due to the living organization which is continued from
one generation to the next. But "hereditary" is then taken in a very
broad sense indeed. Some biologists distinguish "general" heredity
and "specific" heredity, the former characterizing general traits of
organization common to living beings of several levels, the latter
characterizing species or races. Originally Piaget thought that logico-
mathematical structures might belong to these general characteristics
in contrast to specific properties like spatial perception in two or three
dimensions. But there are several arguments against this supposition
(**32**, p.448/p.324), and Piaget now prefers to distinguish organization
as such in its permanent functioning from any hereditarily transmitted
characteristic, either general or specific.

Being neither learnt nor inherited, logico-mathematical structures
are the result of progressive equilibrations by reflective abstraction
and, at higher levels, reflexive thought. There is no need to repeat the
mechanisms of this process nor the self-regulating processes in general.

The fact that instincts "explode" in this way, might give the impression that there is no real link between the biological and the higher
levels of intelligence. However, there are clearly common characteris-

tics: organization, logic, etc. But in order to make such comparisons profitable one has to realize that there is *a fundamental difference between instincts and intelligence. This difference is found in the fact that forms of thought can be applied to ever greater distances in space and time, and thus can create an environment that becomes wider and more stable.* The operational instruments themselves, helped by semiotic instruments (language and writing), have a greater continuity because they can retain the past, and, due to their reversibility, have a dynamic stability that no biological organism can reach.

12.2.2.3 Anticipation

The importance of anticipations is due to the fact that they are based on the conservation of what is inherited, acquired or constructed. Even a simple conditioned reflex, as demonstrated by Pavlov's dog, contains an element of anticipation. The sound of the bell only leads to salivation when it announces food. When the food does not follow any more, there is extinction because the anticipation has not been "confirmed". But at the other extreme of development, anticipations are just as important. In order to test his hypothesis a scientist has to organize his experiments in such a way that predictions or anticipations can be confirmed or disconfirmed.

12.2.2.4 Equilibration

The parallels between organic and cognitive equilibration need only be mentioned for the sake of completeness as there is nothing to add to what has been said in the foregoing sections.
  □This topic is important for some critics, see 23.2.2.

12.3 Structures and the Brain

Though there is not much to say on this topic, it is nevertheless an important one. Piaget emphasizes in many publications that formal logico-mathematical structures are reconstructions of concrete operational structures. These in turn are reconstructions of what has been constructed at the pre-operational stage, and this in turn takes us back to the coordinations of actions. Furthermore, Piaget emphasizes repeatedly that the sensorimotor stage is not the beginning. Going back takes him to the hypothesis that these coordinations of actions presuppose neural coordinations. He often quotes an article by McCulloch and Pitts who found, in their analysis of neuronal operators, isomorphisms between the transformations underlying synaptic connections and the logical operators (*32*, p.312/p.222). Within Piaget's theory this is, of course, a hopeful beginning for a further elaboration.

    ☐More recent research is mentioned in 23.2.5.

13 Biological and Cognitive Phenocopies

□The critique of Chapters 12 and 13 is combined in Chapter 23.
The study of many generations of molluscs and sedum plants with their genotypical and/or phenotypical changes forms a natural starting point for speculations on evolution. Piaget admits that his two recent books (**83, 96**) are highly speculative and contain a number of "risky" hypotheses, but he has published them nevertheless in the hope of challenging biologists to a discussion.

In general, Piaget tries to find a middle position between a theory in which the environmental influence is stressed and the other extreme in which the influence of the organism itself is emphasized. This corresponds to his constructivist position in epistemology. Before going into his *tertium quid* between Lamarckism and neo-Darwinism, his arguments against those theories of evolution will be summarized.

13.1 Piaget's Critique of Lamarckism and Neo-Darwinism

13.1.1 Lamarckism

Lamarck developed two fundamental notions that have not been integrated within his theory. In some of Lamarck's writings they are simply mentioned separately while in others they are contradictory.

The first, well-known, idea is that animals form habits under the influence of external circumstances and that these lead to morphological changes. His example of the giraffe with its long neck is most often quoted and easily ridiculed, but in fact Lamarck gave a great number of more plausible examples. Sometimes he writes that there are "needs" relating new behaviour and morphological changes. But he reduces their importance by saying that new needs of longer duration lead to new habits. So Lamarck's fundamental interpretation of the relation between habits and the animal's organs is that circumstances change habits and these in turn change the animal's organs, or may even lead to new ones.

The second idea is that of an organizing process forming the internal driving force of evolution while not being the result of behaviour nor of external circumstances. The main difficulty is that these two causes of changes remain heterogeneous in Lamarck's writings and often even contradictory. Piaget's interpretation, already given in 1967 (32), is that Lamarck's emphasis on the "fact" that habits are due to external circumstances implies that "the growing composition of the organization" must be seen as associationist. This associationist way of organization would tend to be confounded with the coordination of habits. This would be comparable to what Hull has come to call "hierarchic families of habits". However this may be, either Lamarck considers the habits as "acts of organization" (as he does in some texts), and then tends towards a model of organization as a "composition" of habits themselves, or he maintains (as he does in other texts) two separate concepts or causes of change which he does not synthesize.

There are several reasons why Piaget cannot accept Lamarck's ideas, notwithstanding a certain appreciation.

To begin with, Lamarck does not explain why the animal gets into the new circumstances in the first place. Environments rarely change in a fundamental way. Piaget's own explanation is, of course, in accord with Waddington, Monod and others, that the animal "chooses" his new environment.

□ Monod is attacked by Piaget when he stresses the importance of chance in his theory of evolution, but other ideas of Monod are much appreciated by Piaget. The interested reader is referred to Piaget's chapter (50) on Monod's book.

More fundamental than this point is the fact that Piaget cannot accept purely environmental influences. As I have said in several of the foregoing chapters, any influence of the environment consists of an assimilation into a scheme, that is to say, a combination of the external and the internal. Any change through accommodation is therefore, as well, a combination of the external (exogenous) that could be assimilated, and the internal (endogenous) that has assimilated.

The second point of criticism is the fact that Lamarck does not succeed in integrating the two causes mentioned. This is due, according to Piaget, to the empiricist interpretation of behaviour implied in the idea that the environment alone can influence behaviour. At the same time, many confusions arise from the fact that Lamarck did not clearly identify what he meant by "habits", using a global term at the same time for what is in fact due to hereditary instincts and for purely phenotypical habits—in the belief that the second are a prolongation of the first.

As for Lamarck's organization, this can only be seen as an associationist whole and there is hardly any need to say that this is unacceptable to Piaget.

For Piaget the value of Lamarckism is to be found in the fact that Lamarck did emphasize the importance of the animal's behaviour in the environment, while mentioning the internal organization. But he certainly does not consider himself a Lamarckist or neo-Lamarckist.

13.1.2 Neo-Darwinism

The two central ideas in Darwin's conception of evolution were: small variations and their progressive selection. These notions were not fundamentally changed by the fact that he integrated the essence of Lamarckism into his theory in the sixth edition of *The Origin of Species*.

After the rediscovery of Mendel's laws and the discovery of mutations, Darwinism was revived as neo-Darwinism, called "classical neo-Darwinism" by Piaget. Classical neo-Darwinism or "mutationism", stresses the internal structures of the organism because mutations have their starting point in the organism, and selection by the environment only follows at the end stage. Another characteristic of mutationism is its atomism. Genes are considered independent units and selection ends up by singling out individual genes as if they were adult or complete units (**32**, p.162/p.112).

Though Piaget cannot accept any form of atomism, his main argument against classical neo-Darwinism is that it accepts far too many accidental events that are then combined by a favourable chance. Suppose that new behaviour is the result of mutations that can survive and are then selected after the event. This origin of new behaviour would have to be accepted as a chance result. Then it meets—by chance—an environment favouring its survival. This means already two favourable results of chance that are independent of each other. Then there is a structural modification of an organ—once more the result of a chance mutation—and selective adjustment in which chance must play a role. This implies two new influences due to chance. So many chance effects in cumulation are completely unacceptable to Piaget.

☐There are probably many other arguments against mutationism, but they are no longer important because in this century evolutionists have developed a new synthesis, or synthetic theory of evolution. This is often called "neo-Darwinism" as well. One of these neo-Darwinists was Waddington, but Piaget prefers to see Waddington's theory as quite different, calling it a *tertium quid* between Lamarckism and neo-Darwinism. In this way he could admire Waddington and "assimilate" his notions without "accommodating" his own theory, as I mentioned in the context of the epigenetic system.

13.2 Piaget's Theory of Evolution

Piaget's theory of evolution (**83, 96**) concentrates on small changes in evolution. He develops a hypothesis for explaining phenocopies which is important because he then looks for isomorphisms with what he calls "cognitive phenocopies" (**83, 91**).

13.2.1 Phenocopies

There are different definitions of what is meant by *"phenocopy"*. *Piaget prefers to define it as a "replacement of an initial phenotype by a subsequent genotype presenting the same characteristics"* (**91**, p.809).

☐The definition most often given is "a phenotypic change that simulates a genotypic change." Waddington introduced another term "genetic assimilation". The process of genetic assimilation is defined by him as "one by which a phenotypic character, which initially is produced only in response to some environmental influence, becomes, through a process of selection, taken over by the genotype, so that it is formed even in the absence of the environmental influence which had at first been necessary" (**452**, p.91).

Piaget's hypotheses on phenocopies were inspired by his research on pond snails, already mentioned several times. The essential data are that *Limnaea stagnalis* usually has an elongated shell but gets a much shorter shell with a broader opening in water troubled by strong wind and waves. This is a morphological difference, and even a behavioural one, as the organism has chosen the running water—thus Piaget. The observed and carefully measured differences in shell raise the question of how it can be explained and above all whether it is a phenotypical or a genotypical difference.

Analogous differences were found in the alpine plant, sedum, also studied by Piaget for many years. Here again the question is whether changes are phenotypical or genotypical (**25, 83**).

Both studies showed that certain organisms have a very constant variety in comparison to the normal phenotype as long as they develop in the same, originally unusual, environment. When the organism is returned to its original habitat, it should follow its usual chreod in the next generation if the variety is no more than a phenotypical change, repeating itself in every generation because this happens to be the best adaptation to these circumstances. This is in fact what happens sometimes. But it was also found that the next generations continued to show the same changed variety though there was no longer an adaptive "reason" for it. One has to conclude that the genotype changed.

The following summarizes Piaget's explanation of these changes, called "phenocopies". Piaget uses the name though he believes that it is misleading as there is no copy at all.

The normal construction of a phenotype from a given genotype is indicated by Piaget as "$\uparrow a$". This hereditarily programmed movement starts from the DNA of the genome, passes on to the RNA, then to the entire system of the germinal cell with its regulations, and so on until the level of behaviour is reached. Each of those systems has its own regulations within the system but there are also autoregulations within the total system (**83**, p.57). When an organism is transplanted into a different environment "$\downarrow b$" indicates the influence of the changes imposed by the environment. If the environment has the unusual characteristics x, y, z, the phenotype finds a compromise between its original epigenetic development and these characteristics by producing the phenotypic variations x', y', z'. These new characteristics then cause a disequilibrium at a lower level of the organism indicated as x'', y'' and z''. According to Piaget, there is an essential difference between $\uparrow a$ and $\downarrow b$. While $\uparrow a$ carries the information contained in the DNA, the vector $\downarrow b$ only gives feedback that something has gone wrong, without specifying in any way what has gone wrong. This message leads to a third force $\uparrow c$ consisting of "gropings" or exploratory efforts. In other words, the characteristics x', y', z' are the result of the conjunction $(\downarrow b) \times (\uparrow c)$. In the case of x'', y'' and z'', the message that something is wrong is transmitted by $\downarrow b$ to ever deeper levels of the organism until the regulating genes, responsible for the realization of the epigenetic program become sensitized to the fact that something has gone wrong. The result is that the genes will react with different ''gropings'', either consisting in efforts to return to the former equilibrium without mutations or by producing a number of mutations. Those mutations will, in part, be due to chance but not entirely, as they are limited within the field where disequilibriums have occurred. The mutations themselves are therefore considered a kind of explorations. The final question is how those mutations that lead to a better equilibrium will be selected. The first internal or organic selection must exclude those variations that might be lethal or pathogenic as well as those that conflict with the stable system of the organism. The remaining variations, concerned with regions of disequilibrium—as in the case of new phenotypes—will be selected in a second round by the criterion of equilibration. These variations that increase the disequilibrium will be barred from the higher level, while those that decrease the disequilibrium reach a higher level and so on. The end result of this reequilibration will be very similar to that of a simple phenotypic change of the type x', y', z' because the mutations are not taking place in just any directions but are gropings resulting from the disequilibrium x'', y'', z'', and the organic selection sees to it that a choice is made compatible with the external characteristics x, y, z.

But though the end result of a phenotypic change and of a phenocopy may look very much alike, their mechanisms are completely different. In a phenotypic change the environmental characteristics x, y, z are a direct cause of the phenotypic characteristics x', y', z'. In the case of genetic variations due to the disequilibrium x'', y'', z'' the environment is no more than a mould into which the mutations have to fit. This difference is more than playing with words as the causal effect is a positive one, while the influence of a mould is only a negative elimination of those variations that do not fit. The mutations are not caused by the environment, either internal or external, but are entirely endogenous. They explore the zones of disequilibrium until the mould accepts them as adequate solutions. In other words, new phenotypes x', y', z' are no more than temporary compromises between the epigenetic program and the environment. As long as this does not lead to disequilibrium x'', y'', z'', there is no need for further change. As soon as the organism is returned to its original environment the phenotype will be normal in the next generation. In contrast, the phenocopy is a new program that does not lead to a return to its former phenotype when the organism finds itself again in its original environment.

The elaboration of phenocopies given in the foregoing rests on the ''risky'' hypothesis that the process of the phenocopy is a rather general one. It is as though every new adaptation must begin by explorations and phenotypic trials. But notwithstanding the importance of phenocopies resulting from such an assumption, Piaget readily admits that they might explain no more than "elementary" changes. There must, therefore, be higher levels of evolution, but there is no need to summarize Piaget's hypotheses elaborated in **96**.

Though theorizing about phenocopies may seem a long way from epistemology, there is a clear link for Piaget. His hypothesis is one more effort to refute the importance of mutational chance, on the one hand, and Lamarckism or neo-Lamarckism on the other. He is a constructivist, whether as epistemologist, psychologist or biologist.

13.2.2 The Cognitive Equivalent of Phenocopies

13.2.2.1 The general development from exogenous to endogenous

Piaget's second hypothesis concerning phenocopies is that there is a certain relationship between organic and cognitive phenocopies, as though the properties of equilibration and autoregulation found in all domains of life would bring with them a general tendency to reconstruct internally the unstable acquisitions of an exogenous nature (**83**, p.103).

In comparing biological phenocopies and cognitive processes, Piaget is only interested in higher levels of cognition, i.e. intelligence, and not in perception, etc.

In biological phenocopies the main characteristic is that something exogenous is replaced by something endogenous. Looking for an analogous characteristic in cognitive development, the first question is, "What is endogenous where intelligence is concerned?"

In intelligence "endogenous" describes the structures elaborated by regulations and operations of the subject (**83**, p.74). This extension of the term "endogenous" is justified because logico-mathematical structures are based upon the coordinations of actions, and not on experience. It is necessary for two reasons. In the first place, intellectual structures are not innate, and in the second place, the coordinations of actions—though not hereditary—form a continuation of organic regulations. Thus "exogenous" can be used for knowledge taken from physical experience and "endogenous" for knowledge due to logico-mathematical structures.

The development from exogenous to endogenous can best be illustrated by the science of physics. Though trying to understand and to explain the external world of objects, the physicist has recourse to axioms, deductions and mathematical models as if he were trying to get away as much as possible from the world of objects. An explanation of this situation is found in the fact that logico-mathematical structures allow the scientist to introduce an intrinsic necessity into a system that was no more than locally coherent. Here we see a first analogy with phenocopies, where the contingency of environment × epigenesis is replaced by an internal genetic determination. But there is a second analogy as well. In the phenocopy, the characteristics x, y, z of the environment play at first a direct causal role while being no more than a frame posing a limit to the selections of changes once a genotypical change is taking place. Comparing mathematics and physics we find an analogous situation. The physicist-mathematician knows that his deductive laws and principles have to fit experimental data, though these have no causal influence on the mechanisms of his deductions. The third analogy is seen in the fact that the details of the mechanisms which construct the final level are to be found in a succession of disequilibriums and reequilibrations.

Piaget believes that if one still finds the comparison artificial his theory of causality should make his notions more convincing. At all psychogenetic levels, and at all levels of the history of physics, causality consists of attributing our operations and logico-mathematical structures to objects. This implies, again, that empirical knowledge about external objects is replaced by the necessary compositions of internal operational structures, and this replacement is, of course, a reconstruction.

13.2.2.2 The detailed comparison of cognitive development and phenocopies

Cognitive development proceeds by empirical and reflective abstraction. In the context of this chapter, the mechanisms of empirical abstraction are analogous to phenotypical variations, and reflective abstraction is analogous to the nature of genotypes. This analogy is especially clear at the level of "pseudo-empirical abstraction". However, there are two fundamental differences between cognitive activities as the source of endogenous forms and the formative mechanism of genotypes. The first difference is that cognitive structures are not determined in detail by a program of the genome, and the second, related one, that reflective abstraction finally functions at a level of "pure" forms while a pure genotype without a realization in a geno-type is no more than a theoretical abstraction.

The question is, then, whether these differences are so fundamental as to invalidate the analogy or not. In a more concrete form: pheno-copies are only present when there is a change in the environment. In the cognitive domain, on the contrary, knowledge of objects is no more than a limited sector of all knowledge. "Cognitive phenocopies", there-fore, only seem to play a role in physical knowledge, excluding the vast field of logico-mathematical knowledge. A closer analysis of the cogni-tive process will show whether this limitation is justified or not.

In the description of the phenocopy the vectors $\uparrow a$, $\downarrow b$ and $\uparrow c$ were distinguished. In cognitive development $\uparrow a$ characterizes the successive hierarchical levels of cognitive structures. These levels can be charac-terized as a widening spiral in which the spiral represents reflective abstraction. The spiral is "surrounded" by empirical abstractions which also widen (**83**, p.86). The interactions between empirical abstraction and reality are the vectors $\rightarrow b$ and $\leftarrow c$. While the cogni-tive vector $\uparrow a$ closely resembles the biological vector $\uparrow a$, there is more of a difference where $\downarrow b$ and $\uparrow c$ are concerned. In the cognitive epi-genesis $\downarrow b$ does not reach down to the genome, but has rather a "hori-zontal" influence, $\rightarrow b$, or sometimes $\nearrow b$ or $\searrow b$. This means that the actions of objects or the events in the environment only influence the endogenous processes of the same level, possibly with repercussions on the immediately lower level or on that which is being constructed. Analogously c must be symmetrical with b and therefore, on average, $\leftarrow c$.

The comparison thus shows a relationship between organic and cognitive epigenesis, but it is clear that this is limited to physical knowl-edge. Logico-mathematical knowledge becomes freed of the relation-ship with the external world and is therefore not in need of cognitive phenocopies.

The notion of a development from exogenous to endogenous is also essential in the analogy between biological and cognitive equilibration.

In *Biology and Knowledge* Piaget described biological development as a process of "convergent resconstructions with overtaking" ("récon-structions convergentes avec dépassements"). Convergent reconstruc-tions consist of endogenous reconstructions of what has been given at the level of the genes, recombining them according to needs and lacunae in an interaction of the interior milieu and epigenetic syntheses. Such reconstructions that lead to a higher level must be assumed in order to explain the instincts that cannot be due to simple phenocopies. But the more limited scope of phenocopies does not exclude a close relationship with convergent reconstructions. The route to new and higher combinations might be opened up by originally simple schemes resulting from phenocopies. In phenocopies there is also a replacement from exogenous to endogenous and a reconstruction. The general mechanism of reequilibration found in phenocopies and in the more general convergent reconstructions is that of improving equilibration. This same form of general equilibration is found in cognitive development. So, whether one looks at biological or at cognitive processes, one always finds an ''overtaking'' by a reorganization containing new combinations but using elements taken from an earlier system.

References

The references in Volume I give Piaget's publications, while other authors are found in Volume II, whether their work is quoted in Volume I or in Volume II.

The numbers **1-14** give those early books that were used for this text. The numbers from **15-121** give Piaget's publications from 1965 on, as far as they were used for this text. This means that some prefaces and small contributions to congresses were left out, as well as specifically educational papers. A complete bibliography can be found in the catalogue of the Archives Jean Piaget.

Because I consider the chronological order of Piaget's work very important, I have followed that order as much as possible. In consequence all publications to which he has contributed have been entered under his name, whether he was the only author, the senior author, the last one mentioned in a team or an interviewee. Originally I planned to add the dates at which papers were read but this proved technically impossible. One exception has been made for a paper read in 1971 and published in 1977. If English readers miss a book, this will probably be due to the fact that it was translated during the period reviewed but published before 1965, e.g. the book on chance was published in 1951 and in English translation in 1975. The same is true for articles or papers. In the French volumes with reprints the first date of publication is given, and I think that the publishers of the translations did their readers a poor service by leaving them out.

In Volume II the numbers from **150** on are used, the order being that generally in use. (Please note that there are no numbers **122-149.**)

Some abbreviations
The following abbreviations might puzzle some readers:

E.E.G. = *Etudes d'épistémologie génétique*
P.U.F. = Presses Universitaires de France
Note: In Volume II *The Genetic Epistemologist* is mentioned as a journal.
This is a quarterly publication of the Jean Piaget Society.

1 Piaget, J. *La représentation du monde chez l'enfant.* Paris: Alcan, 1926. Translated: *The Child's Conception of the World.* New York: Harcourt & Brace, 1929.

2 Piaget, J. *La causalité physique chez l'enfant.* Paris: Alcan, 1927. Translated: *The Child's Conception of Physical Causality.* Totowa, N.J.: Littlefield, Adams, Patterson, 1960.

3 Piaget, J. Logique génétique et sociologie. *Revue philos. France l'Etranger,* 3/4, 161-205, 1928.

4 Piaget, J. *Le jugement moral chez l'enfant.* Paris: Alcan, 1932. Translated: *The Moral Judgment of the Child.* Glencoe, Illinois: The Free Press, 1948.

5 Piaget, J. *La naissance de l'intelligence chez l'enfant.* Neuchâtel: Delachaux & Niestlé, 1936. Translated: *The Origin of Intelligence in the Child.* London: Routledge & Kegan Paul, 1953.

6 Piaget, J. *La construction du réel chez l'enfant.* Neuchâtel: Delachaux & Niestlé, 1937. Translated: *The Construction of Reality in the Child.* New York: Basic Books, 1954.

7 Piaget, J. & Inhelder, B. *Le développement des quantités chez l'enfant.* Neuchâtel: Delachaux & Niestlé, 1941.

8 Piaget, J. *La formation du symbole chez l'enfant: Conservation et atomisme.* Neuchâtel: Delachaux & Niestlé, 1945. Translated: *Play, Dreams, Imitation in Childhood.* New York: Norton, 1951.

9 Piaget, J. & Inhelder, B. *La représentation de l'espace chez l'enfant.* Paris: P.U.F., 1948. Translated: *The Child's Conception of Space.* London: Routledge & Kegan Paul, 1956.

10 Piaget, J. *Traité de logique. Essai de logistique opératoire.* Paris: A.Colin, 1949. (2.ed. slightly revised by J.B. Grize, *Essai de logique opératoire.* Paris: Dunod, 1972.)

11 Piaget, J. *Logic and Psychology.* Manchester: Manchester University Press, 1953.

12 Inhelder, B. & Piaget, J. *De la logique de l'enfant à la logique de l'adolescent.* Paris: P.U.F., 1955. Translated: *The Growth of Logical Thinking from Childhood to Adolescence.* New York: Basic Books, 1958.

13 Piaget, J. Logique et équilibre dans les comportements du sujet. In L.Apostel, B.Mandelbrot & J. Piaget, *Logique et équilibre. E.E.G.* Vol.II. Paris: P.U.F., 1957.

14 Piaget, J. L'explication en psychologie et parallélisme psychophysiologique. In P.Fraisse & J.Piaget (Eds) *Traité de psychologie expérimentale,* Vol.I. Paris: P.U.F., 1963. Translated: *Experimental Psychology: its Scope and Method.* London: Routledge & Kegan Paul, 1968.

15 Piaget, J. *Sagesse et illusion de la philosophie.* Paris: P.U.F., 1965; 2.ed. (avec critique et réponses), 1968; 3.ed. (avec nouvelle préface), 1972. Translated (2.ed.): *Insights and Illusions of Philosophy.* London: Routledge & Kegan Paul, 1972.

16 Piaget, J. Psychology and Philosophy. In B.B.Wolman & E.Nagel (Eds), *Scientific Psychology.* New York: Basic Books, 1965.

17 Piaget, J. & Mayer, R. L'explication d'une situation d'équilibre avec variations du centre de gravité. *Arch. de Psychol.*, 40, 1-18, 1965.

18 Piaget, J. & Papert, A. L'explication du retour sur elle-même d'une balle de ping-pong. *Arch. de Psychol.,* 40, 20-29, 1965.

19 Piaget, J. & Mounoud, P. L'explication d'un mécanisme de rotation et d'enroulement. *Arch. de Psychol.,* 40, 30-39, 1965.

20 Piaget, J. & Fot, C. L'explication de la montée de l'eau dans un tube héloïdical. *Arch. de Psychol.*, 40, 40-56, 1965.

21 Piaget, J. & Mounoud, P. L'explication d'une coordination des mouvements d'un jouet. *Arch. de Psychol.,* 40, 56-71, 1965.

22 Piaget, J. Note sur des Limnaea stagnalis, L.var. lacustris Stud. élevées dans une mare du plateau vaudois. *Revue suisse Zool.*, 72, 769-787, 1965.

23 Piaget, J. & Inhelder, B. *La psychologie de l'enfant.* Paris: P.U.F., 1966. Translated: *The Psychology of the Child.* London: Routledge & Kegan Paul, 1969.

24 Piaget, J. & Inhelder, B. *L'image mental chez l'enfant: Etude sur le développement des représentations imagées.* Paris: P.U.F., 1966. Translated: *Mental Imagery in the Child: A Study of the Development of Imaginal Representation.* London: Routledge & Kegan Paul, 1971. New York: Basic Books, 1971.

25 Piaget, J. Observations sur le mode d'insertion de la chute des ramaux secondaires chez les Sedum. *Condollea,* 21/22, 137-139, 1966.

26 Piaget, J. Biologie et connaissance. *Diogène,* 54, 3-26, 1966. Translated: Biology and Cognition. *Diogenes,* 54, 1-22, 1966. Reprinted as Conclusion of **32** and in **298**.

27 Piaget, J. Nécessité et signification des recherches comparatives en psychologie génétique. *J. Int. de Psychol.,* 1, 1-13, 1966. Reprinted in J.Piaget, *Psychologie et épistémologie.* Paris: Gonthier, 1970 (quoted from this edition) and in J.Piaget, *Problèmes de psychologie génétique.* Paris: Denoël/Gonthier, 1972. Translated: The necessity and significance of comparative research in developmental psychology. In J.Piaget, *Psychology and Epistemology.* London: Penguin University Books, 1972 (quoted from this edition). Reprinted in J.Piaget, *The Child and Reality: Problems of Genetic Psychology.* New York: Grossman, 1973.

28 Piaget, J. L'initation aux mathématiques, les mathématiques modernes et la psychologie de l'enfant. *L'enseign. math.,* 12, 289-292, 1966.

29 Piaget, J.   La psychologie, les relations interdisciplinaires et le système des sciences. *Bull. de Psych.*, XX, 242-254, 1966.

30 Piaget, J.   Résponse à P. Moessinger. La polémique Piaget-Hersch. *ISE-Echo*, 8, 7-8, 1966.

31 Piaget, J.   Le problème des méchanismes communs dans les sciences de l'homme. *L'Homme et la Société*, 2, 3-23, 1966. Translated: The problem of common mechanisms in the human sciences. *The Human Context*, 1, 163-185, 1968.

32 Piaget, J.   *Biologie et connaissance.* Paris: Gallimard, 1967. Translated: *Biology and Knowledge.* Chicago/London: The University Press, 1971.

33 Piaget, J. (Ed.)   *Logique et connaissance scientifique. Encyclopédie de la Pléiade.* Paris: Gallimard, 1967 (several chapters by J. Piaget).

34 Piaget, J.   Logique formelle et psychologie génétique. Les modèles et la formalization du comportement. *Intern. Colloq. Nat. Center Scient. Res. Paris, July 5-10, 1965.* Paris: 1967, 269-283.

35 Piaget, J.   Book Review of J.S. Bruner, R.R. Oliver & M. Greenfield, *Studies in Cognitive Growth.* In *Cont. Psychol.*, 12, 532-533, 1967.

36 Piaget, J. & Inhelder, B.   *Mémoire et intelligence.* Paris: P.U.F., 1968. Translated: *Memory and Intelligence.* London: Routledge & Kegan Paul, 1973.

37 Piaget, J. *et al.   Epistémologie et psychologie de la fonction. E.E.G.,* Vol.XXIII. Paris: P.U.F., 1968. Translated: *Epistemology and Psychology of Functions.* Dordrecht, Netherlands: Reidel, 1977.

38 Piaget, J. *et al.   Epistémologie et psychologie de l'identité. E.E.G.,* Vol.XXIV. Paris: P.U.F., 1968.

39 Piaget, J.   *Le structuralisme.* Paris: P.U.F., 1968. Translated: *Structuralism.* New York: Basic Books, 1970.

40 Piaget, J.   *Memory and identity.* Barre, Mass.: Clark University Press, 1968. The lecture on identity and conservation is reprinted in **298**.

41 Piaget, J.   Quantification, conservation and nativism. *Science,* 162(3657), 976-979, 1968.

42 Piaget, J.   Psychologie du psychologue. In *L'aventure humaine, encyclopédie des sciences de l'homme.* Geneva: Kister, 1968.

43 Piaget, J.   La conscience. In *L'aventure humaine, encyclopédie des sciences de l'homme.* Geneva: Kister, 1968.

44 Piaget, J.   A theory of development. In D.L. Sills (Ed.), *International Encyclopedia of the Social Sciences,* Vol.4. New York: Macmillan & The Free Press, 1968.

45 Piaget, J.   Introduction. In M. Laurendeau & A. Pinard, *Les premières notions spatiales de l'enfant.* Neuchâtel: Delachaux & Niestlé, 1968.

46 Piaget, J. & Inhelder, B.   The gaps in empiricism. In A. Koestler & J.R.Smithies (Eds), *Beyond Reductionism.* London: Hutchinson, 1969. Reprinted in **298**.

47 Piaget, J. L'épistémologie génétique. In R. Klibansky (Ed.), *Contemporary Philosophy*. Florence: La nuova italia editrice, 1969.

48 Piaget, J. *L'épistémologie génétique*. Paris: P.U.F., 1970. Translated: *The Principles of Genetic Epistemology*. London: Routledge & Kegan Paul, 1972.

49 Piaget, J. *Epistémologie des sciences de l'homme*, chapitre I. Paris: Gallimard, 1972. Translated: *The Place of the Sciences of Man in the System of Sciences*. New York: Harper & Row, 1974.

50 Piaget, J. *Epistémologie des sciences de l'homme*, chapitre II: La psychologie (see **49**). Translated: *Main Trends in Psychology*. London: George Allen & Unwin, 1973.

51 Piaget, J. *Epistémologie des sciences de l'homme*, chapitre III: Problèmes généraux de la recherche interdisciplinaire (see **49**). Translated: *Main Trends in Interdisciplinary Research*. London: George Allen & Unwin, 1973.

52 Piaget, J. *Genetic Epistemology: Four Woodbridge Lectures, 1968*. New York: Columbia University Press, 1970. The first lecture is in part reprinted in **74**. Translated: see **74**.

53 Piaget, J. L'épistémologie génétique. In J. Piaget, *Psychologie et épistémologie*. Paris: Denoël, 1970. Translated: Developmental psychology. In J. Piaget, *Psychology and Epistemology*. London: Penguin University Books, 1972. (The other articles were originally published between 1947 and 1964.)

54 Piaget, J. L'évolution intellectuelle entre l'adolescence et l'âge adulte. Third International Convention and Awarding of Foneme Prizes, 1970. Translated: Intellectual evolution from adolescence to adulthood. *Hum. Dev.*, 15, 1-12, 1972.

55 Piaget, J. Piaget's theory. In P.H.Mussen (Ed.), *Carmichael's Manual of Child Psychology*. London/New York: John Wiley and Sons, 1970.

56 Piaget, J. Mémoire et intelligence. In D. Bovet, A. Fessard, C. Florès, N.H. Frijda, B. Inhelder, B. Milner & J. Piaget. *La mémoire*. Paris: P.U.F., 1970.

57 Piaget, J. Inconscient affectif et inconscient cognitif. *Raison Présente*, 19, 11-20, 1970. Translated: The affective unconscious and the cognitive unconscious. *J. Am. Psychoan. Ass.*, 21, 249-261, 1973. Reprinted in **298**.

58 Piaget, J. with Garcia, R. *Les explications causales*. E.E.G., Vol.XXVI. Paris: P.U.F., 1971. Translated: *Understanding Causality*. New York: Norton, 1974.

59 Piaget, J. The theory of stages. In **271**.

60 Piaget, J. Reaction to Beilin's paper. In **271**.

61 Piaget, J. Hasard et dialectique en épistémologie biologique. *Sciences, revue civilis. scient.*, 71, 29-36, 1971. Translated: Chance and dialectic in biological epistemology: A critical analysis of Jacques Monod's theses. In **386**.

62 Piaget, J. Méthodologie des relations interdisciplinaires. *Arch. de Philos.* 34, 539-549, 1971.

63 Piaget, J. Preface. In E. Ferreiro, *Les relations temporelles dans le language de l'enfant.* Geneva/Paris: Droz, 1971.

64 Piaget, J. Discussion on "Sagesse et Illusion" (1966). In Ch. Bourgois & D. de Roux (Eds), *Psychologie et marxisme.* Paris: Union Générale d'Editions, 1971.

65 Piaget, J. *et al. La transmission des mouvements. E.E.G.,* Vol.XXVII. Paris: P.U.F., 1972.

66 Piaget, J. *et al. La direction lors de chocs et de poussées. E.E.G.,* Vol.XXVIII. Paris: P.U.F., 1972.

67 Piaget, J. Operational structures of the intelligence and organic controls. In A.C. Karczmar & J.C. Eccles (Eds), *Brain and Human Behavior.* New York/Berlin: Springer Verlag, 1972.

68 Piaget, J. The concept of structure. In *Scientific Thought: Some Under-lying Concepts, Methods and Procedures.* New Babylon Studies in the Behavioral Sciences 9. Paris: Unesco/The Hague: Mouton, 1972.

69 Piaget, J. Discours à l'occasion du "Praemium Erasmianum". Amsterdam: 1972.

70 Piaget, J. L'épistémologie des relations interdisciplinaires. In *L'inter-disciplinarité: problèmes d'enseignement et de recherche dans les universités.* Paris: O.C.D.E., 1972.

71 Piaget, J. Physical world of the child. *Physics Today,* 25, 23-27, 1972.

72 Piaget, J. *et al. La formation de la notion de force. E.E.G.,* Vol.XXIX. Paris: P.U.F., 1973.

73 Piaget, J. *et al. La composition des forces et le problème des vecteurs. E.E.G.,* Vol.XXX. Paris: P.U.F., 1973.

74 Piaget, J. In R.L. Evans, *Jean Piaget: The Man and his Ideas.* New York: E.P. Dutton, 1973 (interviews of 1969/1970). Translated: *Mes idées; Le maître de la psychologie de l'enfant.* Paris: Denoël/Gonthier, 1977.

75 Piaget, J. A propos de la généralisation. *Gymnase Cantonal de Neuchâtel, 1873-1973,* 211-233.

76 Piaget, J. Introduction/Remarques finales. In L. Apostel *et al.* (Eds), *L'explication dans les sciences.* Paris: Flammarion, 1973.

77 Piaget, J. Remarques sur l'éducation mathématique. *Math Ecole,* 12, 1-7, 1973.

78 Piaget, J. Introduction générale au dialogue Connaissance scientifique et philosphie. In Académie Royale de Belgique, Connaissance scientifique et philosophie. *Colloque* 16, 17 May, 1973.

79 Piaget, J. Interview by Duckworth: Piaget takes a teacher's look. *Learning,* 1973.

80 Piaget, J. How a child's mind grows. In M. Miller (Ed.), *The Neglected Years: Early Childhood.* United Nations Children's Fund, 1973.

81 Piaget, J. A propos des trois épistémologies. Jean Piaget répond à François Chatelet. *Savoir et action*, 5, 62-64, 1973.

82 Piaget, J. Foreword. In M. Schwebel & J. Ralph (Eds), *Piaget in the Classroom*. New York: Basic Books, 1973.

83 Piaget, J. *Adaptation vitale et psychologie de l'intelligence. Sélection et phénocopie*. Paris: Hermann, 1974.

84 Piaget, J. *Recherches sur la contradiction*. Vol. I (**84a**) et Vol. II (**84b**), E.E.G., Vols XXXI and XXXII. Paris: P.U.F., 1974.

85 Piaget, J. *La prise de conscience*. Paris: P.U.F., 1974. Translated: *The Grasp of Consciousness: Action and Concept in the Young Child*. Cambridge, Mass.: Harvard University Press, 1976.

86 Piaget, J. *Réussir et comprendre*. Paris: P.U.F., 1974. Translated: *Success and Understanding*. London: Routledge & Kegan Paul, 1978.

87 Piaget, J. Structures et catégories. *Logique et analyse*, 17, 223-240, 1974.

88 Piaget, J. The future of developmental child psychology. *J. Youth Adolesc.*, 3, 87-93, 1974.

89 Piaget, J. Histoire et développement de la causalité. *Raison présente*, 30, 5-20, 1974.

90 Piaget, J. *L'équilibration des structures cognitives. Problème central du développement*. E.E.G., Vol.XXXIII. Paris: P.U.F., 1975. Translated: *The Development of Thought*. Oxford: Basil Blackwell, 1978.

91 Piaget, J. Phenocopy in biology and the psychological development of knowledge. *The Urban Review*, 8, 209-218, 1975. Reprinted in **277**.

92 Piaget, J. & Chatillon, J.F. Solubilité, miscibilité et flottaison. *Arch. de Psychol.*, 43, 27-46, 1975.

93 Inhelder, B., Blanchet, A., Sinclair, A. & Piaget, J. Relations entre les conservations d'ensembles d'éléments discrets et celles de quantités continues. *Année Psychol.*, 75, 23-60, 1975.

94 Piaget, J. L'intelligence selon Alfred Binet. *Psych. de l'enfant et Pédag. exp.*, 75, 106-120, 1975.

95 Piaget, J. Le role de l'imitation dans la formation de la représentation. In R. Zazzo, *Psychologie et marxisme: la vie et l'oeuvre de Henri Wallon*. Paris: Denoël/Gonthier, 1975.

96 Piaget, J. *Le comportement, moteur de l'évolution*. Paris: Gallimard, 1976. Translated: *Behavior and Evolution*. New York: Pantheon Books, 1978.

97 Piaget, J. Le possible, l'impossible et le nécessaire. *Arch. de Psychol.*, 44, 281-299, 1976. Translated: Piaget, J. & Voyat, G. The possible, the impossible and the necessary. In **370**.

98 Piaget, J. Postface. *Arch. de Psychol.*, 44, 223-228, 1976.

99 Piaget, J. Autobiographie, partie IX (1966-1976). *Revue europ. sci. soc.*, XIV, 35-43, 1976.

100 Piaget, J. Résponse à François Lurçat. *Cahiers Psychol.*, 19, 284-285, 1976.

101 Piaget, J.   Correspondences and transformations. *The Genetic Epistemologist* (newsletter of the Jean Piaget Society), 1976. Reprinted in **370**.

102 Piaget, J.   *Recherches sur l'abstraction réfléchissante.* Vol. I: *L'abstraction des relations logico-arithmétiques.* Vol. II: *L'abstraction de l'ordre des relations spatiales. E.E.G.,* Vols XXXIV and XXXV. Paris: P.U.F., 1977.

103 Piaget, J.   In B. Inhelder, R. Garcia & J.J. Vonèche (Eds), *Epistémologie génétique et équilibration (colloque de juillet, 1976).* Neuchâtel/Paris: Delachaux & Niestlé, 1977.

104 Piaget, J.   Formulations nouvelles de la structure des "groupements" et des conservations. In *Psychologie expérimentale et comparée. Hommage à Paul Fraisse* (special issue of *Bull. de Psychol.*), 1977. Translated: Some recent research and its link with a new theory of groupings and conservations based on commutability. *Ann. N.Y. Acad. Sci.,* 291, 350-358, 1977.

105 Piaget, J.   Essai sur la nécessité. *Arch. de Psychol.,* 45, 235-251, 1977.

106 Piaget, J.   The role of action in the development of thinking. In **386**.

107 Piaget, J.   Problems of equilibration. In **156** (paper read in 1971). Reprinted in **277**.

108 Piaget, J.   In J. Bringuier, *Conversations libres avec Jean Piaget.* (Interviews of 1969 and 1975/1976.) Paris: Robert Laffon, 1977.

109 Piaget, J.   Preface. In **277**.

110 Piaget, J.   *Recherches sur la généralisation. E.E.G.,* Vol. XXXVI. Paris: P.U.F., 1978.

111 Piaget, J.   What is psychology? *Am. Psychol.,* 33, 648-653, 1978.

112 Piaget, J.   Die historische Entwicklung und die Psychogenese des Impetus-Begriffs. In **438**.

113 Piaget, J. with Sakellaropoulo, M. & Henriques-Christophides, A.   La dialectique des prédicats, concepts, jugements et inférences, étude génétique. *Arch. de Psychol.,* 46, 235-251, 1979.

114 Piaget, J.   Unpublished talks with R. Vuyk 1978/1980.

115 Piaget, J.   Relations between psychology and other sciences. *A. Rev. Psychol.,* 30, 1-9, 1979.

116 Inhelder, B. & Piaget, J.   Procédures et structures. *Arch. de Psychol.,* 47, 165-176, 1979.

117 Piaget, J.   *Les formes élémentaires de la dialectique.* Paris: Gallimard, 1980.

118 Piaget, J.   *Recherches sur le possible et le nécessaire.* Vol.I: *Le développement des possibles.* Paris: P.U.F. In press at time of writing.

119 Piaget, J.   *Recherches sur le possible et le nécessaire.* Vol.II: *Le développement du nécessaire.* Paris: P.U.F. In press at time of writing.

120 Piaget, J.   *Recherches sur les correspondances.* Paris: P.U.F. In press at time of writing.

121 Piaget, J.   *Morphismes et catégories.* In press at time of writing.

List of Translations

Some Piagetian terms have been translated in a number of ways. To avoid confusion I have given a list of the translations I have used, Piaget's terms and other translations. The order is alphabetical (using the first substantive) for my translations.

My translation	Piaget's terms	Other translations
reflected abstraction	abstraction réfléchie	—
reflective abstraction	abstraction réfléchissante	reflexive abstraction
reflexive abstraction	abstraction réflexive	—
centration-decentration = centring-decentring	centration-décentration	centering-decentering
class	classe	category
grasp of consciousness = cognizance	prise de conscience	—
constructivism	constructivisme	constructionism
dialectic, dialectic(al)	une dialectique, dialectique	—
equilibration	équilibration	balancing
improving equilibration	équilibration majorante	heightening, augmentative, incremental, improved equilibration

My translation	Piaget's terms	Other translations
equilibrium	équilibre	balance
constituent function	fonction constituante	constituting function
grouping	groupement	groupoïd
signifying implication	implication signifiante	—
index	indice	indicator
mapping	application	—
metareflexion	métaréflexion	—
necessitation	nécessitation	—
operational	opératoir	operatory, operative
operative	opératif	—
the possible, possibilities, a possibility	le possible, les possibles, une possibilité	the possibility, the possibilities
projective reflection	réfléchissement	—
reconstructive reflection	réflexion	—
empirical reversibility	renversabilité	revertibility
schema	schéma	—
scheme	schème	schema (schemata), pattern
presentative scheme	schème présentatif	—
signification	signification	meaning
signifier-signified	signifiant-signifié	signifier-significant
epistemic subject	sujet épistémique	epistemological subject
tableau	tableau	picture
thematization	thématisation	—